CABINET CONSTRUCTION

The Woodworker Series

Edited By
J.C.S. Brough
(James Carruthers Smith Brough)

Evans Bros., London
c1930

The Toolemera Press

From Our Personal Library To Yours

www.toolemera.com

Cabinet Construction
Edited By James Carruthers Smith Brough (J. C. S. Brough)
c1930

No part of this book may be reproduced, stored in an electronic retrieval system, or transmitted in any form or by an means, electronic, mechanical, photocopy, photographic or otherwise without the written permission of the publisher.

Excerpts of one page or less for the purposes of review and comment are permissible.

Copyright © 2011 The Toolemera Press
All rights reserved.

International Standard Book Number
ISBN: 978-0-9831500-2-2

Published by
The Toolemera Press
Dedham, Massachusetts
U.S.A. 02026

http://toolemera.com

Manufactured in the United States of America

Introduction
by Gary Roberts

"This book deals exhaustively and in a thoroughly practical way with all methods of cabinet construction. Each detail is treated in a way that will guide the reader through it's construction in any size and in any style. The volume enables the woodworker to tackle successfully any design of which he has the scale drawing or even the dimensioned sketch. Fully illustrated with over 300 drawings."
From the dust jacket flyleaf.

Cabinet Construction

An earlier edition of this book was published under the title *Details Of Cabinet Construction. Cabinet Construction*, c1920. This, the later edition, c1930, features larger and more detailed drawings as well as additional descriptions of various woodworking processes.

Evans Bros., London, publishers of *The Woodworker Magazine*, offered a variety of books in The Woodworker Series. J. C. S. Brough (James Carruthers Smith Brough) served as editor of this hugely popular series.

Coming at the end of the Manual Arts education period, The Woodworker Series addressed the functional processes of working wood at a time when those who practiced the craft were passing. Fortunately for the woodworker of today, Evans Bros.

preserved these first hand accounts of hand tool woodworking.

Manual Arts and the Arts & Crafts Period

The Arts & Crafts Period in North America (often known as Craftsman style) was a predominant design aesthetic from the end of the 19th Century on through the beginning of the 20th Century. At the same time, the influence of the Manual Arts movement on educational theory and practice was peaking. Manual Arts, the predecessor to Vocational Education, emphasized the importance of craft in the intellectual, social and physical development of students of both genders.

Often deceptively simple in appearance, but complex in the visual and practical interactions of the various design elements, Arts & Crafts style furnishings represented a departure from the excessive ornamentation of the Gothic, Eastlake, Victorian and Arte Nouveau periods. Manual Arts educators applied the design and process elements of the Arts & Crafts ethos to the requirements of curriculum development: the item created should be doable by students possessed of increasing skill levels as well as being an object which could be put to use in every day life, thereby enhancing the relationships between craft, intellect, and society.

Toolemera Press Reprints

The Toolemera Press reprints classic books and ephemera on early tools, trades and industries. We only reprint items held in our personal library. We will never use a source document from any online document depository. The Toolemera Press manages every aspect of the publishing process.

www.toolemera.com

CABINET CONSTRUCTION
(*THE WOODWORKER SERIES*)

THE WOODWORKER SERIES

PRACTICAL VENEERING.

ENGLISH PERIOD FURNITURE.

WOODWORK JOINTS.

CABINET CONSTRUCTION.

STAINING AND POLISHING.

WOODWORK TOOLS.

TIMBERS FOR WOODWORK.

CARPENTRY FOR BEGINNERS.

WOOD TURNING.

WOODCARVING.

FURNITURE REPAIRING AND RE-UPHOLSTERY.

HOUSEHOLD REPAIRS AND RENOVATIONS.

KITCHEN FURNITURE DESIGNS.

BUREAU AND BOOKCASE DESIGNS.

LIGHT CARPENTRY DESIGNS.

DOOR MAKING.

EVANS BROTHERS, LIMITED,
MONTAGUE HOUSE, RUSSELL SQUARE,
LONDON, W.C.1.

CABINET
CONSTRUCTION
(*THE WOODWORKER SERIES*)

LONDON
EVANS BROTHERS, LIMITED
MONTAGUE HOUSE, RUSSELL SQUARE, W.C. 1

CONTENTS

	PAGE
JOINTS IN CARCASE WORK	1

Framing Joints—Matching Joints—Tenon Joints—Dowelled Joints—Dovetail Joints—Housing Joints—Corner Cabinet Joints—Bureau Ends—Fitting Shelves.

CABINET AND TABLE TOPS 24

Glue-jointed Tops—Grooved and Tongued Tops—Slot-screwed and Dowelled Tops—Battened Tops—Lined Tops—Dovetail-housed Tops—Fixing Tops—Framed and Inlaid Tops—Moulded Edges.

TABLE AND CHAIR LEGS 31

Straight and Tapered Legs—Setting out for Legs—Fixing legs—Tenoning—Buttoning—Pocket-screwing—Notching and Dowelling—Neckings—Underframing—Shelves fitted to Legs—Portable Legs, etc.—Cabriole Legs.

CABINET DOORS 45

Setting out Stiles and Rails—Cutting Mortises and Tenons—Dowelled Framing—Meeting Stiles—Astragals—Panels—Mouldings—Laminating.

BARRED DOORS AND LEADED LIGHTS . . 59

Examples of Barred Doors—Details of Joints—Examples of Leaded Lights—Cutting Glass—Fitting Glass.

HOW TO MAKE DRAWERS 66

Dovetail Joints for Drawers—Setting out—Fronts, Sides, Back and Bottom—Drawers with Mouldings—Veneered Fronts.

DRAWER RAILS AND RUNNERS 78

Jewel Drawer Cases—Writing and other Table Drawers—Runners, Rails and Dustboard—Larger Drawer Framing.

CONTENTS (*Continued*)

	PAGE
HOW TO FIT CORNICES AND CAPPINGS	85

Tenoned Cappings — Screwed Cappings — Dowelled Cappings—Cappings for Screens—Shaped Cappings—Built-up Cornices — Cabinet and Sideboard Cornices—Loose Wardrobe and Bookcase Cornices—Fixing Cornices—Receding Cornices.

SHAPINGS IN CABINET WORK 99

Setting out Shapings from Scale Drawings—Transferring to Wood—Shaped Rails and Aprons—Shaped Pediments—Shaped Brackets—Fret-cut Shapings—How to Cut Shapings—Fitting Shaped Work.

FACING, LINING, AND LIPPING 110

Facing-up for Mirror or Door Frame—Lining-up Cabinet Tops—Lipping for Tops or Shelves.

RULE JOINT FOR DROP LEAVES . . . 113

The Circles—Hinges—Fitting.

HOW TO WORK MOULDINGS WITH PLANES . . 117

Round and Hollow Planes—Method of using Plane—Working a Scotia—Working an Ovolo—Working an Architrave Moulding.

INLAID STRINGS AND BANDINGS. . . . 124

Cutters and Scribers—Stringings for Inlaying—Types of Bandings—Laying—Design Suggestions—Taping for Shaped Edges.

METAL FITTINGS ON FURNITURE . . . 137

Various Hinges—Catches, Bolts, Handles and Castors—Locks. (See also pp. 206–211).

CABINET BACKS AND BACK FRAMING . . 149

Three-ply Backs—Thin Backing—Matched Backs—Framed Sides and Backs—Bookcase and Wardrobe Backs—Panelled Backs—Mirror Backs—Frameless Mirrors.

SETTING-OUT BOARDS 167

Method of Setting out a Board for Small Cupboard.

VENEERING 171

Tools—Veneers—Ground Wood—Cutting—Glueing—Pattern Veneering—Defects and their Remedies.

EXAMPLES OF PERIOD FURNITURE AND METALWORK—TWENTY-FOUR PLATES . . . 189

INDEX 213

FOREWORD

THIS Volume is the first of its kind. It neither competes with nor supersedes any existing guide to cabinet-making; and, as the Publishers believe, it should meet a want long experienced by the home and shop cabinet-maker. Books on general cabinet construction, however excellent when examples similar to those illustrated are being made, do not always help the worker who is engaged on a piece of work different in character. On the other hand, an instructive volume on the setting out and making of joints, whilst essential to every wood-worker, necessarily deals with joints alone and cannot pretend to encroach on the general constructive work.

Here the Authors' aim has been to deal specifically with the separate and distinct detail parts which go to make up pieces of ordinary furniture, and to treat each detail in a way that will guide the reader through its construction in any style and in any size. If, for example, a table is being made, there is a chapter on table and chair legs, another on tops, and a third on drawer-making. Should it, again, be a cabinet that is under construction, the chapters on carcase joints, on cabinet doors, on shapings and on metal furniture will enable the worker to follow the making and fitting of each detail as he encounters it. The details, moreover, cover large furniture as well as small, ornamental as well as plain, and the directions—it is hoped—will thus be of service alike to the advanced craftsman and to the comparatively inexperienced reader.

J. C. S. BROUGH.

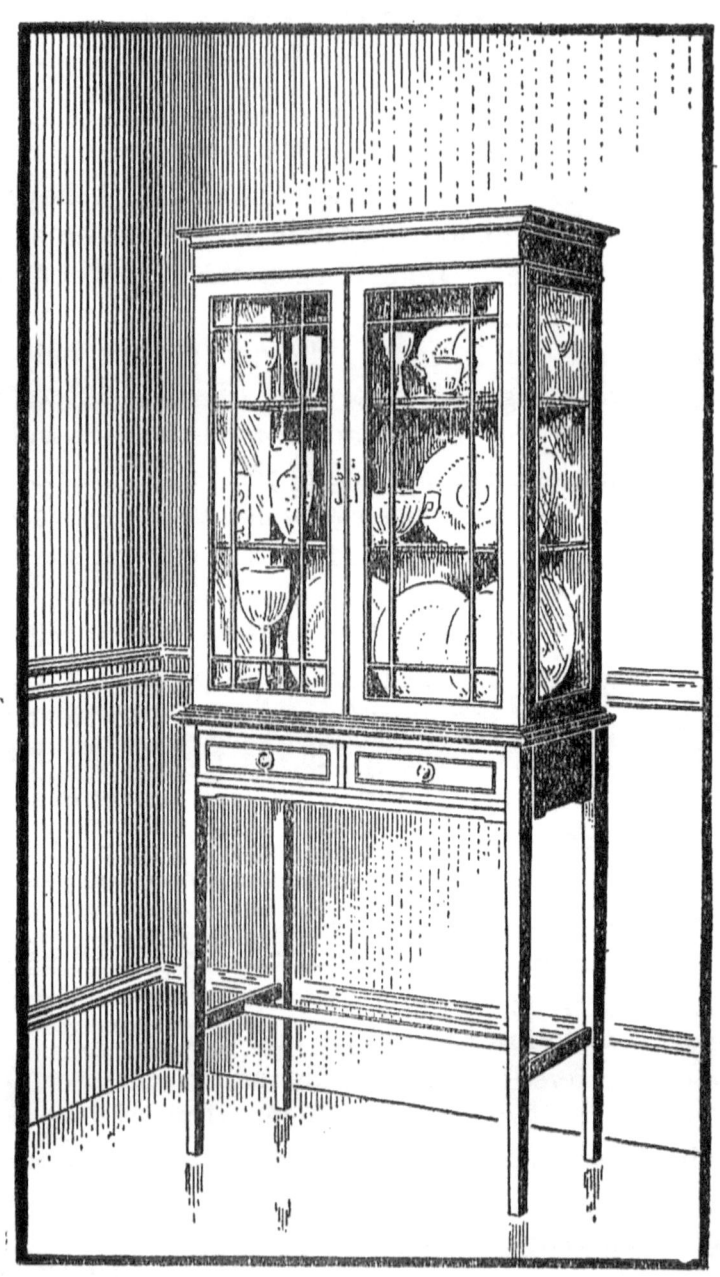

Plate I.—Design for a Display Cabinet.

JOINTS IN CARCASE WORK

IN cabinet-making, the first essential is to have a clear idea of the various joints required for the carcase work. By "carcase" is meant, of course, the main body of the article, which, if it is to stand the wear and tear of everyday use, must be securely put together.

FRAMING.

A Plain Rebated or Lapped Corner (Fig. 1) is useful for small work where a neat, strong and simple joint is desired. The rebate is deep, and the pieces are glued and nailed as shown. It is often used in wireless cabinets and is simpler to make than the tongued corner shown at Fig. 4.

Mitred Rebate (Fig. 2).—Framing can be put together at varying angles by means of the mitred and rebated joint. This joint is in frequent use; it is sometimes glue-blocked behind in the angles, but more frequently nailed or screwed. An application of it would be in connecting flush edges of a bureau top and sides, corners of small carcase work, plinths, panelling, etc.

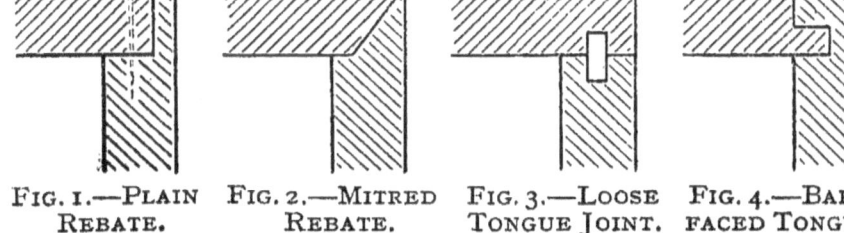

FIG. 1.—PLAIN REBATE.   FIG. 2.—MITRED REBATE.   FIG. 3.—LOOSE TONGUE JOINT.   FIG. 4.—BAREFACED TONGUE JOINT.

Loose Tongued Joint (Fig. 3).—This is a good join to use in connecting sides to a front of same thickness, or to a pilaster or angle corners of framing, and should have the tongue cut cross grain for additional strength.

Cabinet Construction

A Plain or Barefaced Tongue (Fig. 4) is sometimes used for connecting drawer fronts to sides, but the result is of course inferior to dovetailing. It is often used in plinths and framing of similar type—jambs of a mantel and return work of the kind—with or without a bead on the tongued portion in order to mask the joint.

The Rebated Round (Fig. 5) affords a neat and simple finish to small cabinet work, where it is desirable

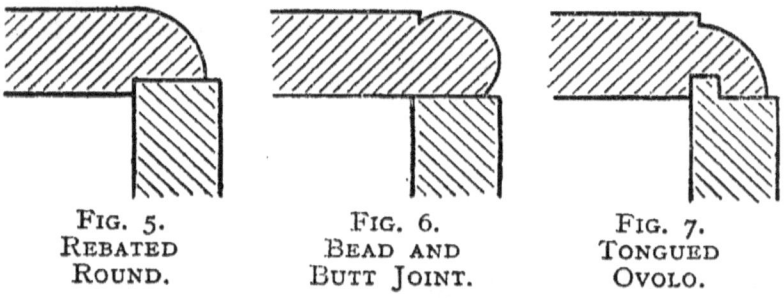

FIG. 5. REBATED ROUND. FIG. 6. BEAD AND BUTT JOINT. FIG. 7. TONGUED OVOLO.

that no sharp edges should exist. It is merely the usual rebated joint with the edge rounded away, or the edge may show a break up to $\frac{1}{8}$ in. wide (as shown) if preferred.

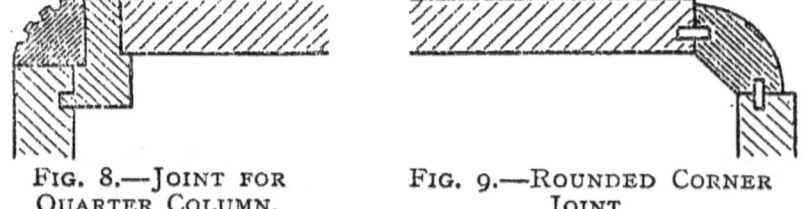

FIG. 8.—JOINT FOR QUARTER COLUMN. FIG. 9.—ROUNDED CORNER JOINT.

The Staff Bead and Butt Joint (Fig. 6) is used for such work as the corner finish of a plain cupboard or wardrobe, the staff or rule bead being worked on the front panels, between which the door shuts. The carcase sides are butted and glued up to the staff, and the sides are often tongued into the staff.

Joints in Carcase Work

The Tongued Ovolo or Round (Fig. 7) is a good corner joint for similar purposes and has a neat finished appearance. A set of round, hollow and canted external corners of carcases, any of which are an advance on the usual square corner, are shown (Figs. 8, 9, 10, 11). In most cases mouldings of other sections can be used with these joints.

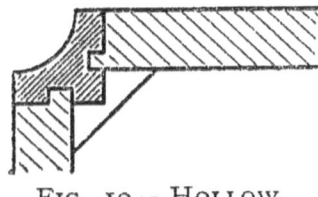

FIG. 10.—HOLLOW EXTERNAL JOINT.

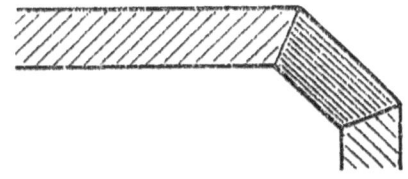

FIG. 11.—PLAIN CANTED CORNER.

Joint for Quarter Column.—Fig. 8 shows a quarter column, fluted and glued into an angle formed for it by tongueing a stile into the side, the door being hinged to the other rebated external edge of the stile. Such a feature would be found in a Chippendale cabinet or bookcase, and affords a rich effect. Alternatively, the turned portion of column might be fluted or carved, and may extend from two-thirds to the full height of the carcase angle. Quarter or half columns are turned up from four or two lengths of stuff glued up with paper between to form a square section, so that all can be turned under one operation. The paper between the glueings enables the parts to be separated easily.

Rounded Corner Joint.—Fig. 9 is a rounded corner bevel, jointed up, which may be either plain glued or cross tongued and glued as indicated. Such a joint may be braced by glue blocking behind, if the angle is convenient for this. The joint would be commonly used for rounded corner work, such as is met with in old style commodes, wardrobes, etc.; also in round or serpentine-shaped work, as carved or kidney-shaped

Cabinet Construction

writing tables. In round work or cylinder falls each length glued up is edge bevelled at a definite angle, and cross tongued together for strength.

Hollow External Joint.—Fig. 10 shows a hollow external corner joint, the corner post being hollowed out with front and sides tongued into it, and the parts glued and braced behind.

Canted Corner.—Fig. 11 is a plain bevelled or canted corner glue-jointed up, and is very suitable for soft stuff. The joint requires that the meeting edges shall be shot perfectly true, so that they engage their whole length when rubbed. It is often met with in small cabinet work and home carpentry.

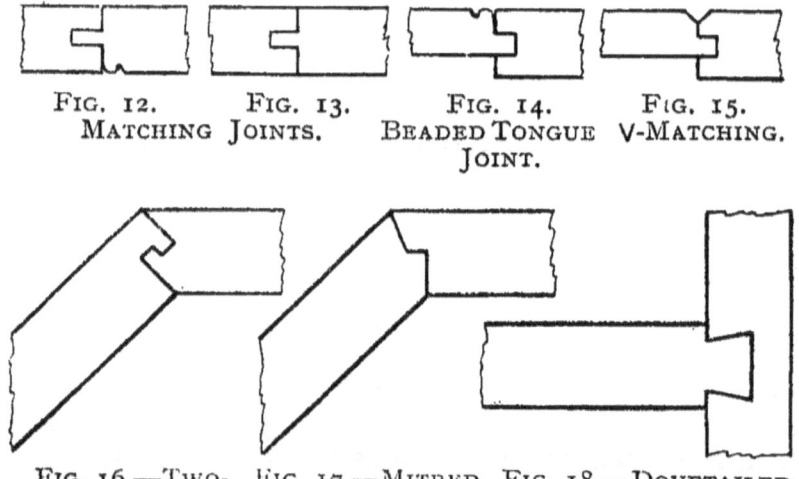

FIG. 12.   FIG. 13.   FIG. 14.   FIG. 15.
MATCHING JOINTS.   BEADED TONGUE JOINT.   V-MATCHING.

FIG. 16.—TWO-TONGUE MITRE.   FIG. 17.—MITRED REBATE.   FIG. 18.—DOVETAILED STRETCHER RAIL.

MATCHING JOINTS.

The ordinary Joint for Matchboarding (Fig. 12) has a bead worked on the tongued board, and is used for the partition and backs of carcase work, as also in the beaded panels of doors, etc.

Joints in Carcase Work

Fig. 13.—Alternatively the flush-tongued joint is used for sides or panelling where the bead is not required.

Fig. 14.—The beaded tongue and groove joint is useful in putting together the mounted backs of carcase work.

Fig. 15.—V-matching is preferred by some to the beaded variety for similar purposes, the difference being merely that the meeting edges are bevelled away slightly, thus forming a V-groove.

The Two-Tongued Mitre (Fig. 16) is not so often met with, but it is a strong joint and repays for the extra trouble of working. As it will sometimes displace itself slightly when the wood has become thoroughly dry, a nail is usually driven in the parts when home.

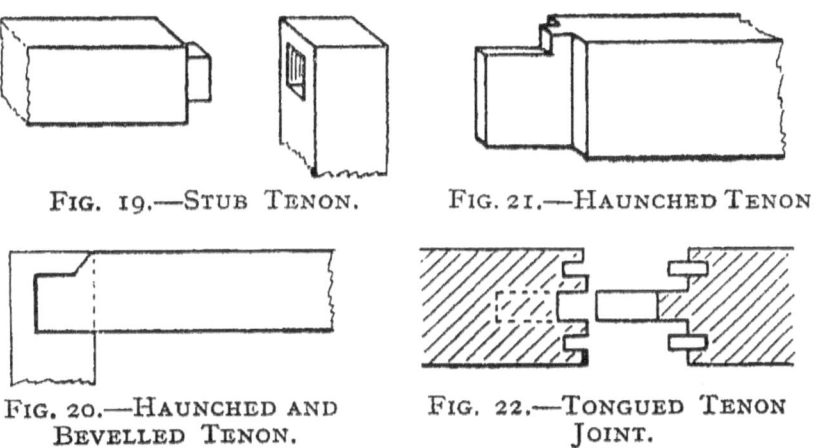

FIG. 19.—STUB TENON.   FIG. 21.—HAUNCHED TENON.

FIG. 20.—HAUNCHED AND BEVELLED TENON.   FIG. 22.—TONGUED TENON JOINT.

Fig. 17 indicates a mitred rebate for canted corners, a neat joint, which can also be nailed.

A Stretcher Rail (Fig. 18) is often needed in the construction of a framing or carcase, and this can be dovetailed each end into front and back rails, and nailed or screwed through if necessary. In cheaper work the rail is often butted into position and held by glue-blocking at each side.

Cabinet Construction

TENONS.

A Stub-Tenon (Fig. 19) is the joint in general use in framing up carcase work in furniture. It may be cut the full width of stuff in use, or be shouldered on both sides (as indicated), according as circumstances may suggest. In order not to render the edge of stile unsightly the tenon does not enter right through in framing up. The depth of mortise must therefore be gauged, a simple method of doing which is to gum or glue a strip of paper temporarily across the mortise chisel, which will save constant measuring.

Haunched and Bevelled Tenon (Fig. 20).—When the tenon comes to the end of a frame it is cut with a bevelled haunch, as shown, the cutting of which necessarily reduces the tenon. A corresponding haunching is cut in the mortise for the joint to bed home. The haunch affords a better holding to the parts brought together.

Haunched Tenon (Fig. 21).—When the stile or upright is required to receive a panel it is grooved throughout its full length, and the haunch of the tenon is cut to fit the groove. The tenon, in the case of a door, is preferably cut to enter right through the stile and be wedged.

Tongued Tenon (Fig. 22).—Where heavy work is concerned an extra stiffening hold can be given to a mortise and tenon joint by tongueing the shoulders as indicated at Fig. 22. In addition to the haunched tenon, each shoulder is grooved to receive a cross tongue, the mortised upright being correspondingly grooved to receive the tongues. The glueing surface is thereby increased and the joint rendered more secure.

Partition Joints (Fig. 23).—The division which parts the two small drawers in a dressing chest is put together as shown here. An upright piece, finishing the

Joints in Carcase Work

same width as the rails, is cut with a pair of tenons or pins each end, to enter corresponding mortises above and below. (A single tenon is often used for the lower end of division.) A continuation piece is tongued on the end grain to enter a groove in upright, and, when home, will

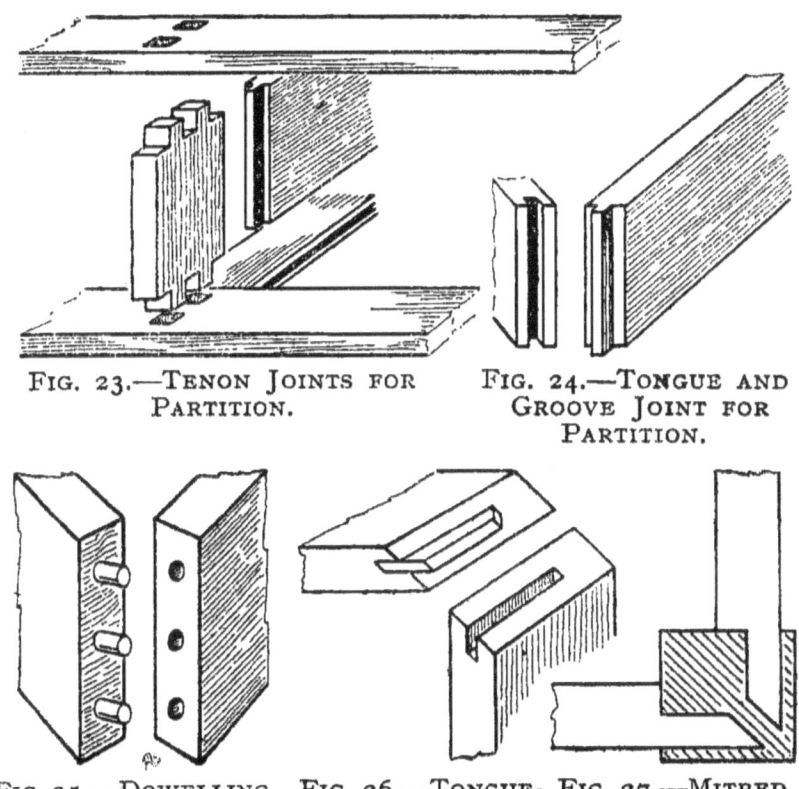

FIG. 23.—TENON JOINTS FOR PARTITION.

FIG. 24.—TONGUE AND GROOVE JOINT FOR PARTITION.

FIG. 25.—DOWELLING END GRAIN.

FIG. 26.—TONGUE-ING END GRAIN.

FIG. 27.—MITRED TENON JOINT.

be screwed through from under the runner upon which the drawer travels. The slide is tongued into the drawer rail, and the latter enters the leg or upright, usually with a couple of tenons. Fig. 24 shows the tongued and grooved parts.

Dowelled Joints.—Where it is required to mitre end grain, as in an arch, or to form a framing, this may

Cabinet Construction

be done by either dowelling or tongueing, the former being indicated at Fig. 25 and the latter at Fig. 26. The tongue should be cut cross grain for extra strength, and may enter the mitre its full length, or be stopped short as shown. Alternatively, the mitre may be screwed through one edge across the join, and in heavy work the mitre is often bolted together, a special double threaded bolt and nuts being procurable.

Joints other than a plain glue-blocked mitre are the veneer keyed, mitred and rebated, and double keyed mitre, useful for plinth or cornice work.

A Mitred Tenon Joint (Fig. 27) is used for rails entering a leg, as in the case of a table. The mortises are cut through the leg till they meet, the tenons being of a length to approach nearly together without meeting.

DOVETAIL JOINTS.

Through Dovetailing (Fig. 28).—Carcase work in general (plinths, cornices, cases, etc.) is, in its simplest form, put together by through or common dovetailing—called " through " owing to both sides of the meeting angles showing end grain. In cabinet work the showing of the joint is usually covered in, except in the case of the back of the job intended to stand against a wall. In some instances, such as kit chests, scientific instrument cases, photographic boxes, etc., however, the end grain is left exposed. In setting out, the pins are kept of neat proportion and the tails much larger, except in the case of large work, where, for the sake of extra strength and to secure a greater equality of shrinkage, the spacing allotted to the parts of the joint more nearly approach equality in size.

Stopped Dovetails (Fig. 29).—An improved appearance is obtained by stopping the dovetails, which, when home, are concealed from sight by a lap on the pin piece,

Joints in Carcase Work

thus masking the end grain. Fig. 29 illustrates this, the joint being in universal use for connecting a drawer side to the front. The angle for cutting a dovetail should lie between one in six and one in eight, the latter being the usually conceded limit of inclination, which, in a common way, may be expressed by saying "the least bit." Practice will often make the worker expert

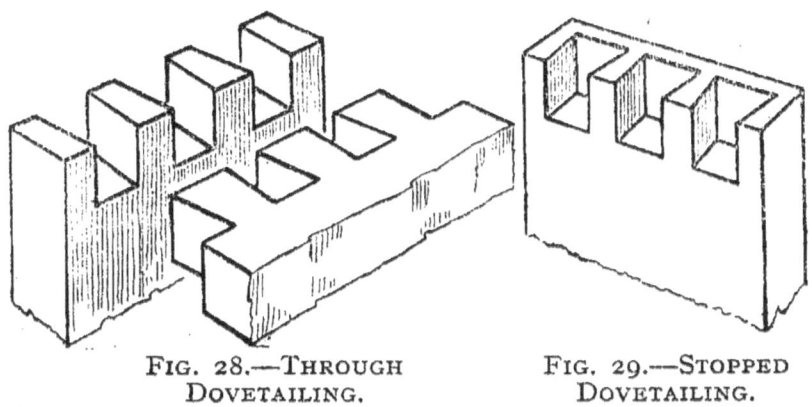

FIG. 28.—THROUGH DOVETAILING.

FIG. 29.—STOPPED DOVETAILING.

in cutting the joint, and there are makers of work-boxes, tea caddies, etc., who can dovetail these articles together practically without measuring at all. Where pieces of similar size are to be jointed in the same way three or four may be put in the vice and have the dovetails sawn at one time. The pins to fit them should be very carefully cut, keeping the saw kerf always on the outside of the set out; otherwise the parts will not properly engage when brought together. Wardrobe and cupboard sides and tops are generally put together by lap dovetailing. In order to prevent any tendency for the ends to warp, it is advisable to cut small dovetails at the sides as shown at B, Fig. 30. These firmly hold in the sides and stop them curling outwards. C shows the tendency for the ends to turn outwards when the end dovetails are large.

To prevent dovetails breaking off at the corners, it is

Cabinet Construction

a good plan to place a batten across them (as at Fig. 31) and lightly hammer them. This applies specially to the dovetails of drawers.

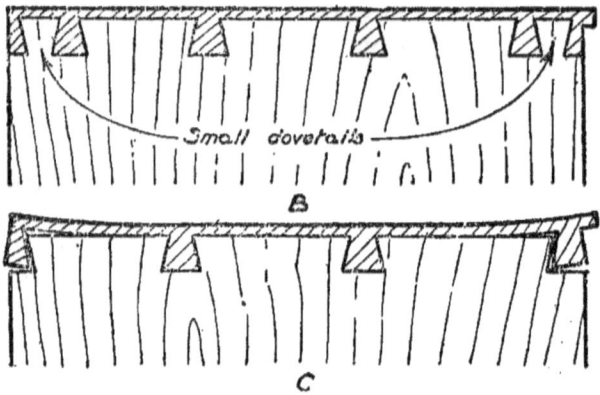

FIG. 30.—B, SMALL END DOVETAILS TO PREVENT CURLING. C, EXAGGERATED EXAMPLE OF CURLING THROUGH LACK OF END DOVETAILS.

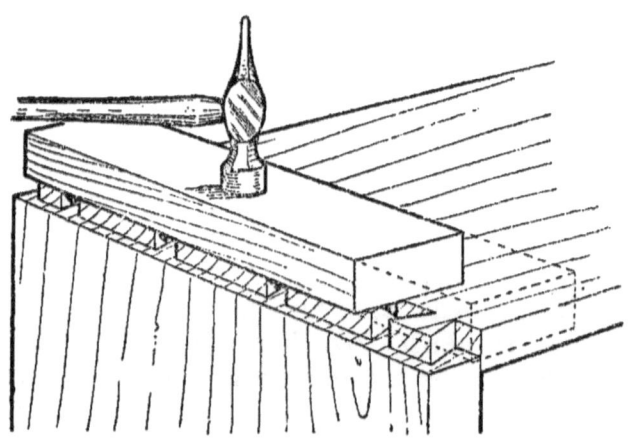

FIG. 31.—USE OF BATTEN WHEN ASSEMBLING TO PREVENT SPLITTING.

Blind or Secret Lap Dovetailing (Fig. 32) is a variation of the foregoing joint, with the possible disadvantage of leaving the lap end grain showing. This,

Joints in Carcase Work

however, is often rounded off at the angle for finish, and has then a neat appearance. Small cabinet work (boxes, plinths, cornices, etc.) has this joint in frequent use.

A useful method of jointing an upright to a horizontal piece, where a hanging strain is concerned, is indicated in Fig. 33, the dovetail being sometimes nailed or pinned through from the sides. Shaped frames of suitable angle may be dovetailed together in a similar manner.

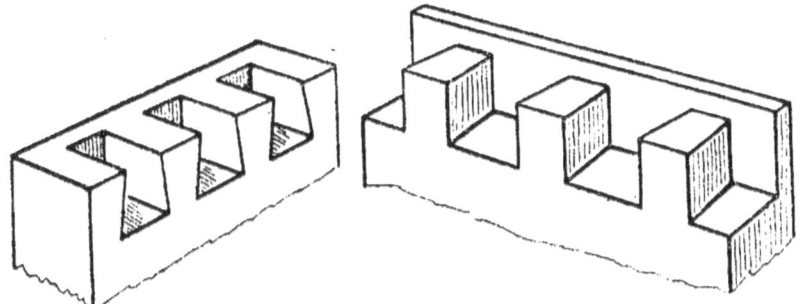

FIG. 32.—SECRET LAP-DOVETAILING.

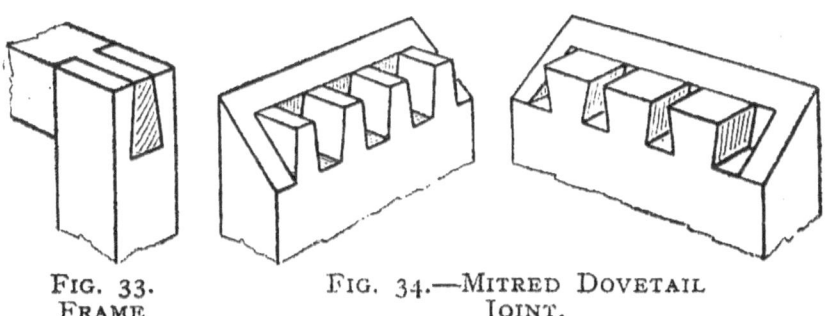

FIG. 33. FRAME DOVETAIL.

FIG. 34.—MITRED DOVETAIL JOINT.

Mitred Dovetail (Fig. 34).—An improved secret joint is the mitred dovetail, the effect being of the neatest. The joint occurs in cabinet work of the highest class and is useful for fitting flush top to sides, as in a bureau, special cases, plinths, and framework that is afterwards to be veneered.

Cabinet Construction

Portions of work, such as panels or pediments of larger and heavier kind, are sometimes stiffened against warping by fitting a dovetail key behind. This consists of a slip of hardwood, tapered as a dovetail in the direction of its length from top to bottom and also bevelled at its sides. This is inserted into a corresponding socket at the back of the part to be stiffened.

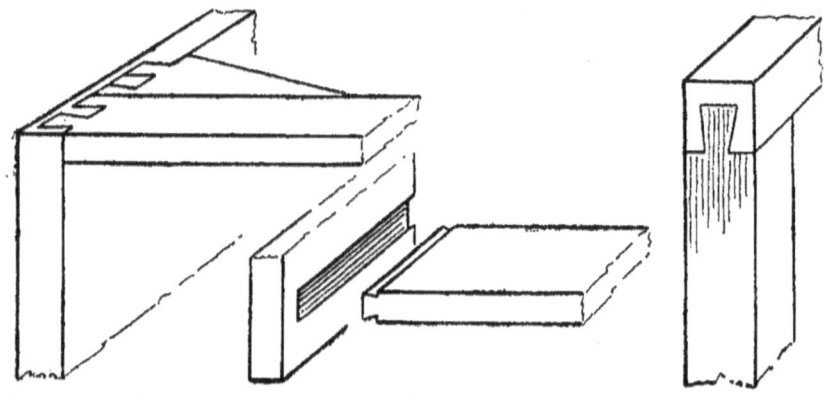

FIG. 35.—CONNECTING BEARER RAIL TO CARCASE END.

FIG. 36.—HOUSED DOVETAIL JOINT.

FIG. 37.—DOVETAIL JOINT FOR TOP RAILS. (See also FIG. 33.)

Bearer Rail Dovetail.—Fig. 35 indicates the usual method of connecting a top rail of carcase to its side, an angle brace of deal being added as a stiffener. This occurs in sideboards, dressers, dressing-tables, washstands, etc., when the parts are masked by the later fixing of the table top.

Figs. 36 and 37.— A bearer rail may be dovetailed into leg or pilaster and side in the manner indicated at Fig. 36, as instanced in a leg table or bookcase. Alternatively, a pilaster may be dowelled or tongued to sides or may be plain glued into position. A slight variation of the dovetailing of leg or post and rail is shown at Fig. 37.

Joints in Carcase Work

Housed Dovetail.—Fig. 36 shows a housed dovetail cut into carcase sides and stopped back from the front edge to the thickness of the door, which is to be hinged inside ends or sides of the job.

The joint is often cut with a half instead of a full dovetail (as indicated), and, where the shelf is to finish flush with the front edge of carcase sides, the dovetail is notched back ⅜ in. to mask the joint. (See Fig. 42.)

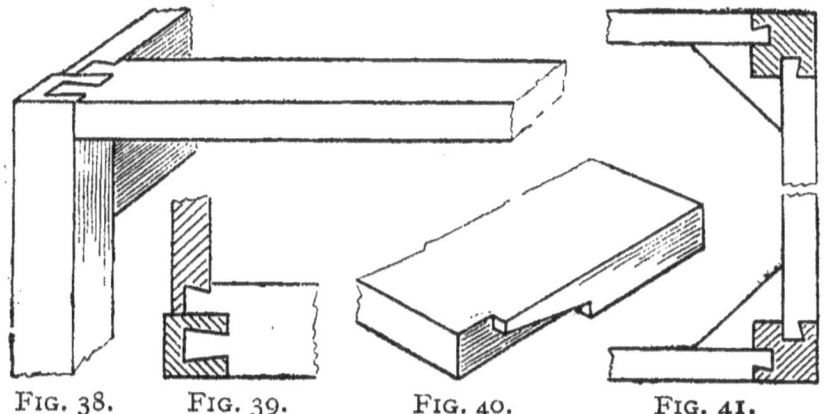

Fig. 38.   Fig. 39.   Fig. 40.   Fig. 41.

FIGS. 38 AND 39.—CONNECTING BEARER RAIL TO LEG AND END.
FIG. 40.—SHOULDERED DOVETAIL HOUSED JOINT.
FIG. 41.—JOINT FOR FLUSH FRONT AND SIDE RAILS.

Fig. 37 is a variation of Fig. 33, the tail in this case being cut to taper from front to back, as well as being bevelled at sides. It is specially useful where the top rail is used for lifting the whole article, and is sometimes cut in pair tails instead of a single tail. A joint of similar kind is used in connecting the inner side to bottom of the lower drawer case of Queen Anne semi-pedestal dressing and writing-tables.

A Shouldered and Dovetail Housed Joint is indicated at Fig. 40. In small carcase work the diminishing dovetail may be cut the full width of the shelf and fitted in this manner. In larger work the diminishing dovetail

Cabinet Construction

may be as shown, this being stopped back ⅜ in. from front edge of carcase, the portion of shelf not dovetailed being housed into sides to its full thickness. Another name for the joint is barefaced housed dovetail. It may be dovetailed on one side only, or on both sides, with the tail either to taper or be parallel its full length. It is a safe stiffening joint, and if properly cut and fitted will make a carcase as firm as a rock. False bottoms, divisions, plinths, fixed shelves, stretcher frames, etc., are put together in this way.

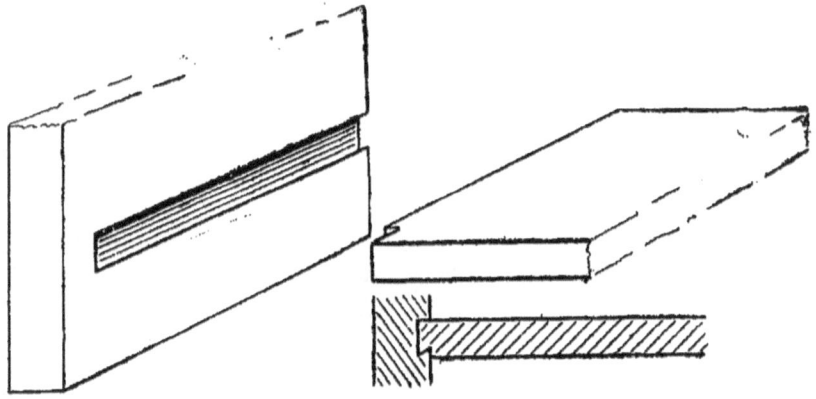

Fig. 42.—Sketch and Section of Stopped Dovetail Housing.

Another method of fixing flush front and side rails to a leg or upright is indicated at Fig. 41, the parts being semi-dovetailed into the leg and braced in the angle behind. This is a frequent joint in the case of "stool" bases fitted below Jacobean cupboards and chests of drawers.

CORNER CABINET JOINTS.

Corner Cabinet Joints.—In the fitting of corner cabinet work it is advisable to fix scribing pieces at the sides so that the back of the job does not actually touch the walls. Fig. 43 makes this clear. The plan to the left shows a square cabinet standing in a corner of over

Joints in Carcase Work

90 degrees, resulting in an open gap at one side. To the right is the same corner, but with a cabinet fitted with scribing pieces. The back of the job does not quite touch the walls and there is no gap. Another advantage is that, when the walls have a skirting and dado or just a chair rail, the scribing pieces can be cut away, *i.e.*, scribed to fit over these members, an impossibility when the front of the job finishes flush with the backs.

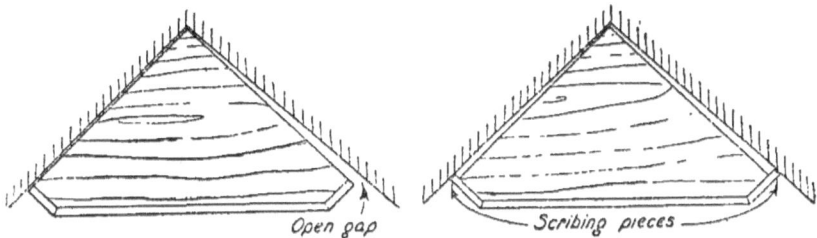

FIG. 43.—USE OF SCRIBING PIECES IN CORNER WHICH IS NOT TRUE.

The addition of these scribing pieces offers little difficulty from either the practical point of view or in the design, because corner furniture is invariably fitted with pilasters to which the door is hinged. The backs are at an angle of 45 degrees with the front, and it would be unsatisfactory to plane the edges of the doors at this angle and hinge them. As the inner edges of the pilasters are square there is no difficulty.

Plain Dovetailed Cabinet.—Fig. 44 shows in plan one of the simplest kinds of corner cabinets. The top and bottom are dovetailed to solid backs, and the front edges are square and faced with pilasters. The method of setting out the dovetails should be noticed. Their slope is the same as if they were being joined to pieces at right angles. The object of this is to obtain the maximum strength. If they were cut to run square into the backs, as at B, one corner of each dovetail would inevitably break off, as shown by the dotted line, owing to the

Cabinet Construction

short grain. Another point to notice is the provision of small dovetails at the front. These are far more effec-

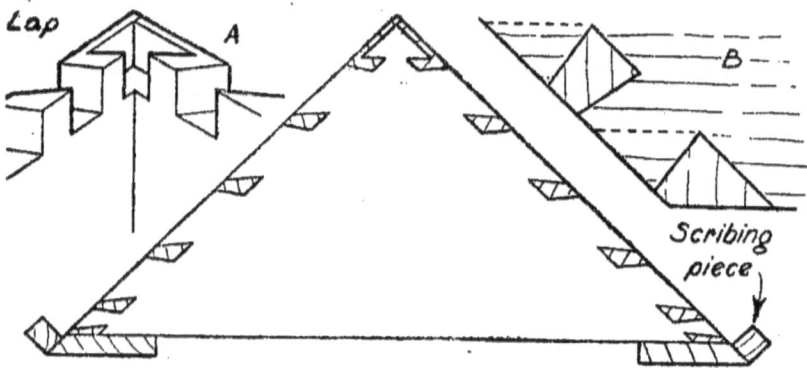

Fig. 44.—Plan of Plain-Dovetailed Corner Cabinet.

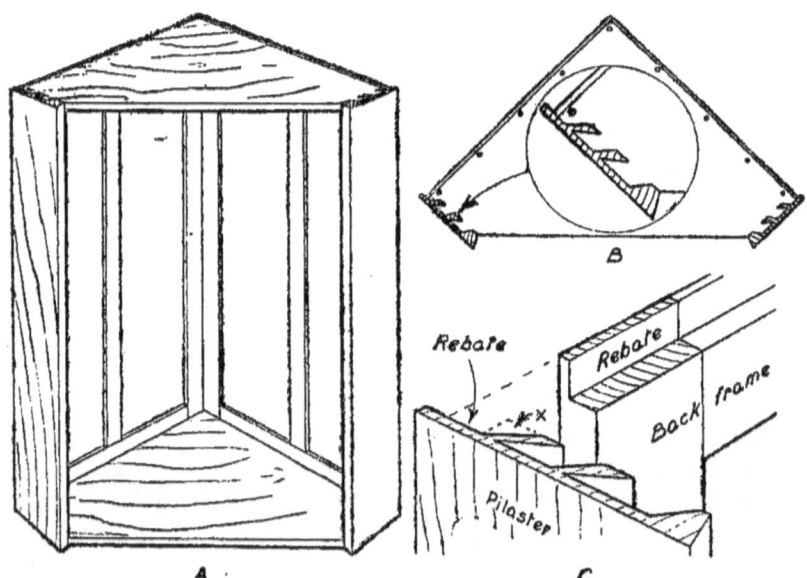

Fig. 45.—Corner Carcase Type with Panelled Back and Pilasters.

tive in preventing the backs from curling outwards through warping than big dovetails. They take no longer to cut and they go a long way in making a strong

Joints in Carcase Work

reliable job. One other feature is the lap introduced at the back dovetail in the angle. If this is not provided the extreme corner has little or no support. It would be free to twist upwards and be liable to break off. The lap gives it full support (see A, Fig. 44).

Another kind of carcase is that in which panelled backs are used, as in Fig. 45. Here the pilasters are at right angles with the backs. A shows a general view of the carcase, B a plan at top, and C a detail sketch of the joint. The backs are simple frames with rebates to take

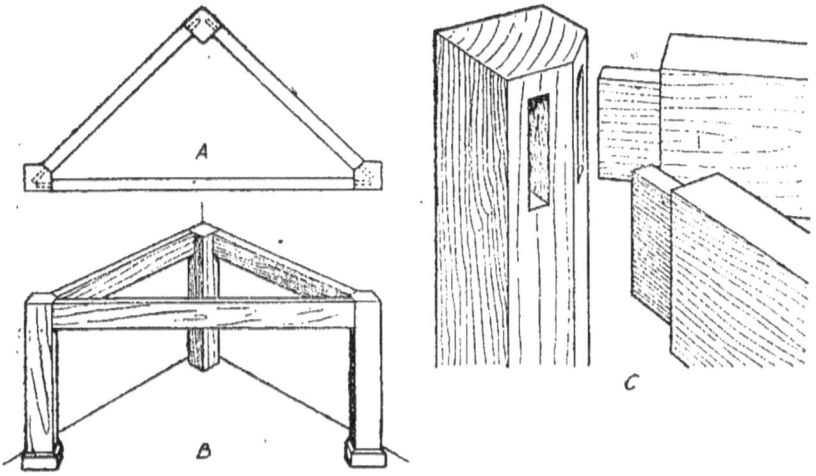

Fig. 46.—Method of Making Stand for Corner Cabinet. (A) Plan. (B) Perspective. (C) Front Joint.

the top and bottom. One is rebated down the back edge, and the other is screwed into it. The pilasters are rebated at their outer edges to fit over the ends of the backs. The rebates are cut extra deep so that the pilasters project, thus forming scribing pieces (B). The top is dovetailed into the pilasters and is screwed into the rebates in the back. B (inset sketch) shows the method of setting out the dovetails; C is a perspective view of the joint. Note the rebate in the pilaster, and how the top corner (X) is cut away, forming the dovetails. It is

Cabinet Construction

usual in most work to make the pilasters the same thickness as the doors.

Corner Cabinet Stand.—Fig. 46 gives the method of making a stand for a corner cabinet. There is no difficulty about the back legs, since the rails are tenoned into it at right angles as dotted lines at A. At the front the legs are set square and the front rail is tenoned in the usual way, but as the back rails are set at 45 degrees the

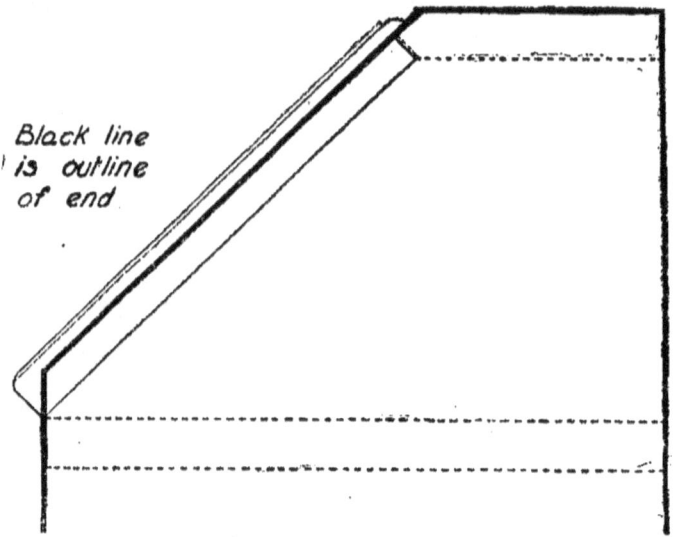

FIG. 47.—SETTING OUT A BUREAU END.

front legs must be bevelled to accommodate them. A detailed view of the joint is given at C. The front legs stand out so that the cabinet fits easily into any corner. It is usual for the upper carcase of such a stand to be fitted with scribing pieces to fill in the rather awkward gaps formed above the sides of the legs.

The Setting out of Bureau Ends (Fig. 47) is a job over which many come to grief. The best procedure is to first mark the mortises and grooves for the writing top (this is always 30 ins. from the floor), and then set

Joints in Carcase Work

out the sloping part. It will be realised that the point at which this begins depends partly upon the depth of the fall rebate; but the distance between the writing top and the beginning of the slope does not equal this depth. It is greater, because the face of the end runs obliquely across the rebate. To ensure accuracy, a job of the kind should always be set out full size.

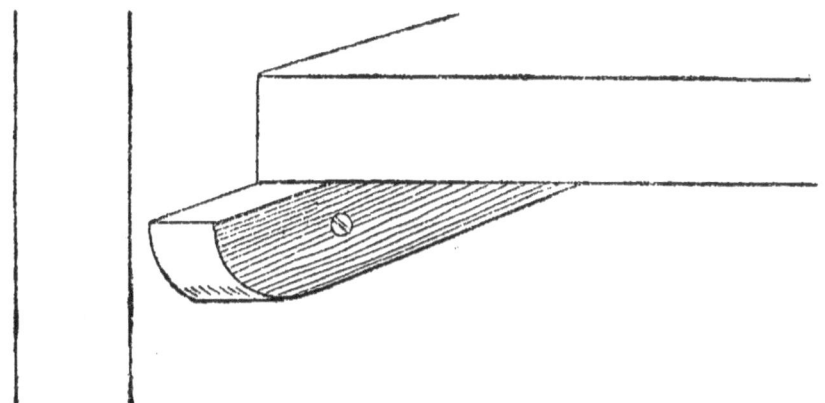

FIG. 48.—SHELVES SUPPORTED LOOSE ON FILLETS.

THE FITTING OF SHELVES.

There are several methods in common use of mounting shelves, either loosely or fixed. The commonest and simplest way is to screw fillets to the sides, for a shelf to rest loosely upon as Fig. 48. Where shelves have to take books it should be remembered that these are dead weight, and in any length over 2 ft. it is best to fit these of $\frac{7}{8}$ in. net thickness. The supporting fillets may be of $\frac{1}{2}$ in. thickness × $\frac{7}{8}$ in. wide. An alternative arrangement for fitting shelves loosely to slide into position is indicated in Fig. 49. Where 1 in. ends are provided, a series of grooves $\frac{7}{8}$ × $\frac{1}{4}$ in. deep may be cut, for the shelves to push home; or, with $\frac{3}{4}$ in. thickness for ends,

Cabinet Construction

slips $\frac{7}{8} \times \frac{3}{8}$ in. may be screwed and glue-dabbed to sides, taking care that the two slips to take the same shelf are perfectly horizontal when in position.

An alternative method is to support the shelves on saw-tooth ratchets, as indicated in Fig. 50. These can be made by cutting slips about $\frac{7}{8}$ in. wide $\times \frac{3}{8}$ in. at spaced intervals as indicated. A space of at least 1 in.

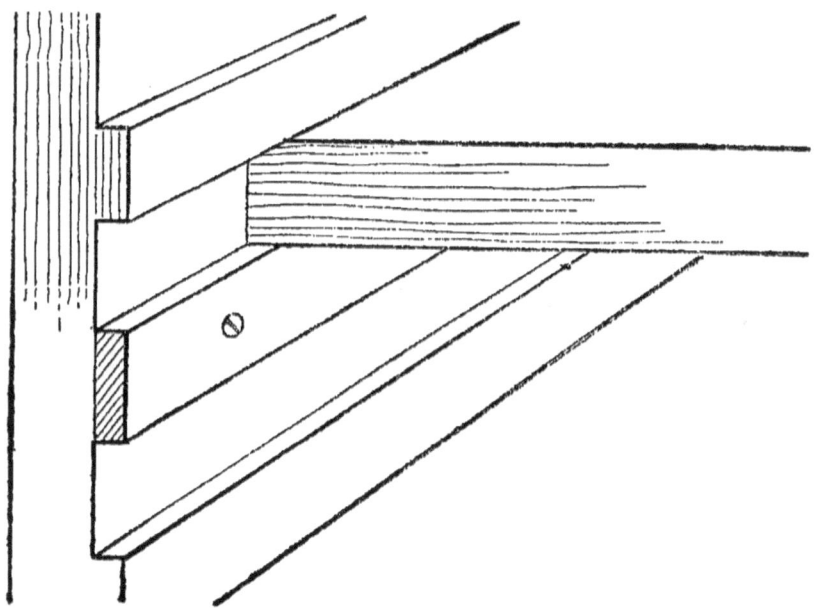

FIG. 49.—ALTERNATIVE METHOD OF FITTING SHELVES IN GROOVES.

between each step should be allowed. A pair of these ratchet fillets is fitted, one at front and one at back of interior casing. A slip, $\frac{3}{8} \times \frac{7}{8}$ in., bevelled at each end to agree with the saw-tooth, will be required for the shelves to rest upon, the arrangement affording a satisfactory and efficient result.

Still another method is to support a loose shelf on pins similar to those indicated in Figs. 51–53, these being intended to fit into corresponding holes in sides for

Joints in Carcase Work

supporting purposes. Where turned wooden pins are used, the circular portion of the pin head may have a corresponding notching made for it in the edge of shelf, as at Fig. 53, so that the latter cannot press out of posi-

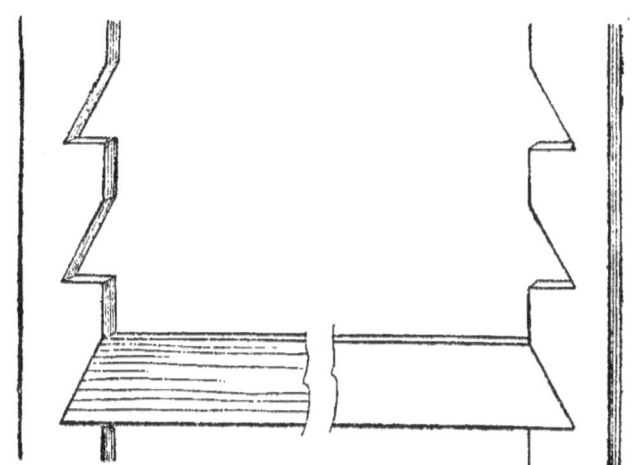

FIG. 50.—SAW-TOOTHED RATCHETS FOR HOLDING MOVEABLE FILLETS FOR SHELVES.

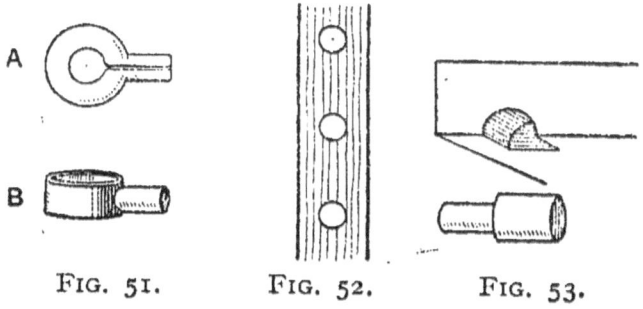

FIG. 51.   FIG. 52.   FIG. 53.

tion. The adjustment holes for pins may either be bored at spaced intervals in solid ends, to a gauged depth, or they may be bored in a separate slip as Fig. 52, to be afterwards fitted in position front and back of the ends.

Cabinet Construction

A fixed shelf can be let into sides or ends by means of slot-dovetailing, or dovetailed-housing as Fig. 54.

In showcases for china or silverware the shelves are often lined with silk or other material, the portion to be lined being sunk about $\frac{1}{16}$ in. below the shelf surface, leaving a lipping along the front edge as a finish to the material used.

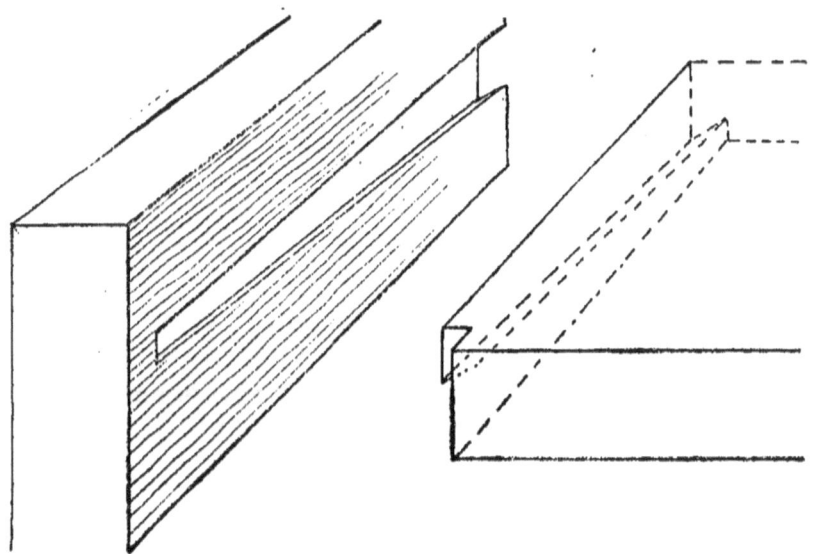

FIG. 54.—SHELF SLOT-DOVETAILED TO END.

Alternatively, a cabinet may be fitted with plate glass shelves, $\frac{1}{4}$ in. thick, with ground edges. In this case the shelves may be supported on lugs, having a pin similar to Fig. 51B, to enter corresponding holes spaced about $1\frac{1}{2}$ ins. apart in the carcase sides. There are several substitutes for these lugs in a cheaper form, now procurable in stamped brass, one of which is indicated in Fig. 51A, this generally being inserted in a metal-bushed hole with firm holding. Another kind sometimes used is similar to Fig. 51B, but fitted with a felt or rubber buffer for direct contact with the glass. In cruder

Joints in Carcase Work

fashion and with a slight element of risk, a small brass screw eye inserted at each corner is used for supporting

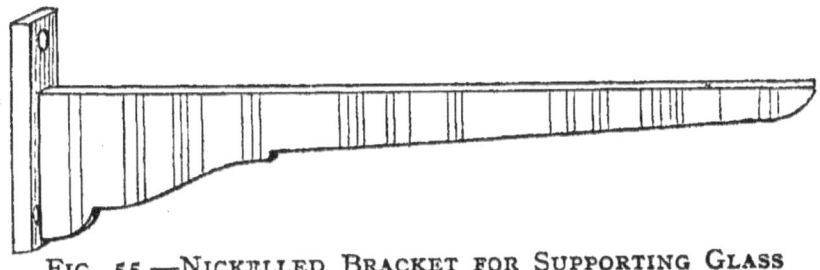

FIG. 55.—NICKELLED BRACKET FOR SUPPORTING GLASS SHELVES.

glass shelves, whilst, where fixing from one position only is possible, an oxydised or nickelled bracket, as Fig. 55, may be screwed to the back for support.

CABINET AND TABLE TOPS

VARIOUS TOPS.

THE simplest and probably most frequent joint met with in the piecing up of table or cabinet tops is the plain glued joint (Fig. 56), generally termed the "rubbed" joint, on account of having the glued edges rubbed against each other lengthwise to squeeze out excess glue and secure a surer holding of the parts brought together. It is about the best joint for stuff that is soft in texture and thin, and it is essential that the edges be planed up perfectly true. If the stuff be slightly in winding, the parts can be cramped after glueing and the irregularity then be planed out. When glueing up, narrow widths are preferable, and are best jointed together with the grain alternately reversed, thus equalising the "pull."

Matched Tops.—Tops may be "matched" together, this joint having the tongue worked on the solid (Fig. 57) and glued into a corresponding groove in the meeting board; properly done the joint stands well. In some instances the glueing can be dispensed with and the boards be cleated by screwing lengths of stuff crosswise to the under side, the screw holes being slotted to allow of any expansion or contraction that may take place in any of the boards. A cleat is sometimes rebated on edges, and the top attached by means of wood buttons screwed on. Alternatively, metal shrinkage plates may be used.

Grooved and Tongued Jointing (Fig. 58) is also in common use. Both meeting edges are grooved to about one-third of the thickness of the stuff, and a loose tongue is glued and laid therein. The tongue may be "feathered" or cut with the grain running in the direction of its length, but is stronger if cut across the grain.

Cabinet and Table Tops

The fitting of this tongue affords an extra glueing surface, and the joint is usually a strong one, although it at times will open where a rubbed joint will stand. In thicker stuff twin grooves and tongues are sometimes used. Fig. 59 shows the twin boards together.

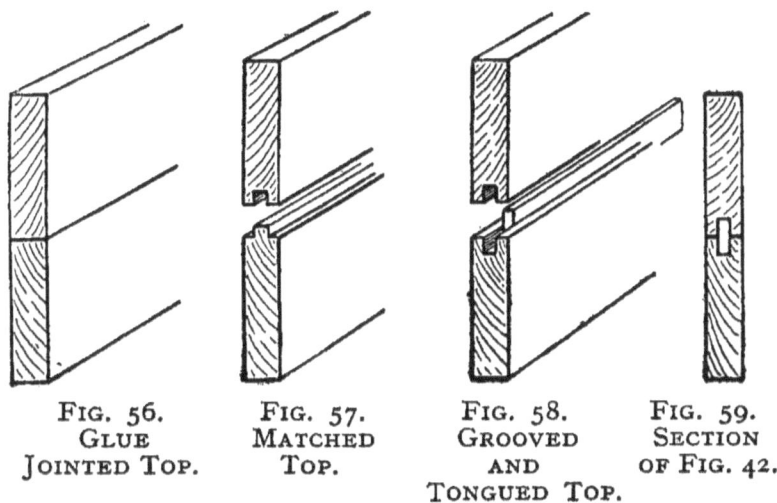

FIG. 56. GLUE JOINTED TOP. FIG. 57. MATCHED TOP. FIG. 58. GROOVED AND TONGUED TOP. FIG. 59. SECTION OF FIG. 42.

Slot-screwed and Dowelled Top.—Another method of bringing the boards together is by means of the secret slot screw joint, in which slots are cut in the one edge for the reception of a screw head in the other, as indicated at Figs. 60 and 61. A more usual way is to dowel the boards together (Fig. 62), but the joint has some tendency to open and requires the edges to be shot perfectly true and square.

Battened and other Tops.—With regard to stiffening small deal tops, whether in one piece or jointed up, these may be merely battened under, as indicated at Fig. 63, the legs being sometimes tapped into the battens with a cross rail underframing. The battens are cut back to about 2 ins. from edge of top if this is to be fastened down to a squared leg and rail framing.

Cabinet Construction

The ordinary small table top, with a centre leg and splayed toes, is battened across as Fig. 64, and the support tapped into this. If the parts do not screw up

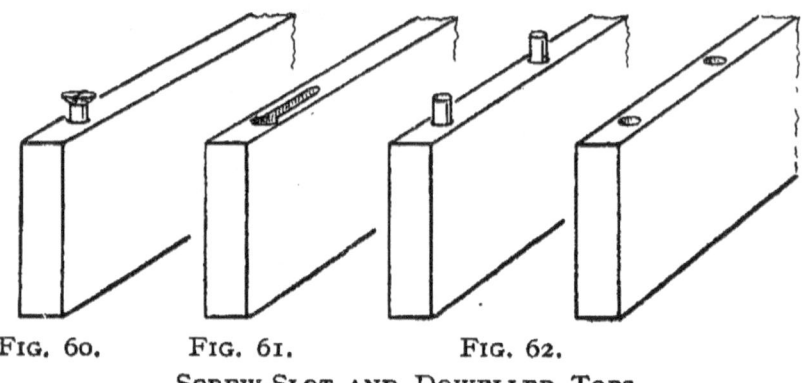

Fig. 60.   Fig. 61.   Fig. 62.
Screw-Slot and Dowelled Tops.

tightly this can be remedied by wrapping a piece of linen round the thread of the top or screwed portion.

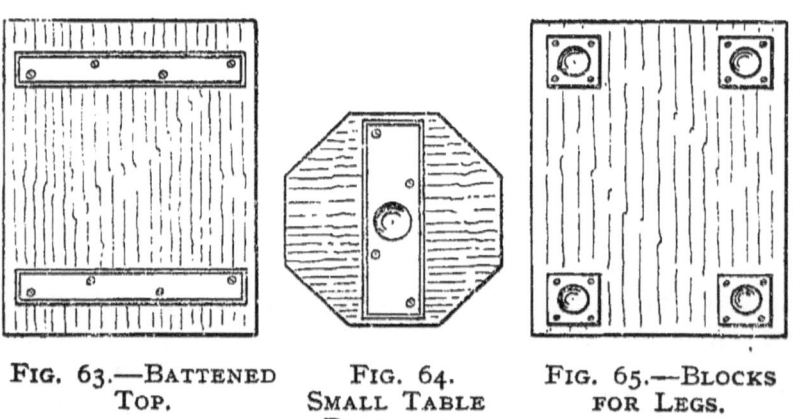

Fig. 63.—Battened Top.   Fig. 64. Small Table Battened.   Fig. 65.—Blocks for Legs.

In some cases the top of a light table can be supported on legs glued into blocks fitted under, as Fig. 65.

A small circular top can have a lining under, as Fig. 66, glued or screwed to it to receive the centre leg. If glued,

Cabinet and Table Tops

the grain of the lining piece—1¼ ins. or so thick—should run in same direction as that of the top.

Lined Top.—Generally a top such as that of a kitchen table is lined up as a stiffening as at Fig. 67; the lining slips across the ends, being cut across the grain so that, if any more shrinkage in the wood takes place, all goes together.

Dovetail Housing.—In instances where a table or cabinet top is connected to an upright side instead of legs, as indicated in Figs. 68 and 70, these may be jointed by dovetail housing, stopped back ½ in. from front (Fig. 69), or by a diminishing dovetail. Alternatively, the parts may be dowelled or grooved and dowelled together, but jointing is the better joint.

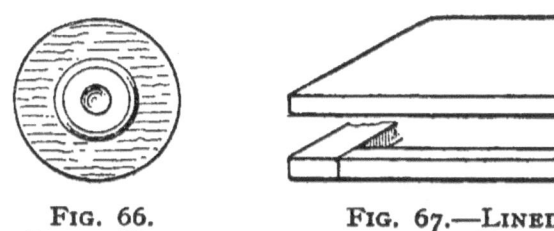

Fig. 66. Lined Top.

Fig. 67.—Lined Kitchen Table.

FIXING TABLE AND CABINET TOPS.

Pocket Screwing.—Usually a top is secured to its underframing by screwing through thumb slots, as Fig. 71, and the legs may have a stub-tenon cut on the upper end as an extra hold.

Glue blocking, however, is the most favoured method by some, as at Fig. 72, but the blocks should be of sound stuff, and fit well into the angles. The grain of the blocks should agree with that of the parts they are to stiffen.

Wood buttoning (Fig. 90A) ranks as a better finish, whilst in some cases metal shrinkage plates are used instead.

Cabinet Construction

Dowelled Framing.—In the making of a small writing table top (Fig. 73), which has to be leather-lined, the recess for the leather to be in is obtained by finishing the centre of the table a bare $\frac{1}{16}$ in. less in thickness than the clamping, the latter being dowelled and cut with the grain in the same direction.

Inlaid Tops.—In the matter of inlaid tops the groove to receive the stringing (Fig. 74) can be routed out. Care must be taken to obtain an even depth and clean corners, and the width of the cutter must, of course, be exact to that of the stringing.

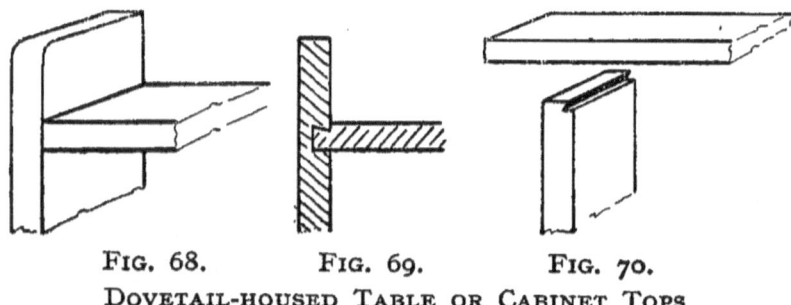

Fig. 68.   Fig. 69.   Fig. 70.
Dovetail-housed Table or Cabinet Tops.

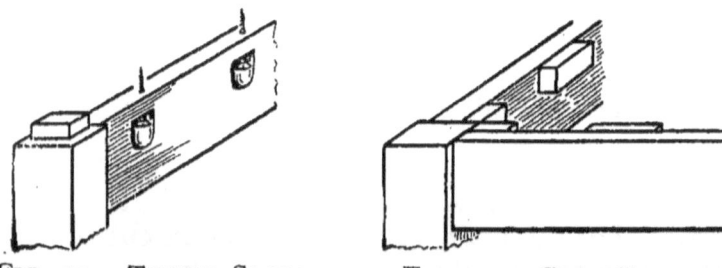

Fig. 71.—Thumb Slots.   Fig. 72.—Glue-Blocking.

The end of an ordinary hammer is generally used to press the stringing into place, the lengths being lightly touched with glue previous to insertion. For satinwood or chequered banding the same applies if set in an inch or so from outer edge of top. If the banding is to be up to edge of top (as Fig. 75) a carefully cut rebate to the

Cabinet and Table Tops

required depth will be necessary to avoid the extra trouble of cleaning up afterwards.

Moulded Edges to the top often appear to present difficulties which fade away surprisingly with a careful attempt to overcome them.

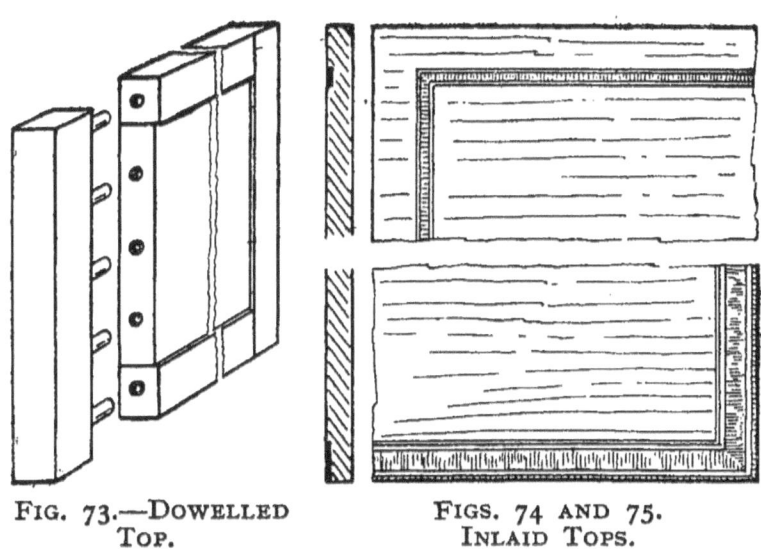

FIG. 73.—DOWELLED TOP.

FIGS. 74 AND 75. INLAID TOPS.

Fig. 76 shows an edge finished with four beads which means three quirks with the scratch; or a quickly-made tool that will do the work nicely is to insert a suitable screw into a spare block something after the manner indicated in Fig. 60, using the screw head as a cutter and the block as a fence. A turn of the screw will easily adjust the head to the right position.

Figs 77 and 78 need no reference. Fig. 79 shows a thumb mould, which can be obtained by rebating and bevelling as Fig. 83, afterwards finishing by scraper or glasspaper on a block hollowed to the shape required.

Similarly, Fig. 80 is arrived at as shown progressively at Figs. 85, 86, 87 and 88. Fig. 81 can be obtained by ploughing and bevelling away the waste as dotted in

Cabinet Construction

Fig. 84, and then finishing with suitable hollow and round planes. Previous to starting, the shape of the members should be carefully marked on each end as a

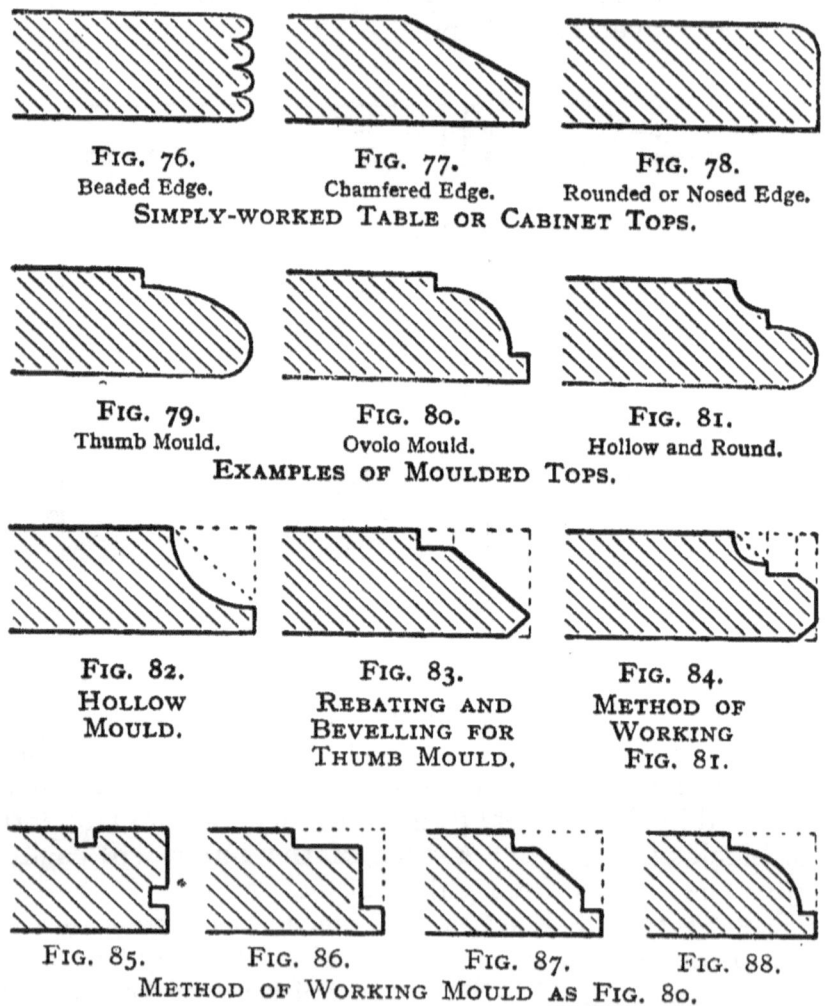

FIG. 76. Beaded Edge. FIG. 77. Chamfered Edge. FIG. 78. Rounded or Nosed Edge.
SIMPLY-WORKED TABLE OR CABINET TOPS.

FIG. 79. Thumb Mould. FIG. 80. Ovolo Mould. FIG. 81. Hollow and Round.
EXAMPLES OF MOULDED TOPS.

FIG. 82. HOLLOW MOULD. FIG. 83. REBATING AND BEVELLING FOR THUMB MOULD. FIG. 84. METHOD OF WORKING FIG. 81.

FIG. 85. FIG. 86. FIG. 87. FIG. 88.
METHOD OF WORKING MOULD AS FIG. 80.

guide in the working. Fig. 82 shows a hollow, the method of working which will be apparent from the dotted lines shown.

TABLE AND CHAIR LEGS

WHEN considering the detail of a table that is about to be made, it soon becomes apparent that the character and finish of the legs will play a noticeable part in the effect. From the plain square kitchen table leg in deal to the elaborately carved, reeded, fluted, or inlaid hardwood leg is a far cry; yet, if the little points of careful finish are studied and carried out, satisfaction ensues as much with the one grade as the other.

Wood.—In selecting wood for legs, sound and well-seasoned stuff only, free from shakes and knots and straight in the grain, should be secured. Where something tougher than deal is required, birch is a very good substitute for the legs in combination with a basswood table top. Birch takes the stain in imitation of hardwoods and replaces walnut or mahogany very well—these latter being considered in a class apart.

Square Legs.— For an ordinary square kitchen table leg as Fig. 89A, the stuff may size up $2\frac{1}{2}$ ins. by $2\frac{1}{2}$ ins. or 3 ins. by 3 ins. according to dimensions of table. Each leg should have the best sides marked for outside and be shot clean and true, each face being planed up perfectly level and with the corners sharp.

Taper Legs.—If a tapered leg is required as Fig. 89B the taper will start about 7 ins. below the top, 3-in. legs being diminished to about $2\frac{1}{4}$ ins. and a $2\frac{1}{2}$-in. leg to about 2 ins. at ground. In preparing the stuff, attention must be given to the 7-in. block into which the rails are framed, to ensure that each side is alike parallel, straight and square. The top must be smoothly faced up and the taper taken off from the two inner sides. A little previous practice is handy here as the tendency will be to make the taper unequal, and in any case it is advisable to pencil in the line of finish as a guide for the planing.

Cabinet Construction

Leg Tapered on all Sides (Fig. 89c).—In some cases, such as for a lamp or plant-stand, where the legs splay out, these are tapered on all four sides. In preparing the legs it is best to mark the lines of taper of opposite faces of the length to be worked, and, after reducing these, to mark the lines for the remaining two faces to be planed; *i.e.*, parallel pairs of faces to be

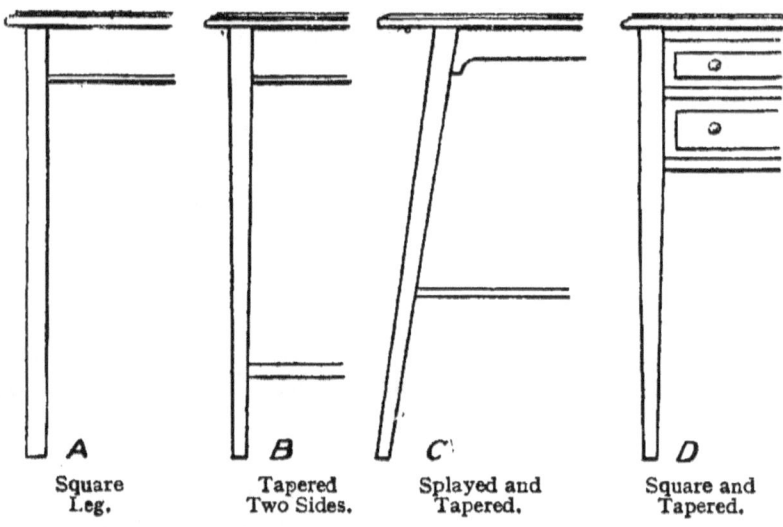

FIG. 89.—TYPES OF TABLE LEGS.
A Square Leg. B Tapered Two Sides. C Splayed and Tapered. D Square and Tapered.

planed up at a time. A leg such as in a dressing-table, generally in hardwood, has the upper portion of leg square for from 6 ins. to 15 ins. and the remainder tapered on all four sides as Fig. 89D, but the procedure is similar to c, starting from a pencilled line marked round the four sides of leg.

Turned Legs.—Turned legs often present difficulties to the amateur who does not happen to possess a lathe, and it may be said that a good selection of suitable legs is obtainable at a moderate price from timber merchants who cater for miscellaneous turnery. The

Table and Chair Legs

legs may be had as plain, turned, reeded, carved and reeded, fluted and partially or all carved, and in mahogany, oak, walnut or birch. Cabriole, tapered and Jacobean twisted legs are also obtainable.

Setting out Legs for Kitchen Table.—Taking the stuff for legs in hand, it is simplest and best to mass the set together and mark all at one time, keeping the best sides outside, as they will show in the finished table. The line at *a*, Fig. 90B, indicates a portion for cutting off as waste. From this line the line *b* is 2 inches, and

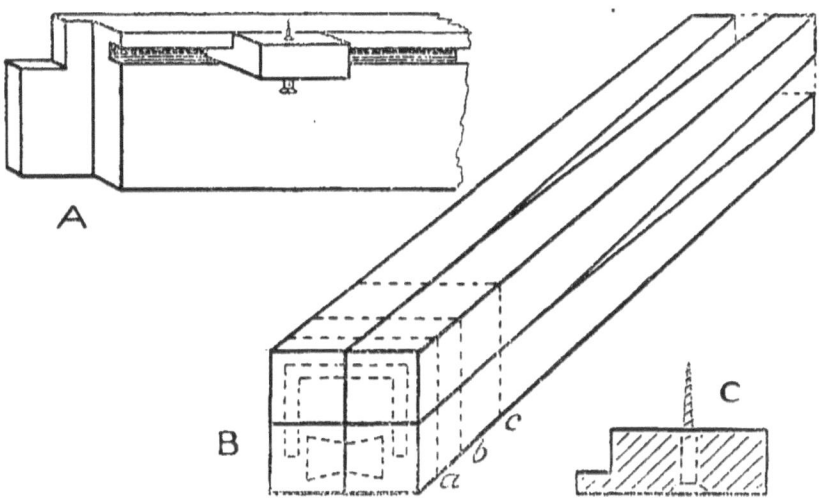

FIG. 90A.—HAUNCHED AND TENONED RAIL, WITH BUTTON.
FIG. 90B.—SETTING OUT FOUR LEGS FOR TENONS AND TAPER.
FIG. 90C.—ENLARGED SECTION OF BUTTON.

beyond this the line *c* is 4 inches, which will mark the widths for haunching and tenon respectively. Before taking the legs apart it is also advisable to mark the positions of mortises on each leg; and, if a drawer is to be fitted to one end, the positions of the dovetails on rails which connect the legs at the drawer end should also be marked. The mortise can be about ½ in. thick, and set in about its own thickness from face of leg; in

Cabinet Construction

gauging for joints the lines should be continued to the tops of legs to mark for the haunchings.

If the legs are to be tapered they can also at same time be squared and quickly marked for the planing. The preliminary identification of legs in this way saves considerable needless comparison of the lengths as the work proceeds.

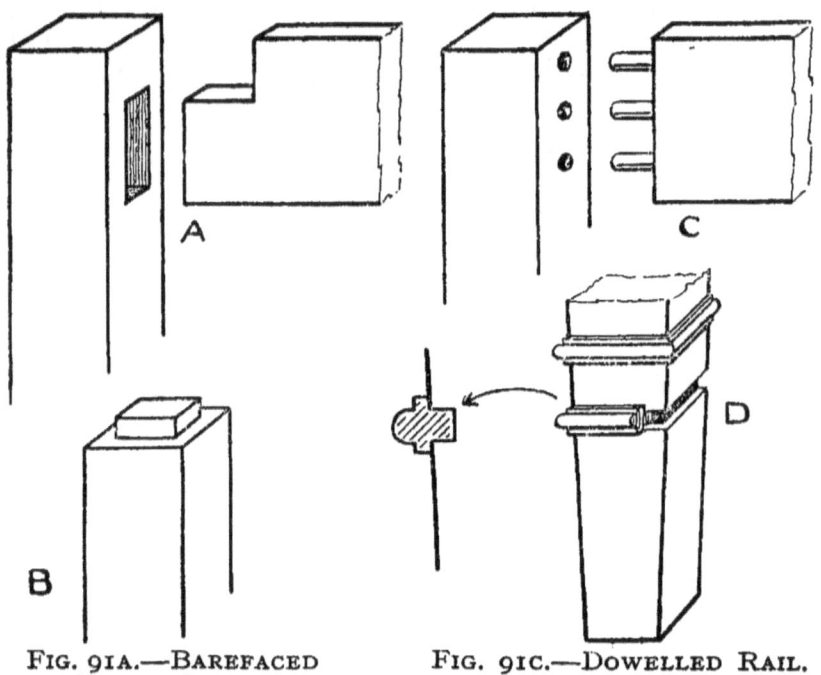

Fig. 91A.—Barefaced Tenon Joint.
Fig. 91B.—Stub-Tenon.
Fig. 91C.—Dowelled Rail.
Fig. 91D.—Necking on Leg.

Cutting Mortises.—The mortises in legs are cut a sufficient depth below the top of the stuff to avoid splitting with the mortising chisel when getting out the waste. It will, however, be found simpler to start the mortises by boring holes between the gauged lines with a brace and suitable twist bit, afterwards carefully chiselling out the waste. The mortises for sides and one end rails should be cut through till they meet, the

Table and Chair Legs

joint being a barefaced tenon as Fig. 91A, or with a bevelled or a square haunching as Fig. 90A. In addition to mortising, the legs are also finished with a stub-tenon as Fig. 91B to enter the table top which is correspondingly mortised to receive same.

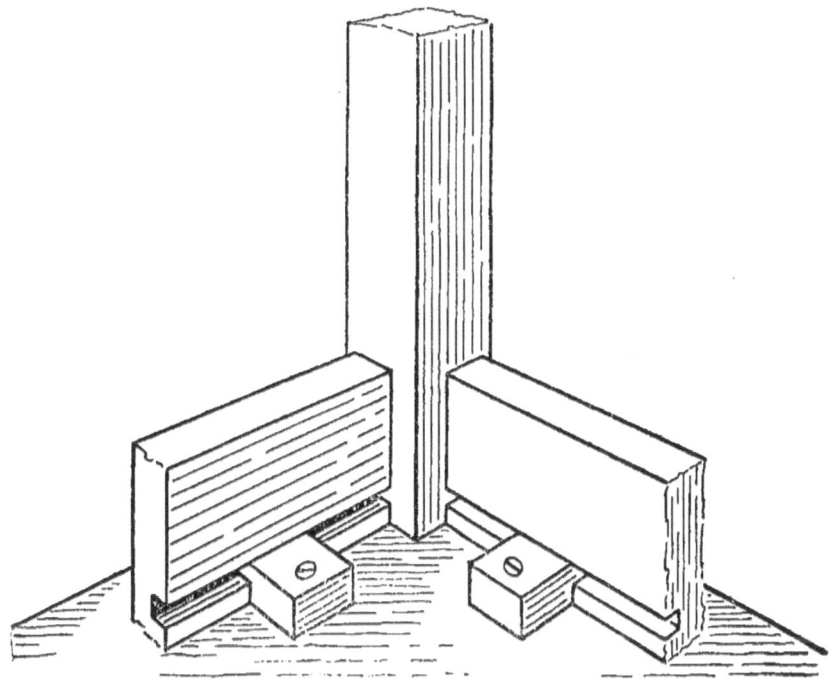

Fig. 92.—View of Buttoned Table Top (Table Reversed).

Dowelling. — The rails of small tables are often dowelled (Fig. 91C), three or more dowels being used according to width of rail; and, if the thickness of rail will permit, the dowels may be zig-zagged—*i.e.*, not exactly in line one under another. The legs and rails of a chair may be jointed in this way. In the case of a kitchen chair the legs are usually finished with a dowel at top which enters the chair seat at an angle so that all legs splay out and are stiffened by underframing.

Cabinet Construction

Beech dowels can be bought cheaply, or hardwood dowels may be made by passing through the dowel plate. The stuff must be carefully planed up before marking and boring the holes, the latter being slightly countersunk with a rosebit, after which the dowels can be glued in.

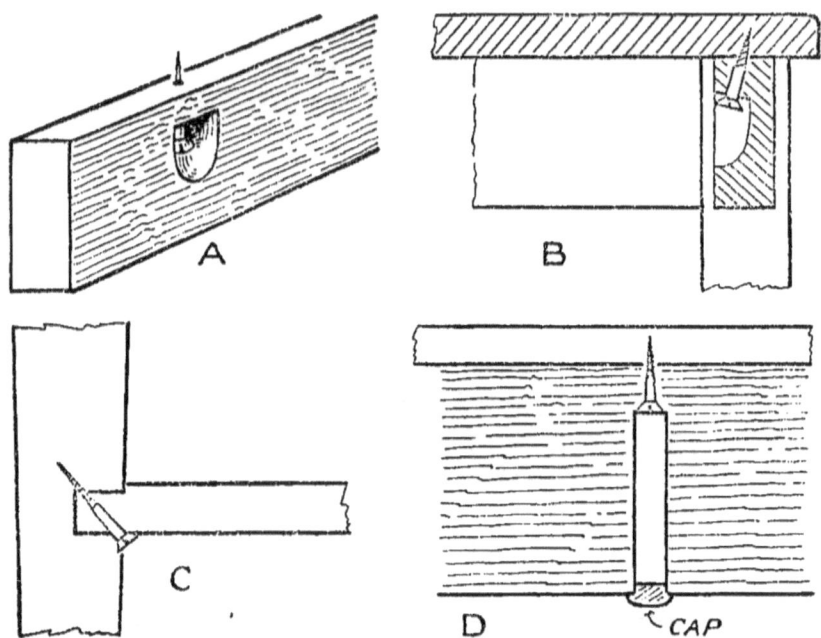

FIGS. 93.—A, B, AND D, METHODS OF POCKET SCREWING. C, SCREWING ASLANT FOR RAIL.

Buttoned Top.—When legs and rails are together the table top is held with hardwood buttons. A view of this buttoning method is given at Fig. 92, looking from under side of table; the detail of rail with button in position is sketched at Fig. 90A, and section of button at Fig. 90C. The rail is grooved $\frac{1}{4}$ in. or $\frac{3}{8}$ in. deep at about $\frac{3}{8}$ in. or $\frac{1}{2}$ in. below top edge to receive the button (size for the buttons is about 2 ins. by 2 ins.), and the position of groove will give thickness of stuff required. In some

Table and Chair Legs

cases metal shrinkage plates are used under a table top these being made with a lengthened hole to allow for any move in the wood owing to atmospheric conditions.

Pocket Screwing.—The legs and framing are often connected by pocket screwing, of which there are two methods. That shown in perspective at Fig. 93A and in section with top at Fig. 93B has the hole for screw bored aslant through the rail to inner side and the thumb

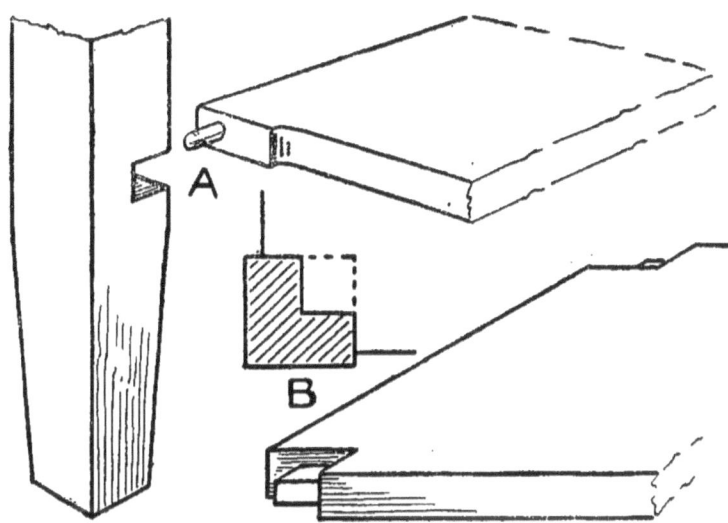

FIG. 94A.—SHELF DOWELLED TO LEG.
FIG. 94B.—SHELF NOTCHED AND LEDGED TO LEG.

notch gouged out for entry of screw head and access for the screwdriver. The method at Fig. 93D has the screw entered at lower edge of rail. For this purpose a hole of suitable diameter (say $\frac{1}{2}$ in.) is bored with brace and bit, to required depth, and the shank hole for screw then bored with gimlet. The entry to hole can be filled in with wax or a small turned button or cap.

Legs and Dovetailed Rails.—Legs are often jointed up by mortise and tenon and dovetailing in combination;

Cabinet Construction

Fig. 95 gives a sketch of this, one rail being entered with a tenon and bevelled haunching and one rail by dovetailing, pocket screwing fixing for top being also indicated. Fig. 96 shows a method of dovetailing the rails into the leg where the drawer is required, the second or bearer rail being entered with a pair of tenons. In passing it may be added that, where a drawer is fitted at

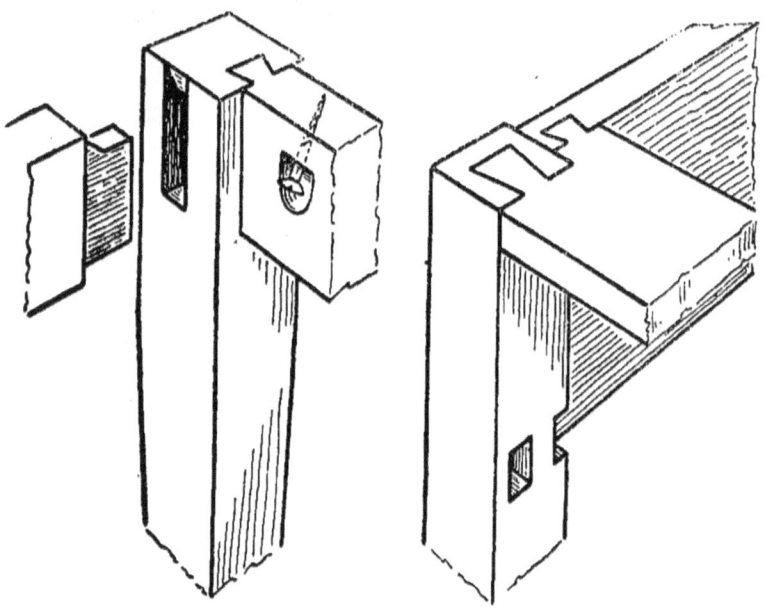

FIG. 95.—SHOWING ONE RAIL TENONED, THE OTHER DOVETAILED.

FIG. 96.—DOVETAILING DRAWER RAILS TO POST AND END.

each end of table, a stretcher rail is generally dovetailed into top of side rails midway, and this may be made to act as a stop for the drawers.

Neckings.—The small mouldings (often astragal in section) seen at times on both upper and lower portions of square legs as Fig. 91D may be ⅜ in. in width or larger, and may be simply mitred round leg and carefully panel-pinned on. It is better, however, to groove them in slightly and mitre up the angles neatly, which will tend

Table and Chair Legs

to prevent them either parting at the angle or being knocked askew (or off) in course of wear. The grooves should be squared carefully and an eye kept on the cutting so that there is no risk of finishing up out of line.

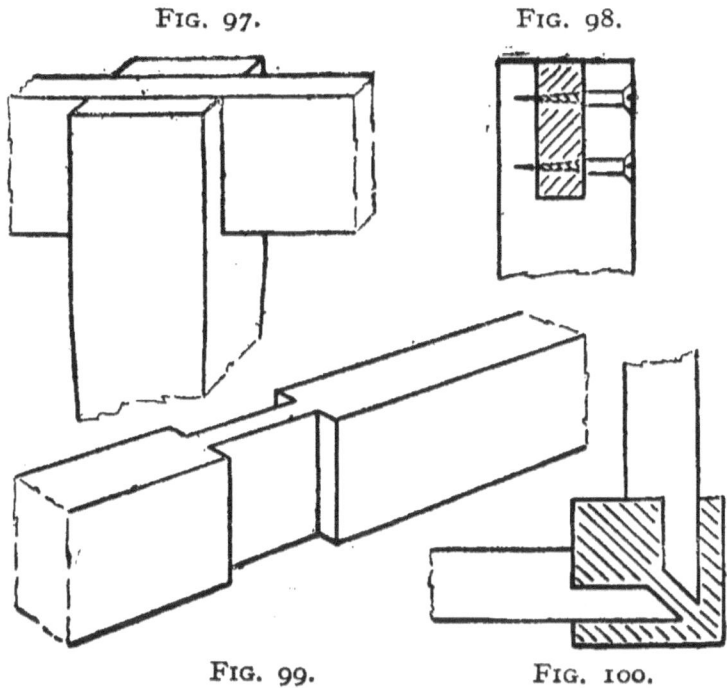

FIG. 97. FIG. 98.

FIG. 99. FIG. 100.

FIGS.—97, 98, AND 99.—BRIDLE JOINTED LEG.
FIG. 100.—SECTION OF RAILS AND LEG AT CORNER.

Underframing.—When fitting an underframing to a table to stiffen the legs the simplest method is the H pattern; *i.e.,* two rails from front to back and one in centre (across) connecting them. The rails can be stub-tenoned into legs and be further held by a fine screw carefully entered up from underside through tenon into leg as at Fig. 93C. The cross rail in centre may be of same thickness and tenoned into the other two, or a slat ¾ in. thick and 2 ins. wide may be screwed up from under side to the rails. If a narrow shelf is

Cabinet Construction

required this slat can be 4 ins. wide. Alternatively, the underframing may be X pattern, being halved together where it crosses and fitted with screw plates inserted in the corners of the legs.

Fitting Shelves to Legs.—In fitting a shelf to the lower portion of a leg the latter will require notching for the entry of the shelf, which is usually dowelled or ledged in addition. If dowelled a shelf may be entered as at Fig. 94A, the notching being sufficiently deep to afford a bearing, but not so deep as to weaken the leg. The centre of the notching is then bored for the dowel which may stop just short of going through, the joint being finally glued up. This method can be used whether the legs are square with the front of the table or on the cant.

With the legs and undershelf square, the two may be jointed as at Fig. 94B, the notching being wide enough to receive a stout ledge or tongue to which the corner of the shelf is reduced, and which may be square as shown or triangular shaped. A screw can be entered upwards from underside through tongue into leg. If the shelf is slight it can be entered to its full thickness and screwed. Occasionally a dowel is fitted instead of the ledging, and at other times the shelf obtains a strengthened bearing by the fitting of steel-plates under the corners. These have a screw at one end to enter the leg; the flat or plate portion has two countersunk holes for shallow screwing into underside of shelf. In light work a screw eye may be entered into leg instead of the plate and screwed with advantage.

Portable Legs.—At times table legs are made portable; *i.e.*, they are made to screw in and out—an arrangement that is very convenient where ample clearance in the house is not available. In some cases iron taps or screws are used for attachment of leg shafts to block, the block being holed and the legs screwed. Hardwood taps are very satisfactory in ordinary wear, a

Table and Chair Legs

piece of linen being wound round the thread of the screw before insertion into block.

Bridle-jointed Legs.—The legs of a table are sometimes bridle-jointed to the framing. This occurs when the framing under top is circular or octagonal, or when it is desired to put a leg in the centre of a rail. If the leg is considerably stouter than the framing it can be entered as Figs. 97 and 98 and screwed from inside. Generally, however, the framing is cut as Fig. 99, which is better, as it offers a stiffening hold apart from pinning or screwing. A shaped framing may be in parts and dovetailed each end into legs.

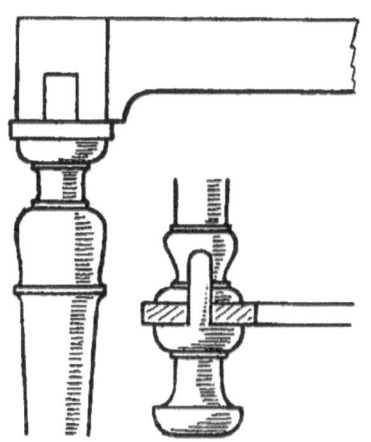

FIG. 101.—DOWELLING TURNED LEGS.

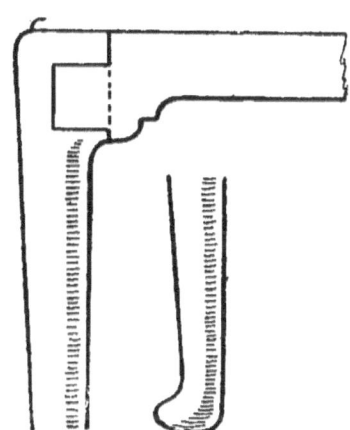

FIG. 102.—FITTING CABRIOLE LEG.

Legs in Antique Style.—Many repeats of antique furniture are made at the present time, and legs of the William and Mary or Jacobean type are frequently fitted with (in many cases) a charmingly quaint effect. As some of these legs are in the nature of their design turned up to somewhat frail and risky dimensions, a shaped underframing usually goes with them as a stiffening. Such legs would be dowelled to the upper block of table framing. The toe portion below the underframing, separately turned, terminates in a dowel which enters the lower part of the main turning above, passing through and pinning the underframing thickness as at Fig. 101. The Queen Anne type of cabriole leg, with toe or club foot, can be turned or pared down from the straight, the finish of the taper being about 2 ins. from the ground to allow for rounding away to the toe. The leg can be fitted as Fig. 102.

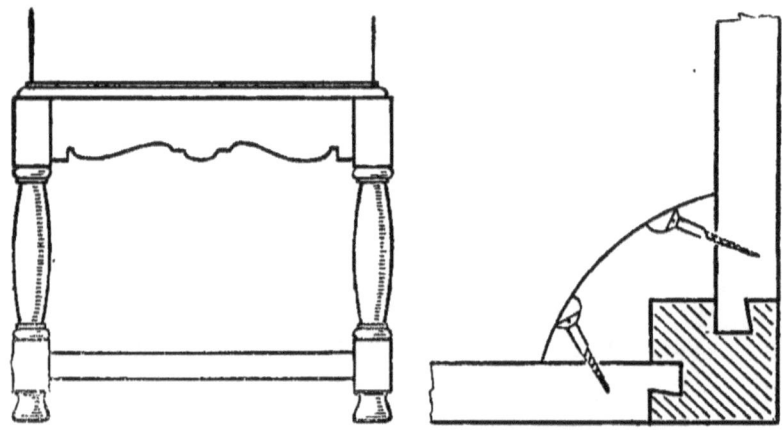

FIG. 103.—LOWER FRAMING FOR CHEST OR CUPBOARD.

In antique style a cupboard wardrobe, dressing-table, bureau, etc., may be mounted upon a base or low table framing, rails and legs finishing flush all round, after the sketch at Fig. 103. Such parts can be assembled in the manner indicated, the rails being dovetailed into leg and the legs and rails braced in the inside angles.

CABRIOLE LEGS.

Most legs of the cabriole type have a square at the top, as at A, Fig. 104, the rails being tenoned into this, as in the side view, B. The tenons should have shoulders on both sides, and should almost meet in the thickness of the square; see section at C. In certain types of

Table and Chair Legs

cabriole legs, however (see D), there is no top square, and, to save the necessity of using very thick stuff for the rails, the mortises can be set askew, as at E. The surplus wood is planed off after the whole has been put together. It is obvious that the jointing faces at the top of the leg must be vertical if the legs are to be square. This is illustrated by the upright dotted lines in E.

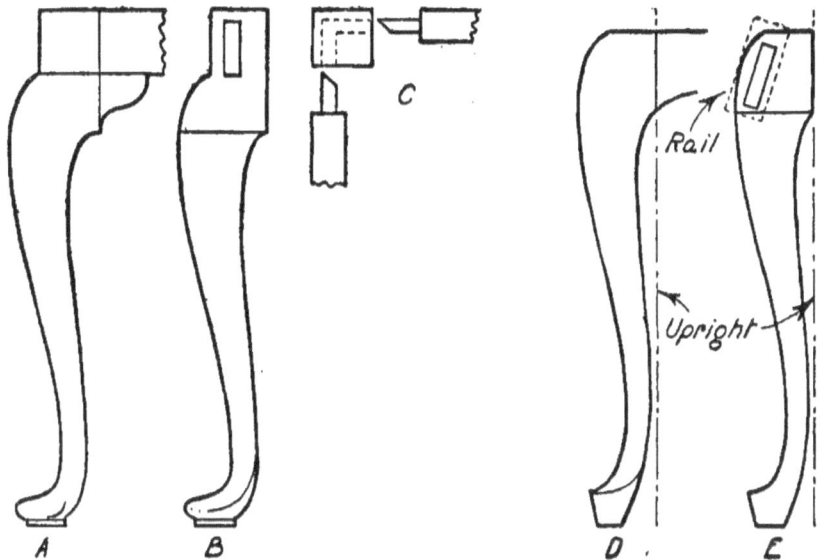

Fig. 104.—Method of Jointing Rails to Cabriole Legs.

The wood selected for the making of cabriole legs should be as straight and regular in grain as possible, free from shakes, knots, or other imperfections, well seasoned, and dry. Stuff for use may be 3 ins. by 3 ins., or as required. Fig. 105 indicates a method of setting out the cabriole shape on the lengths of stuff provided for the purpose. In this diagram the portions for sawing away are marked on the square, a block being allotted to the toe. The latter may either be turned to the extent indicated for a plain toe, or carved up to shape

Cabinet Construction

for finishing to claw and ball detail. When sawn away square to the rough shape, a result similar to Fig. 106 will be obtained. The leg will then require trimming

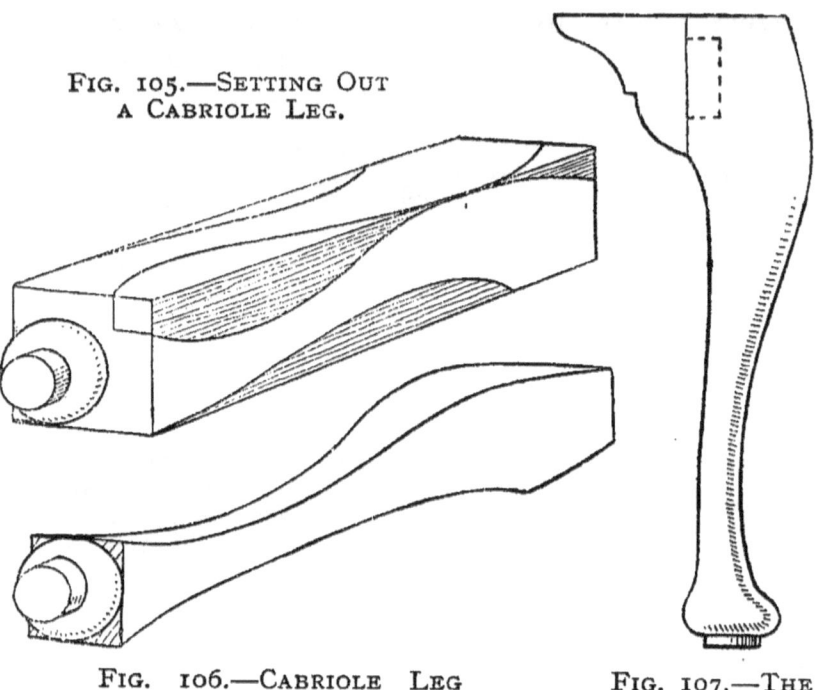

Fig. 105.—Setting Out a Cabriole Leg.

Fig. 106.—Cabriole Leg Roughly Sawn to Shape.

Fig. 107.—The Leg Finished.

with spokeshave and rasp to the curve, all inequalities being pared down with the chisel and finished with glasspaper. Fig. 107 indicates the finished leg at this stage.

CABINET DOORS

ON the subject of the construction of a cabinet door a few points of detail will prove serviceable to the beginner for reference as he proceeds with his work; and, in the first place, stress may be laid upon the desirability of working to a full size set out in order to avoid the little slips and discrepancies that will often creep in even when one is watchful.

Wood.—Oak, walnut, and mahogany are, of course, the prime woods to use, and the timber should be carefully selected as being well seasoned and free from shakes, knots, or other faults. Birch, basswood and satin walnut, in the second grade, will take stain well. Pitch pine is figured and useful for heavier work. Maple and sycamore are not, at present, much in vogue, and the same may be said of ash. It is a good plan, if a friendly cabinet-maker is available, to procure the necessary wood from him, as he will most likely have on hand just the class of stuff required.

Sizes.—For a small door about 16 ins. by 12 ins. stuff of $\frac{3}{4}$-in. thickness (net) may be used; but, as an extra provision against winding, it is advisable to employ for all larger dimensioned doors stuff to hold up $\frac{7}{8}$-in. net. Stiles and rails generally can be from $1\frac{1}{2}$ ins. to $2\frac{1}{4}$ ins. wide, the former for a small plain frame and the latter for a larger frame, with $\frac{1}{4}$ in. or $\frac{3}{8}$ in. allowed for moulding out of the solid. The length of rails should be the full finished width of the doors to allow for tenons. The tenons are sometimes given an extra length beyond this to allow for wedges, but as these can be cut from the haunches the worker can please himself. Using hardwood, a cabinet-maker allows $\frac{1}{4}$ in. or so waste in length on the stiles above the finished height of the door when

Cabinet Construction

cutting the mortises, but the less practised worker may apportion a little more so that he may run less risk of splitting his wood by working so near the ends.

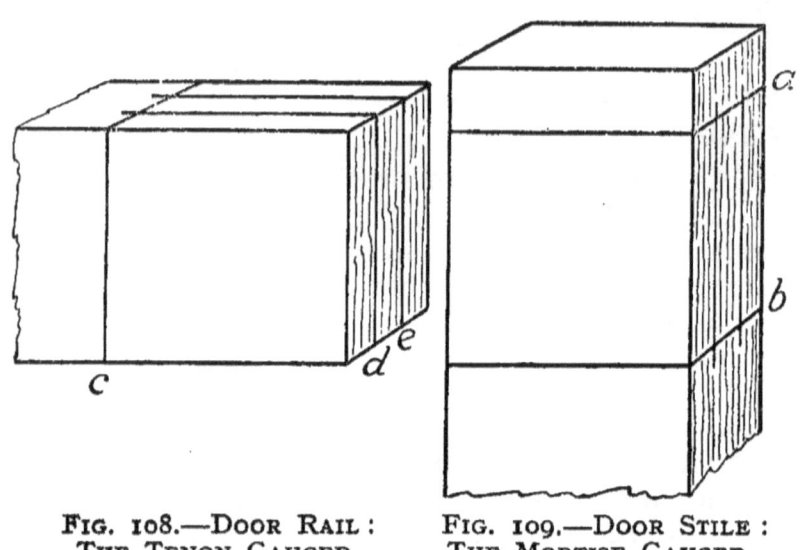

FIG. 108.—DOOR RAIL: THE TENON GAUGED.

FIG. 109.—DOOR STILE: THE MORTISE GAUGED.

SETTING OUT AND CUTTING.

Stiles.—Having cut the respective lengths for stiles and rails, these should be examined and the best side of the wood planed up straight and true. The use of a straight-edge over the face will reveal any tendency to twist, and, if any, this should be carefully planed out. The best edge of each piece can next receive attention, great care being taken to plane them up true and perfectly at right angles with the face, testing continually with the square before reducing the surface. As these edges form the ruling base of all squared and gauged lines, failure to get them true will naturally result in the work being out of square. The prepared face and edge should then be marked with the usual pencilled

Cabinet Doors

hook so that each is known at sight, which will save time in course of handling.

Cutting Mortises.—In jointing the door, mortises are cut in the stiles and tenons on the rails; and, proceeding to set out the mortises, the stile (Fig. 109) should have squared across it (in pencil) on the face side two lines (the width of the stile apart—1½ ins. or 2¼ ins. as the case may be). The lines, in continuation, are then squared across the two edges to give the width and length of the tenon. A mortise gauge, set to about a third of the thickness of the stuff in use, can then be worked along the face, the resulting cuts across the lines *a, b,* giving the net width of mortise. Be careful, of course, to allow for the set-in of mortise.

In making the mortise, these lines must serve rigidly as boundaries of the cuts, and no wood must be removed beyond them. A chisel may be used for the purpose; but, as the tenons are to go right through, it will be preferable to bore with brace and twist bit from each edge of the stile towards the centre of the mortise, thus removing a good portion of the waste with a lesser chance of getting out of truth. A suitable chisel is used afterwards for cleaning up. To allow for wedging, the mortise should be made a cut wider at the outside, *i.e.*, sloping outward $\frac{1}{16}$ in. or so, as Fig. 110, starting midway of the length. When the tenons are finally home, the wedges are tapped in and the waste cut off.

An alternative method of wedging is shown at Fig. 111, a couple of cuts being made in the tenon and wedges inserted, which has a neat appearance. The wedges should be edged with the chisel before entry, as indicated in the enlarged sketch, Fig. 112. At times the wedges are omitted and the outside edge of tenon where it comes through is merely spread by careful tapping.

Rails.—Taking the rails (Fig. 108) the tenons can next be set out. Start on the face side by squaring the

Cabinet Construction

line *c* across it with the striking knife or marking awl. Continue the same line over the face edge, and prolong across the reverse side which will give the length of tenons. With the mortise gauge as previously set, and working from the face side, cut the boundaries of the tenons on both thicknesses and ends, the intersection of lines giving the thickness of tenon.

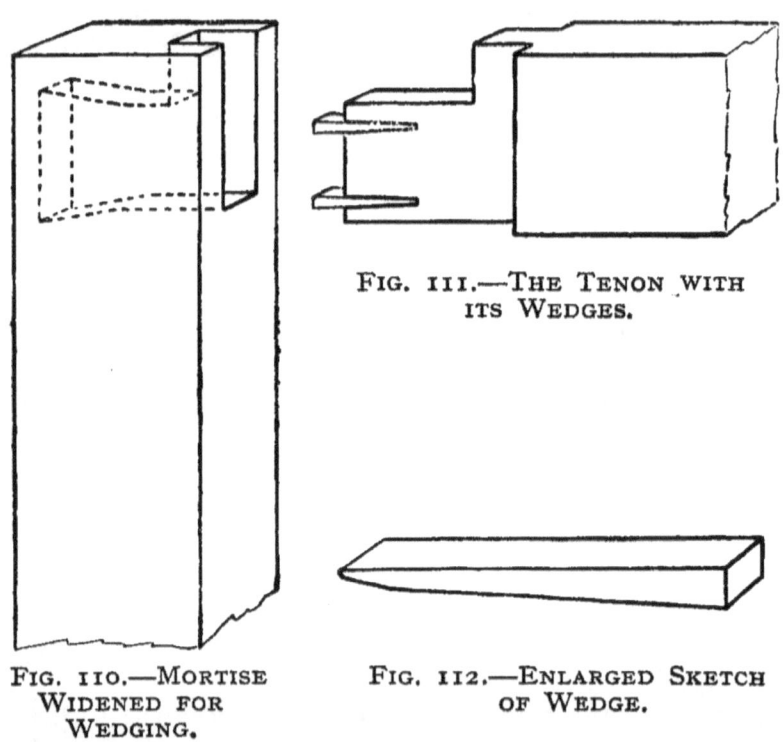

FIG. 111.—THE TENON WITH ITS WEDGES.

FIG. 110.—MORTISE WIDENED FOR WEDGING.

FIG. 112.—ENLARGED SKETCH OF WEDGE.

Cutting Tenons.—Proceeding to cut the tenon, the rail should be firmly held in the vice, end up, and, with the tenon saw, cut down *outside* the lines *d*, *e*. The saw kerf must come out of the waste wood and leave the tenon to the full width cut in by the striking knife. The cuts made with the striking knife can be widened

Cabinet Doors

out on the *waste* side by taking a V out with a chisel and will then give a fair start for the saw. The exact square cutting of the tenon will be facilitated if started diagonally from one corner down to the shoulder, then from the other corner down to the shoulder, so that both cuts cross midway, afterwards cutting with the saw horizontally to the shoulder, and finally cutting the shoulder across carefully to the squared line.

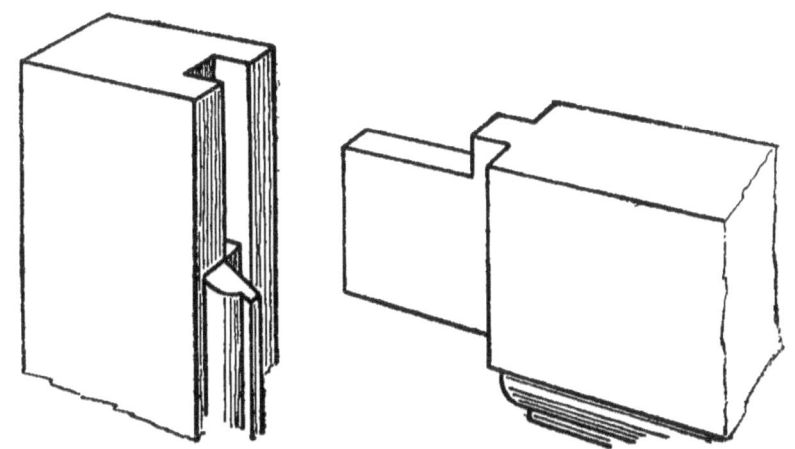

Fig. 113.—Stile and Rail: Showing Mortise, Tenon, Rebate and Moulding.

The shoulder when glued and well home, serves the purpose of keeping the tenon in position and the framing square.

The Rebate on the frame may be $\frac{5}{16}$ in., and is worked with rebate plane or fillister for the fitting of the panel. If this is to be grooved in, a suitable plough will be used, and (if desired) the grooves can be altered to a rebate by planing away one of its cheeks afterwards till flush with the bed. The groove ploughed in the stile will necessitate a square haunch of the same size on the tenon (Fig. 113), so that the portion left of the groove above the entry through of the tenon into the stile will

Cabinet Construction

be neatly filled in. Fig. 113 is slightly exaggerated to show the joint.

If a moulding is to be worked round stiles and rails out of the solid, the section chosen (say ovolo or ogee) may be $\frac{5}{16}$ in. width and will, of course, require mitreing back from the shoulder of the tenon. It can be cut in after the rebate is made, but possibly the worker would manage as well if he worked the mould before the rebate was cut.

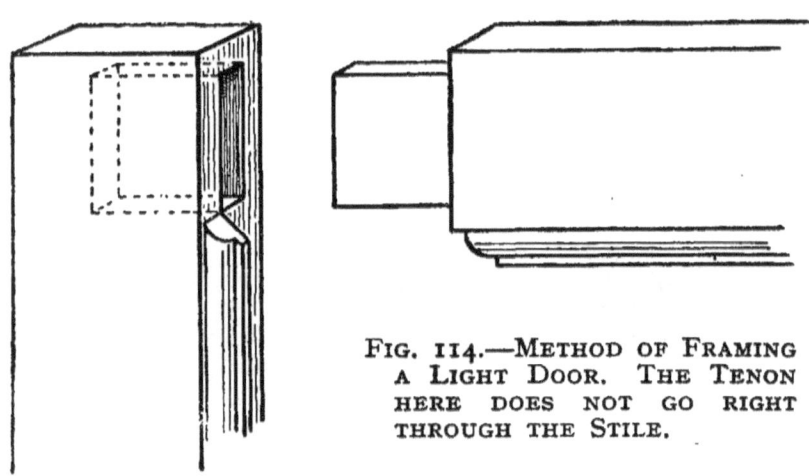

FIG. 114.—METHOD OF FRAMING A LIGHT DOOR. THE TENON HERE DOES NOT GO RIGHT THROUGH THE STILE.

Light Cabinet Doors are often put together by mortise and tenon in the manner indicated at Fig. 114. Such a joint—not going right through—can be merely glued when home, but as an extra hold can be fox-wedged. To do this a couple of saw cuts should be made in the end of each tenon for the entry of small wedges which should be of the same size. With the wedges in position the tenons are entered into the mortises and cramped up, the pressure thus brought to bear on the wedges forcing them home and expanding the tenon at the same time.

In Fig. 114 an ovolo mould, worked in the solid and

Cabinet Doors

mitred, is indicated. Here note that the depth of the moulding should equal that of the rebate as shown. It is essential when marking out the joints to make the distance between the shoulders equal to the length A, not B, in Fig. 115. Many workers go astray here, because the joints are necessarily set out before the moulding and rebate are worked, and the edges are consequently square. The distance is wrongly taken from the edges instead of from the gauge lines marking the depth of the rebate.

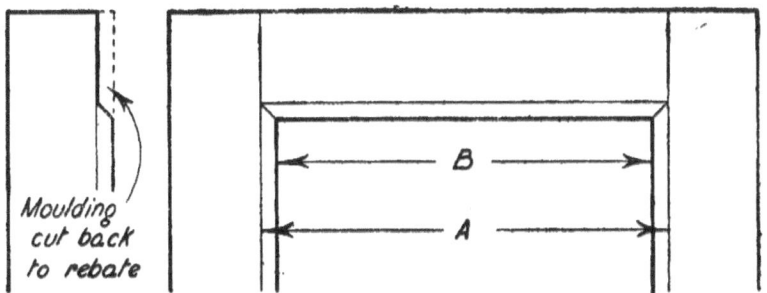

Fig. 115.—Setting Out Shoulders of Rebated and Mitred Frame.

Dowelled Framing.—In most workshops light frames are nowadays put together by dowelling, as Fig. 116. Both stiles and rails are bored to take dowels and are then rebated. In very cheap work the stiles and rails are merely butted together and dowelled, without recourse to the long and short shoulder, but the method is inferior.

Glueing and Cramping.—After glueing and fitting the frame together it should be cramped up. If the ordinary cramps are not to hand a couple of suitable cramps can be made from lengths of $2\frac{1}{2}$ ins. by 1 in. stuff, sufficiently long to project several inches beyond the stiles on either side. Near the ends a thumbscrew and nut can be entered, and a piece of wood the same thickness as the door pushed in between screw and door edge, so that it easily fills the space between them. After tightening the screws a couple of small folding wedges can be made from a rectangular piece of the same thickness, cut diagonally, and knocked in from each side between screw and block until firm.

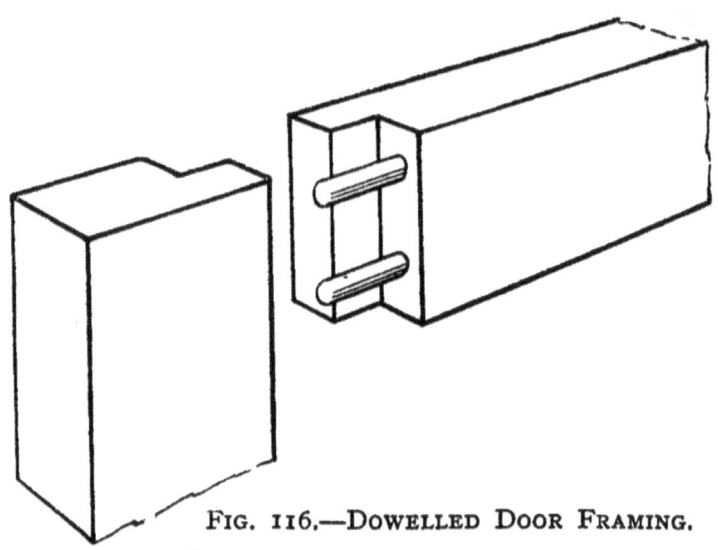

FIG. 116.—DOWELLED DOOR FRAMING.

The Panel should be cut to fit the rebate, well up in height so that it presses in easily to the full width to cover shrinkage. It may be $\frac{5}{16}$ in. thickness for a plain panel, and thicker for a bevelled one. If it be treated as a raised panel the wood should first be squared to size and the line of the raised square then marked with a cutting gauge. Next cut down with a side fillister or plough to the depth of the raising. If preferred a router or chisel can be used instead of the planes for the purpose. A trying or jack plane will take off the bevel, taking care to finish the sloping sides of the panel to the mitre line where they intersect. If in possession

Cabinet Doors

of one, a panel plane should be used for finishing, this being specially fitted with a side iron to do the work.

The panel is usually beaded into position from the back, but (at the worker's choice of mould) can be held by mouldings inserted on the face.

When completed the door can be fitted to the carcase. This may involve a few shavings off the sides by

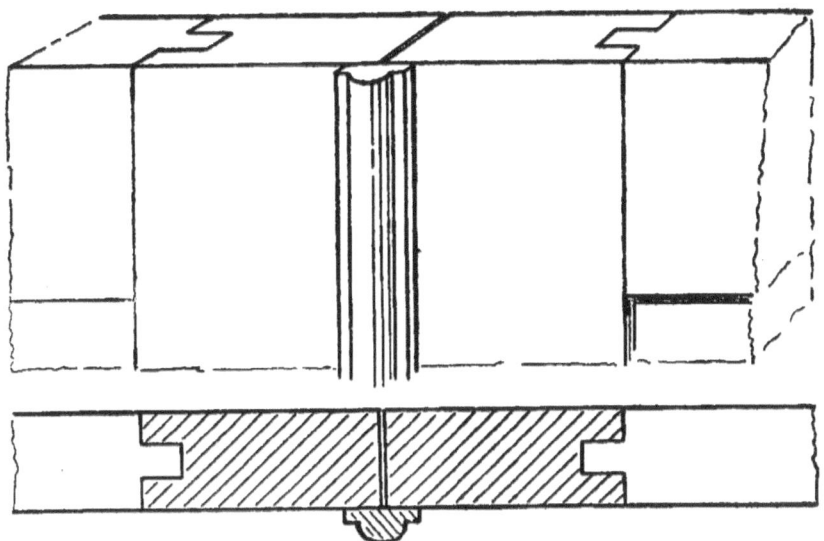

Fig. 117.—Meeting Stiles with Applied Astragal.

way of easing—a point which offers the hint that, as it is easier to take off than to put on, the door should be made on the full side. In high-class work it sometimes happens that the carcase is made to fit the door.

Astragals, etc.—In the case of the single door this may shut upon a fillet nailed to the inside of the pilaster or carcase end to form a stop. Where a pair of doors are fitted to close upon each other the meeting stiles will require a little attention. Fig. 117 shows the meeting stiles closed with an applied length of $\frac{1}{2}$-in. or $\frac{5}{8}$-in. astragal mould—to be neatly glued and pinned on to the

Cabinet Construction

right-hand door as indicated. The centre raised-bead portion can be stopped and rounded off by way of finish —the little detail being very usual on cheap work.

Fig. 118 shows how, instead of the above, the meeting stiles may close upon rebates cut in each to intersect. The face of the overlap on right-hand door is finished with a ⅛-in. quirked bead.

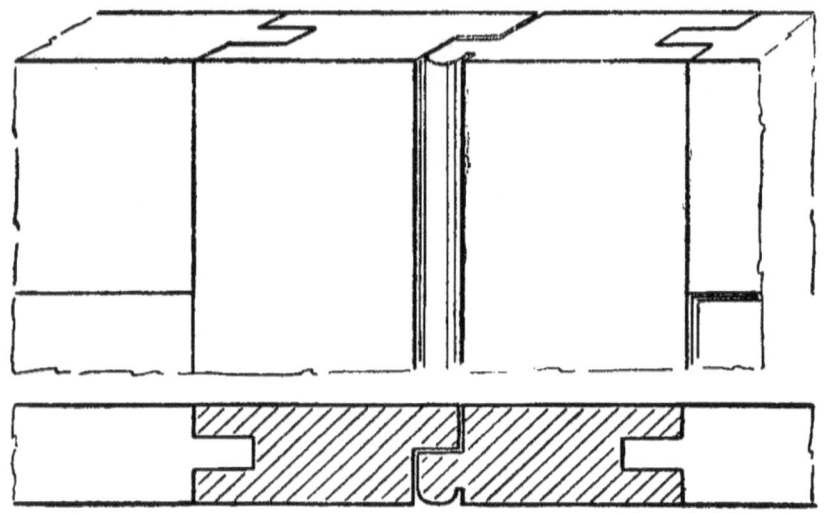

FIG. 118.—MEETING STILES REBATED, WITH BEAD FINISH.

Fig. 119 shows a rebated slip finished on face as a raised bead to overlap the left-hand door stile. Each right-hand stile can be reduced a trifle to allow the slip to be glued and pinned into position, the slip itself being worked from a length of stuff ⅝ in. thick. Instead of a bead the face edge of slip can be worked to an astragal section.

Fig. 120 indicates a slight improvement upon Fig. 119 in the way of finish. It can be effected by reducing the rebate upon the astragal slip and rebating the meeting stile of right-hand door to receive it. This is a detail used in the best work.

Cabinet Doors

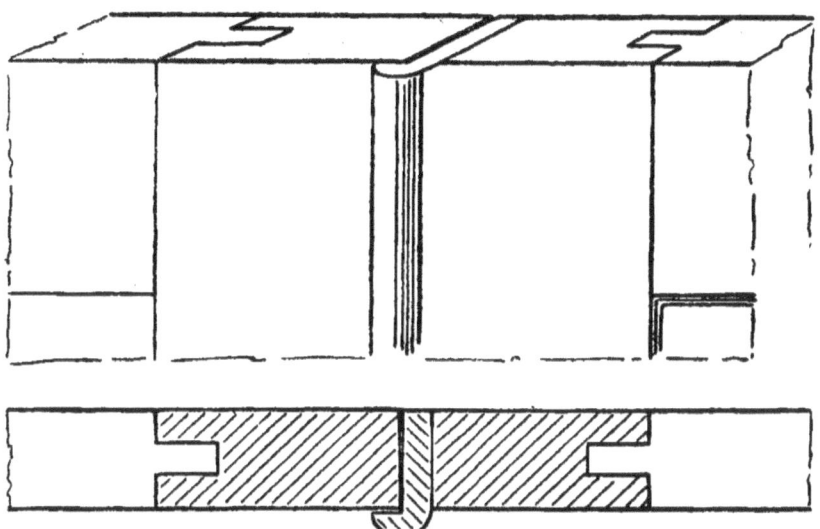

Fig. 119.—Showing Rebated Slip Fixed to Right-Hand Door.

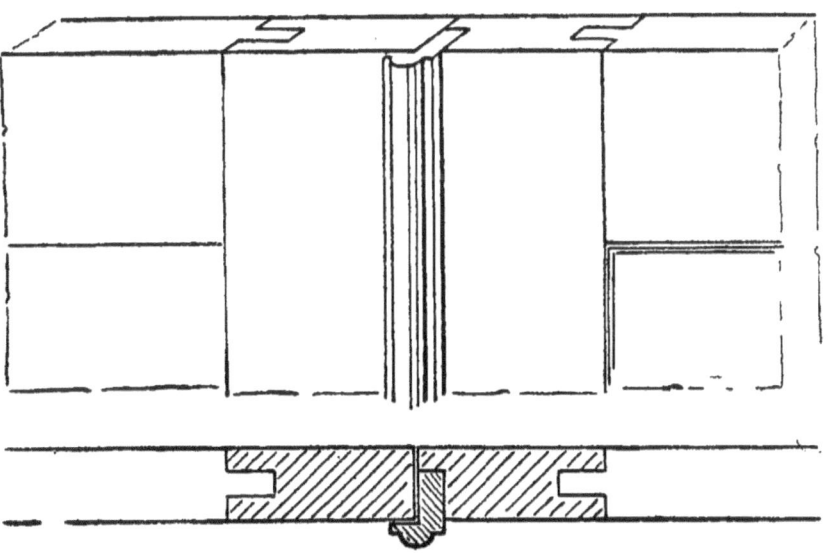

Fig. 120.—Alternative Method to Fig. 119.

Cabinet Construction

Framing.—Fig. 121 gives a section of a plain frame, rebated to receive a plain panel, which is beaded in from the back.

Fig. 122 shows a section with ovolo mould worked out of the solid and a panel bevelled at back to receive the bead.

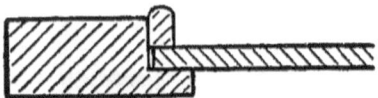

Fig. 121.—Plain Frame Rebated for Panel.

Fig. 124.—Frame with Moulding Drooped into Rebate.

Fig. 122.—Moulded Frame with Panel Bevelled at Back.

Fig. 125.—Treatment for Heavier Doors.

Fig. 123.—Frame with a Hollow and also an Applied Moulding.

Fig. 126.—Effective Treatment for Large Doors.

(*Note.*—The back beads in Figs. 124, 125 and 126 are ornamental, but also useful if shrinkage should take place.)

Fig. 123 is a simple section to work where a heavier moulded effect is desired. The solid wood is worked with a hollow, and lengths of astragal mitred round this on the face of frame, to be glued and pinned. A plain bevelled panel is shown. Fig. 124 shows an ogee mould dropped into the rebate, glued and pinned after the panel has been entered. The mould could be rebated on to the frame if preferred.

Cabinet Doors

Fig. 125 shows a heavier section rebated face of frame and with a raised panel—very effective for a larger size door.

Fig. 126 gives an alternative section with stouter raised panel which, in addition, carries a cocked bead grooved into position as indicated. This bead gives a refined effect to the panel, but calls for some care in the fitting.

Laminating.—Laminating flush doors and surfaces, or the glueing up of several thicknesses of veneer or thicker wood, has certain advantages over the use of a thickness of natural growth, inasmuch as it offers a means of avoiding shrinkage. The process was much favoured by the great cabinet makers of Georgian days, enabling them as it did to obtain unbroken effect with the figured wood used, as well as increasing the space available for flat surface treatment or decoration.

In laminating, either three, five, or seven thicknesses of wood may be glued together, the pieces being laid so that the grain of one crosses the grain of the next piece at or about right angles. The pieces must be thoroughly well glued, and then be placed in a veneering press or between two flat surfaces to be well cramped up or heavily weighted. A couple of sheet zinc squares may be found very handy for the purpose of pressure.

Where a door is mitre-clamped up, it should be veneered both sides after toothing and sizing. In curved work, such as a serpentine or ogee shape, a ground or "core" must be got out. This will require cauls to be first prepared to the exact shape required for each face. Stuff about $\frac{3}{16}$ in. thick can be used for the core, which will require to be steamed till saturated and pliable, and this be repeatedly hand screwed between the heated cauls till dry. Next clean up, tooth and veneer both sides, again using the same cauls until thoroughly dry and hard. Stuff about $\frac{3}{8}$ in. or $\frac{7}{16}$ in. can be bent to a slow curve between shaped cauls, and then be laminated

Cabinet Construction

or veneered both sides, but it will be found easier to make up a ply panel, any slight inequalities in the surface being levelled down and the surfaces toothed before veneering.

A different method of laminating is indicated in Fig. 127. In this manner a sufficient number of segments of the curve required are sawn out as at A. The pieces should be glued down one over the other much in the manner of brick-work bond, to form a rough outline of

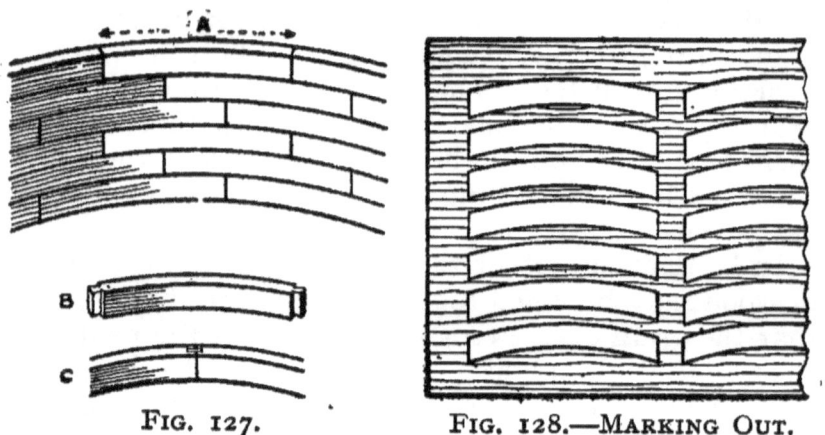

Fig. 127.   Fig. 128.—Marking Out.

curve to be dealt with, the whole then being cleaned up both outside and inside with plane or spokeshave. The part will then be ready for veneering on both sides as a face finish. Stuff 1 in. thick can be used for this segmental laminating, and veneer or saw-cut up to $\frac{1}{16}$ in. thick for facing. Shield, oval and kidney-shaped frames are generally built up in this way. Circles can be built up in quadrant shape pieces, which can also be dovetailed, or pocket-screwed together. Fig. 127B indicates a segment of required curve as dovetailed; C shows a couple of segments joined by tongueing. Fig 128 indicates how the different segments may be marked out on a board for economical cutting.

BARRED DOORS AND LEADED LIGHTS

THE greatly enhanced effect which a barred door has over an entirely plain one is so immediately apparent that it is almost superfluous to comment upon the fact, whilst the charmingly refined effects possible to a simple and pleasing design for leaded-light panels ought to be known to all woodworkers.

FIG. 129.

FIG. 130.

EXAMPLES OF BARRED DOORS WITH CURVES.

Barred Doors are generally identified with furniture in the Chippendale style, the term "barred" being derived from the flat bar upon which the moulding is laid. A section is given at Fig. 137, *a*. In fitting a door in this manner, the bars, which are halved, or tenoned together (Fig. 137, *b* and *c*) should be laid first, The mould, which has a groove on the under side,

Cabinet Construction

drops on to the bar length and is fixed with a light glueing. The completed framing is finally stiffened with strips of black canvas or tape of suitable width, glued on the back.

For the exact cutting of the intersecting joints it will be necessary carefully to mark a centre line, so that the meeting points of the outside parallel lines can be ruled

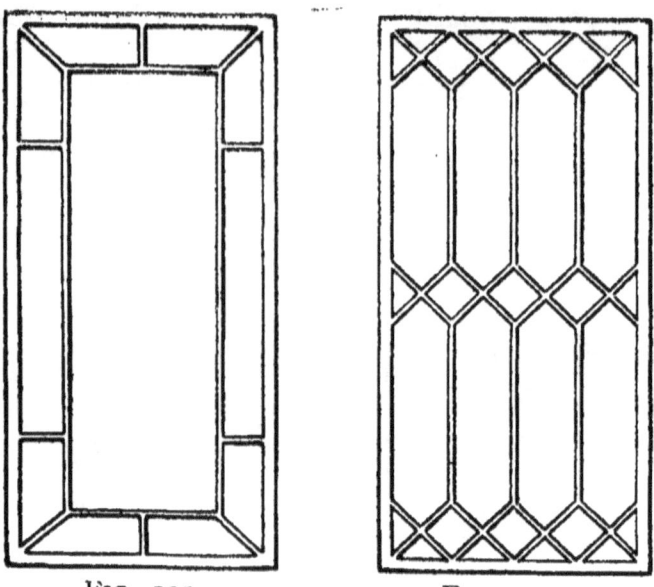

FIG. 131.   FIG. 132.
BARRED DOORS WITH SIMPLE MITRES.

across from it, in order to obtain the bevel and length of the mitres. The mould on the inner edges of the door frame is half the width (Fig. 137, d) of the same section as that in use, and is either worked on the door or rebated in, in the ordinary way. The section of mould varies slightly and can be purchased in lengths ready for cutting up to required sizes.

It is advisable in all cases to set out a sufficient amount of the barred design to full size, so that it may be constantly referred to before cutting up the moulding.

Barred Doors and Leaded Lights

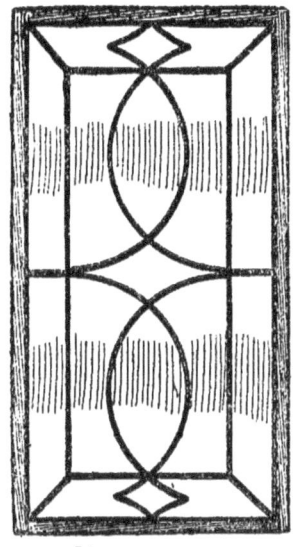 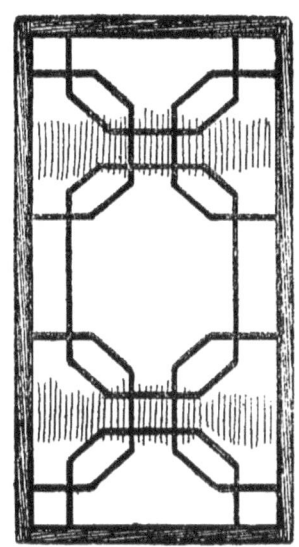

FIG. 133. FIG. 134.
MORE ELABORATE BARRED DESIGNS.
(See also Plates X and XI, pages 197 and 198.)

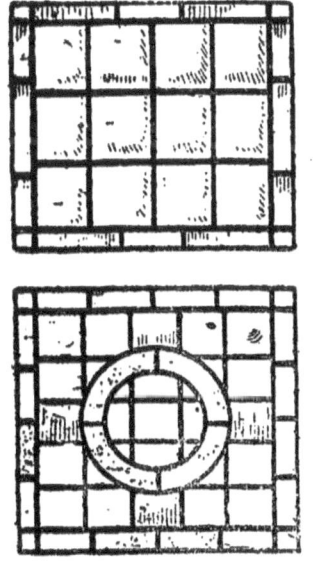 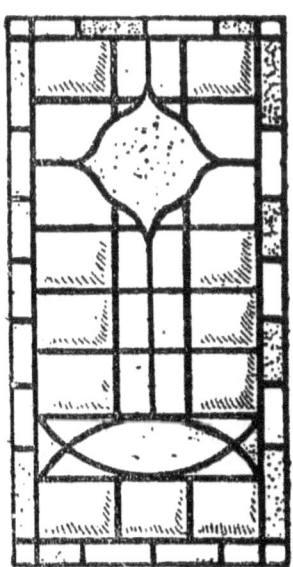

FIG. 135.—EXAMPLES OF LEADED LIGHTS.

Cabinet Construction

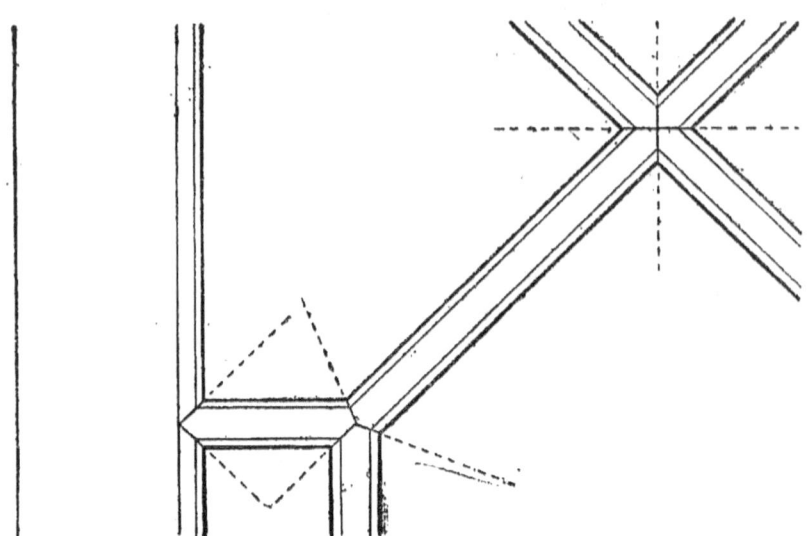

Fig. 136.—How to Find Mitres of Bars.

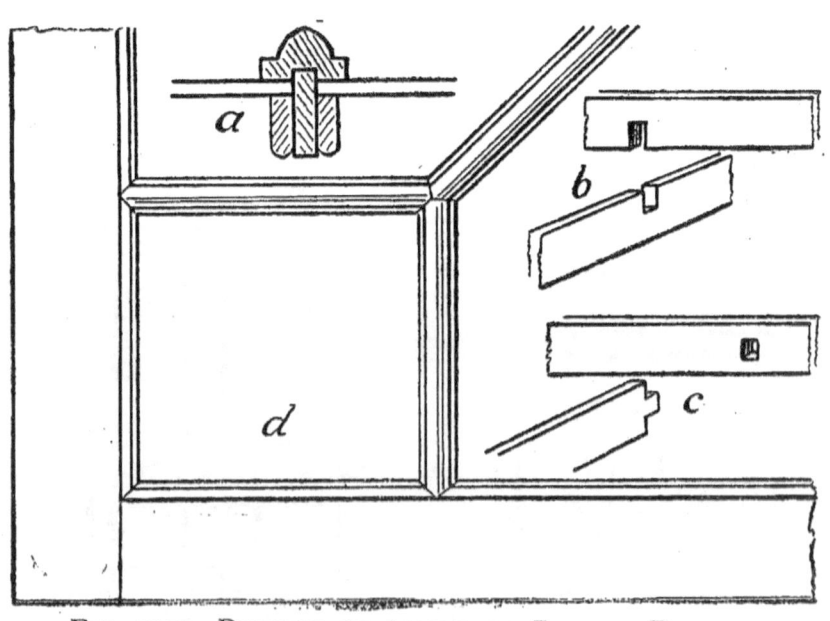

Fig. 137.—Details of Joints of Barred Doors.

Barred Doors and Leaded Lights

Six designs are given in this chapter, graduated from the simple mitreing to curved and more ornate pattern, each having a widely different effect when made up. The curved shapes are sprung, steamed, or bent, in a saddle or caul, to required shape (Figs. 129 to 134). In every case the true angle at which to cut the mitres of the bars is found by halving the angle of intersection. See dotted lines in Fig. 136. Examples of Chippendale and Sheraton barred doors will be found on pages 197 and 198.

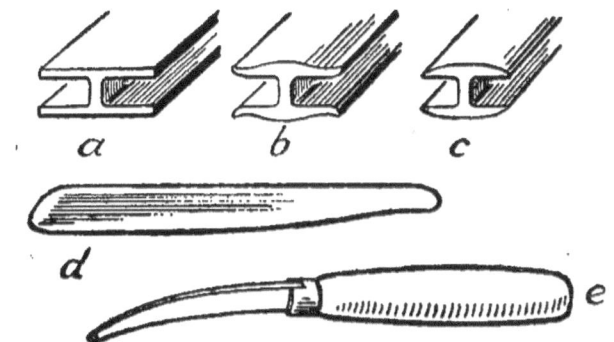

FIG. 138.—LEADED LIGHT MOULDS AND TOOLS.

LEADED LIGHTS.

Tools.—In the making of leaded lights a few special tools will be found necessary, several of which can be home-made: a cutting knife, for cutting the lead and for opening it out, bending, etc., a lever or lathykin, Fig. 138, *d*, a soldering iron and solder, lasting tacks, a stopping knife, *e*, glass cutter, pliers of the square-nosed variety, etc. For glazing (in addition to window glass which, of course, is the cheapest) there are kinds used to achieve a varied and refined effect, such as flashed, rolled, opalescent, bottle glass, muranese, muffled, antique and coloured glass.

The leaded mould into which the glass is fitted is

Cabinet Construction

obtainable in several sections and sizes, three of which are indicated at Fig. 138, *a*, *b* and *c*, *i.e.*, flat, beaded, and round, all adaptable to the thickness of the glass that has to be used, which must enter easily, leaving sufficient space for a final filling of cement to make it damp proof.

Cutting the Glass. — A full-size drawing of the pattern in hand should be made in ink, or a very soft pencil, the drawing then being spread out on a flat board, table, or bench ready for carefully tracing the outlines of the various pieces of glass. For this a glazier's diamond is best, but a very serviceable cutter is obtainable for a few pence. Lay the glass over the drawing and hold the glass cutter between the first and second fingers of the right hand—the handle tilting towards the shoulder slightly and the wheel, in all cases, perfectly upright. Remember to start cutting only on a quite flat surface, with cloth or baize between it and the glass, and do not press too hard. After cutting, the sheet of glass can be raised a little by the left hand and the portion to be removed be pressed downwards with the thumb above and fingers of the right hand below, when it should come away cleanly. Curved shapes, however, will require nursing a trifle and should be dealt with very carefully—tapping with the cutter on the under side occasionally along the line of the cut.

To Assemble the Leads and glass, a couple of square laths can be tacked together to the bench at a true right angle. These will be useful as a guide to squareness and should be fixed as forming the bottom left-hand corner of a frame. A wide lead can be laid close up to this, after being pulled straight and eased.

When starting to cut the lead with a sharp knife note should be taken that the horizontal pieces only are to be cut to fit into the perpendicular uprights, which remain in one piece, top to bottom. The lead must be cut square at ends and to a very near fit, so that careful

Barred Doors and Leaded Lights

measurement should be taken. The parts can be soldered together when square and tight. The outer leads, it might be said, overlap the horizontal pieces—the inner pieces of the latter being merely butted up to the former. Scrape all joints with a knife blade slightly to clean them before soldering. Cement the glass and lead together through the crevices finally remaining, by running in a mixture of black paint and plaster of paris, working in the cement with a hog hair brush thoroughly.

If the doors are fairly large, or the glazing is likely to be subjected to jarring (as in a street door, for instance) support should be provided behind by fitting one or several bars of $\frac{1}{4}$-in. iron, to which the leaded lights can be attached by means of short lengths of copper wire soldered on to the back of the lead framing.

HOW TO MAKE DRAWERS

WHEN setting out a cabinet or other piece of furniture containing drawers, some little thought should be allotted to the finished effect of the drawer fronts, which may be made to play an important part in the decorative appearance of the work when completed. For instance, a plain drawer front is embellished by the addition of mouldings, while the introduction of a little clean-cut carving may prove just the one touch needed to make the finished *tout ensemble* a success. Similarly a plain front can be improved by veneering, and the veneering itself be enhanced by reversing or quartering the grain in conjunction with inlaid lines, chequered or cross-banding, etc. Such treatment, if carefully done, bestows upon the finished article a distinctly refined effect.

Thickness of Wood, etc.—Generally speaking, hardwood to finish $\frac{7}{8}$ in. thick is used for drawer fronts, more especially for those likely to be in constant use. Shallow drawers of medium size are, however, often made with $\frac{3}{4}$-in. (net) fronts, and small drawers, such as those in a dwarf nest of drawers, can have $\frac{5}{8}$-in. fronts. Sides and backs can be $\frac{3}{8}$ in. and $\frac{1}{4}$ in. respectively and bottoms $\frac{1}{4}$ in., sometimes with bevelled edges for fitting.

With regard to the making of a drawer to the carcase opening, the points to remember are that the drawer front should exactly fit the opening, top to bottom; and, as a precaution against unguarded withdrawal, the drawer itself should tighten slightly as it is pulled out. The fronts are connected to the sides by lap-dovetailing to mask the side end grain, and the back and sides are jointed by plain dovetailing where the exposed end grain does not matter.

In a rough and ready way a drawer may be put together as at Fig. 139, with the addition of a couple of

How to Make Drawers

screws or nails as an extra hold ; or, as is often done, with a couple of dovetail pins into sides. In machine work the sides are often jointed to fronts as Fig. 140, but such methods do not rank as good construction. A drawer front exceeding 6 ins. in depth can have three dovetail pins and two half pins as Fig. 141, those of lesser depth usually having two pins between the half pins as Fig. 142.

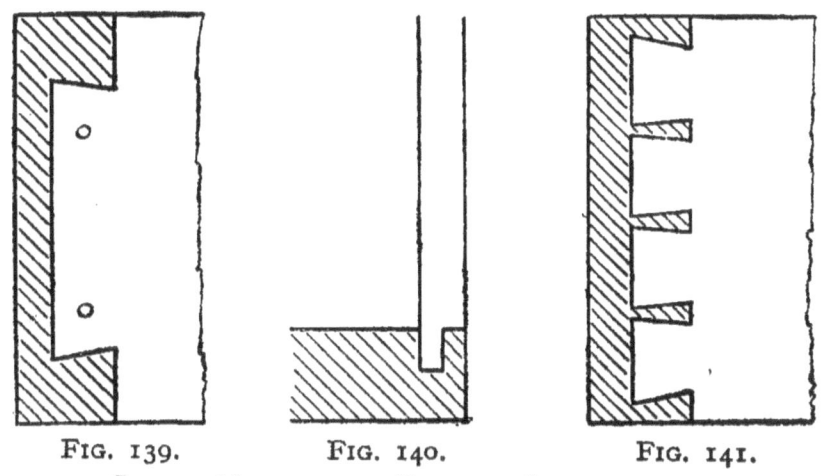

FIG. 139.   FIG. 140.   FIG. 141.
SIMPLE METHODS OF DRAWER CONSTRUCTION.

SETTING OUT FOR DOVETAILING

In setting out the dovetails for drawer work the neatest appearance is obtained by making the tails relatively wide to the pins, which are narrow. The angle of the dovetail is also of importance, that generally adopted as affording the greatest strength being 1 in 8. A ready means of striking this angle is indicated at Fig. 143. Take a spare board, shoot the free edge true and mark off a line AB 8 ins. long. From B draw a line BC, 1 in. long, at right angles to it ; connect AC, which line will serve for adjusting the bevel with which all the dovetails will be set out. A permanent template

Cabinet Construction

in wood or metal is often made for the purpose of setting out, but this is hardly worth while unless a considerable number of drawers have to be made.

Front.—Proceeding to construct the drawer, plane up the front true and to thickness, and square off to the precise length required. It should be fitted on bottom edge and ends to the opening, but the width can be on the full side—say ⅛ in., for easing later.

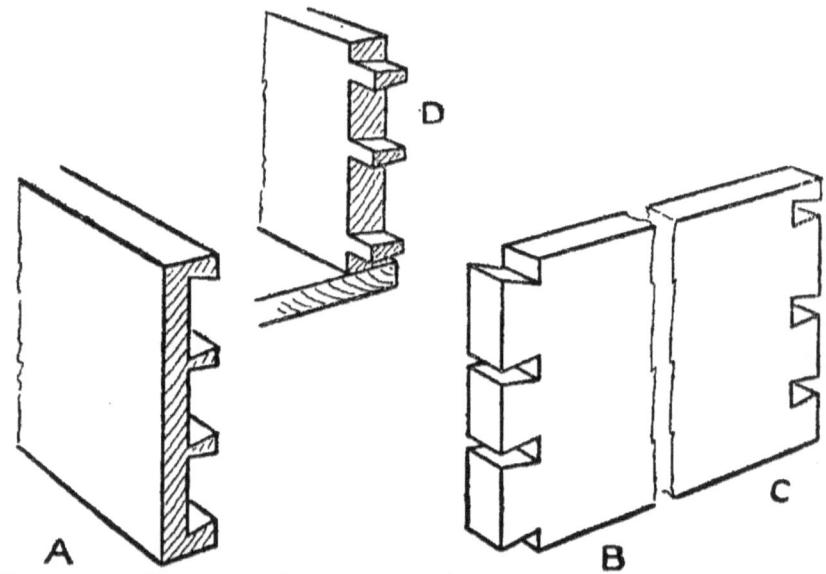

FIG. 142.—DRAWER JOINTS. A, FRONT; B, FRONT END OF SIDE; C, BACK END OF SIDE; D, PINS ON BACK EVENLY SPACED.

The Sides are next planed to width and tested by sliding into carcase, taken out, shot and squared, both to same length, which should allow a full ½-in. clearance behind the completed drawer when inserted home.

The Back can next be fitted to the opening, but should be about ¾ in. narrower than the size. Take the cutting gauge, set it to a shade less than the thickness of the sides and, gauging from the ends, mark a line on the

How to Make Drawers

inside face of front—both sides of back, and likewise back end of sides. Then ⅜ in. up from bottom edge of front plough a groove ³⁄₁₆ in. deep to receive the drawer bottom. The lap-dovetails on sides are allowed a length of full two-thirds the thickness of front, and the gauge line for them is marked on the front ends of sides and end grain of front. A sketch of the joints is given at Fig. 142, A being the front, B the front end of sides, C the back end of same, and D the pins on back,

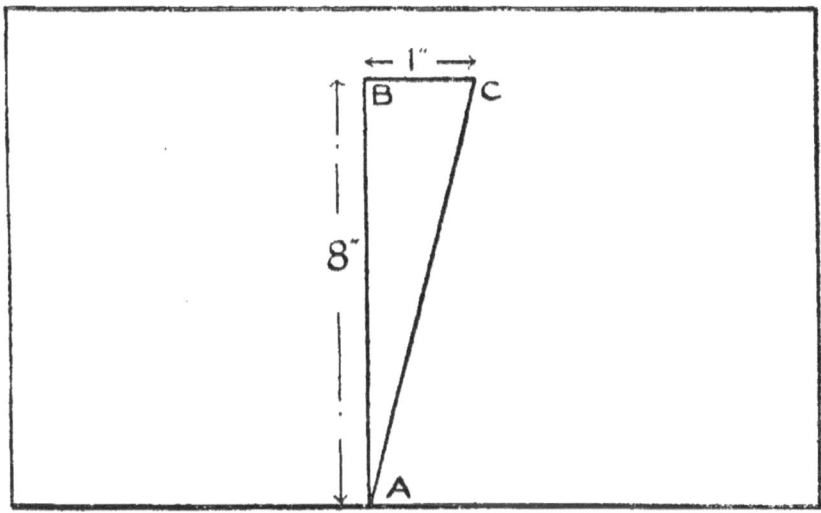

Fig. 143.—How to Strike Dovetail Angle.

all equally spaced. In setting out it is best to square a centre line and mark the pin equally each side of it, using the joiner's bevel for the angles and squaring down to the gauge line with marking awl and try square.

The sockets on the front can be started with the tenon saw and the waste cleared out with a bevelled firmer chisel. When finished the drawer front can be turned over in position on the front end of drawer sides, so that the precise openings for the pins to enter can be carefully scratched with the marking awl into sides as a guide for cutting. The back end of sides can be marked to receive

Cabinet Construction

the pins on drawer back in like manner, or a tenon saw can be used instead of the marking awl.

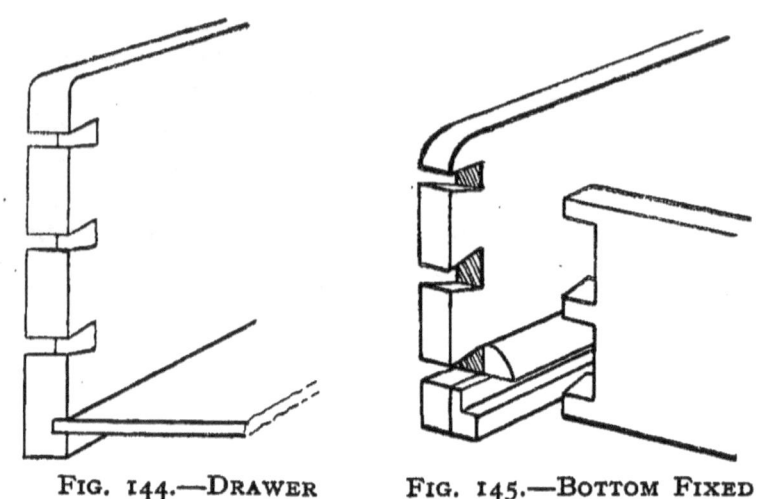

FIG. 144.—DRAWER BOTTOM GROOVED IN.

FIG. 145.—BOTTOM FIXED ON GROOVED SLIPS.

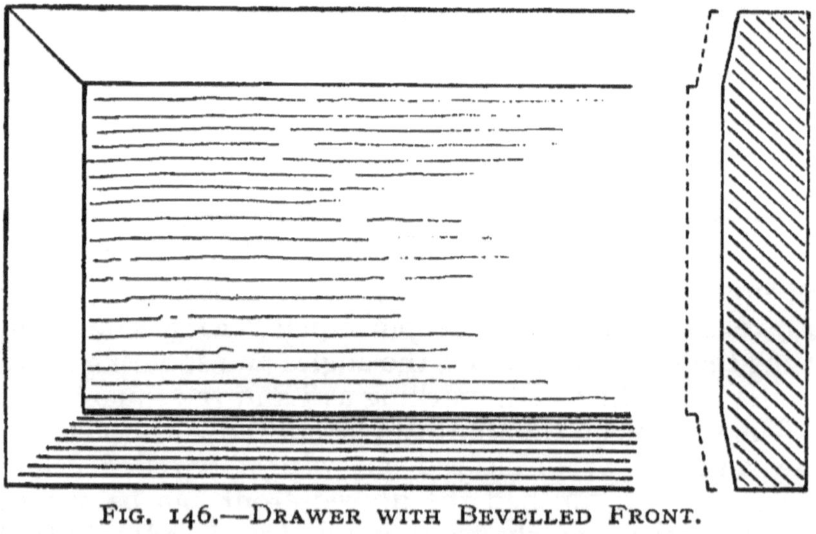

FIG. 146.—DRAWER WITH BEVELLED FRONT.

In Putting Together, one side with the dovetails glued should be laid flat on the bench. The dovetail

How to Make Drawers

sockets in back and front can then be glued and pressed home on the corresponding tails, the remaining side being then glued and tapped into position with a mallet. The operation may possibly cause the drawer to spring

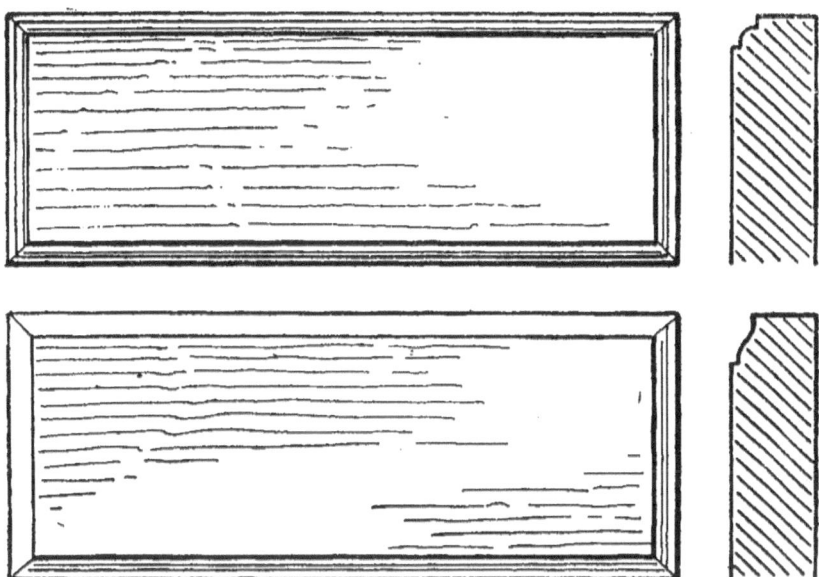

Fig. 147.—Drawer with Applied Solid Mould.

a trifle out of square. If so, the drawer can be laid on a table over a plan drawn to size on stout cartridge paper, and be pressed till the sides and corners agree; or a try square can be used for the purpose.

The Drawer Bottom should be cut with the grain running in the same direction as the front; it should be very carefully cut and squared to fit well home in the grooves, as it plays a part in keeping the whole thing square. The bottom may either be grooved direct into sides (Fig. 144), with the bottom edge mulleted or bevelled away ⅜ in. (being tested on a mullet before finally fitting); or slips grooved to receive the bottom may be fitted to the bottom edge of sides, as Fig. 145,

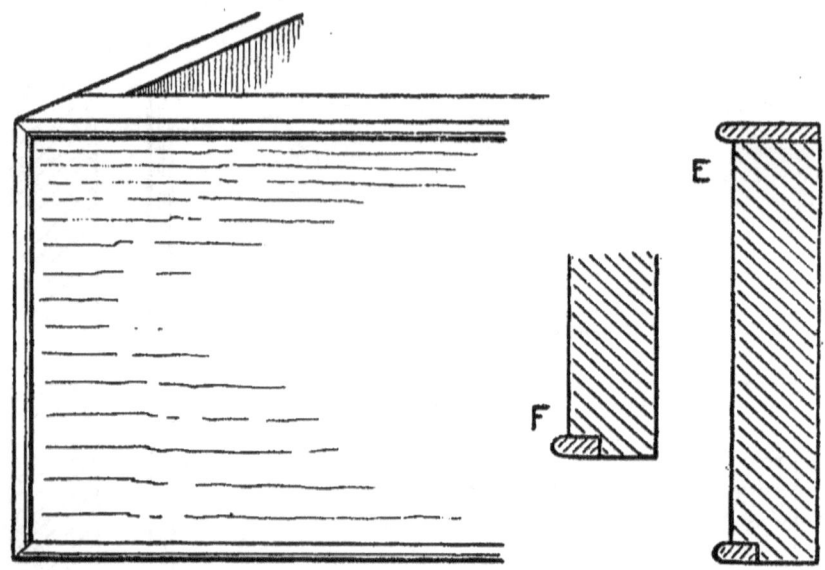

Fig. 148.—Drawer Front with Cocked Bead.

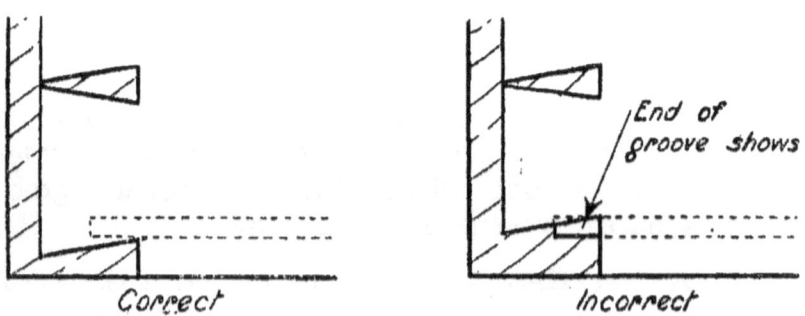

Fig. 149.—Correct and Incorrect Positions of Dovetail in Drawer Front.

a portion of the rounded part of slip being notched away to receive the drawer back.

How to Make Drawers

In most cases, whether slips are used or not the front is grooved to hold the bottom, and this necessitates the lower dovetail being arranged so that the groove is continued within it as shown to the left in Fig. 149. Otherwise the groove will show at the sides as in the incorrect diagram at the right. The bottom should be allowed to project beyond back a trifle to cover shrinkage. Instead of using slips the bottom is sometimes

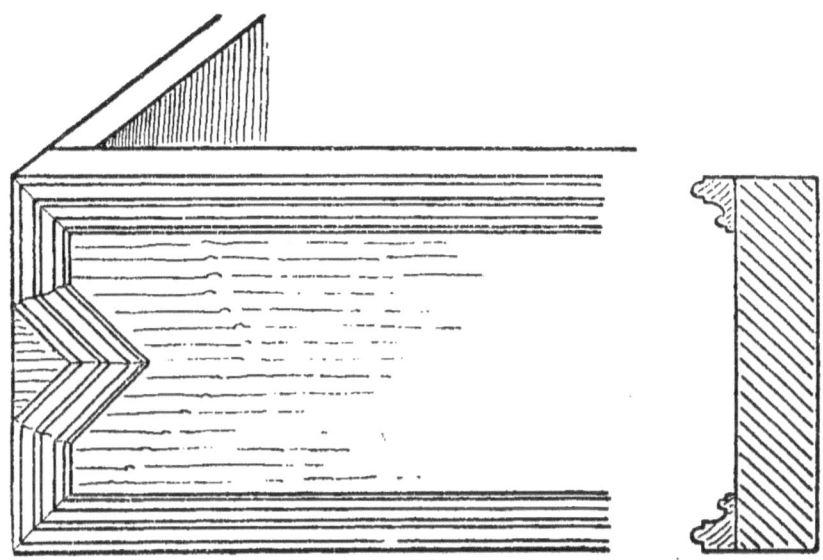

Fig. 150.—Showing Applied Mitred Mould.

rebated on the under side so that, when grooved into sides, the remaining portion of rebate can be filled in with hard wood blocks. The bottom is held in position by tapping a few small brads through into back, and the drawer when inserted into carcase is prevented from pushing in too far by glueing and bradding small cuts of $\frac{1}{8}$ in. stuff so that they stop the front flush with the opening.

Cabinet Construction

Drawers with Mouldings.—Fig. 146 gives a part sketch of small drawer front with bevel as a departure from flatness. If preferred, a raised panel effect may be obtained by finishing as indicated by dotted line.

Fig. 147 shows a drawer front with simple outside mould worked on the solid to $\frac{5}{16}$ in. wide. Additional members to the section are possible, but all should be neat and flat in character.

Fig. 151.—Drawer Front with Applied Mould and a Sunk Panel for Carving.

At Fig. 148 is seen a cocked bead as usually worked upon drawers of the Chippendale period. The bead is formed by the rounded edge of a flat slip, $\frac{1}{8}$ in. thick, with the same projection of $\frac{1}{8}$ in. rounded beyond the front. The flats for ends and bottom edge are rebated (F) into postion, the rebate extending to the dovetails on drawer sides up to which the slips butt. The flat

How to Make Drawers

for the top edge of front is usually finished the full thickness (E) in order to avoid a joint showing, and all slips are mitred at the angles.

Fig. 150 shows a part front with internal mould applied to the front and mitred up to a design in the Jacobean style. The section can be either $\frac{5}{8}$ in. or $\frac{7}{8}$ in. in width as required and is, of course, most suitable for brown or fumed oak.

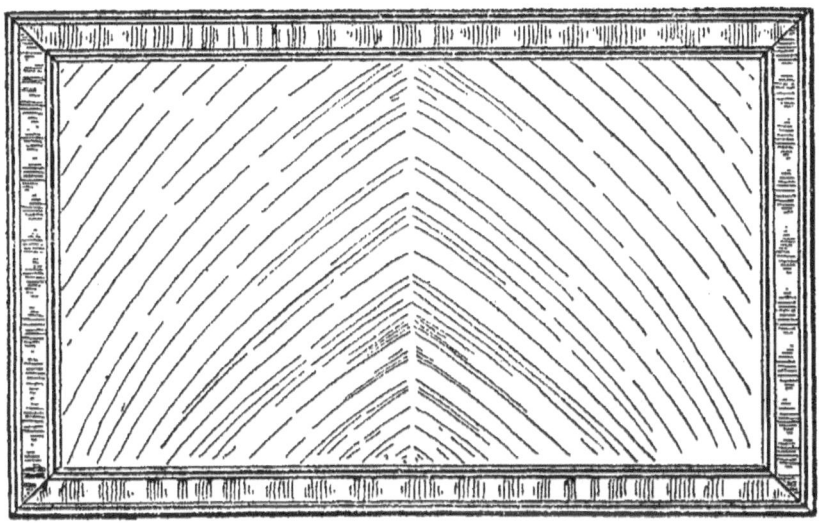

FIG. 152.—VENEERED DRAWER FRONT.

In Fig. 151 we have a front with internal mould which may be either applied to the face or rebated into position. It is suitable for a sideboard or bookcase, and may be elaborated by the introduction of an internal panel grounded into front and carved up to a suitable design.

Veneered Drawer Fronts.—Fig. 152 indicates a front as veneered and edged with cross-banding. The wood in this case can be figured mahogany cut with

Cabinet Construction

the grain reversed from the centre of front and enclosed with ebony, box and satinwood banding $\frac{3}{8}$ in. wide.

Fig. 153 is an alternative front suitable for oak and satinwood. It shows the veneer quartered with a $\frac{3}{16}$ in. banding surround, and edged with cross-banding $\frac{3}{8}$ in. or $\frac{1}{2}$ in. wide, which may, however, be omitted with

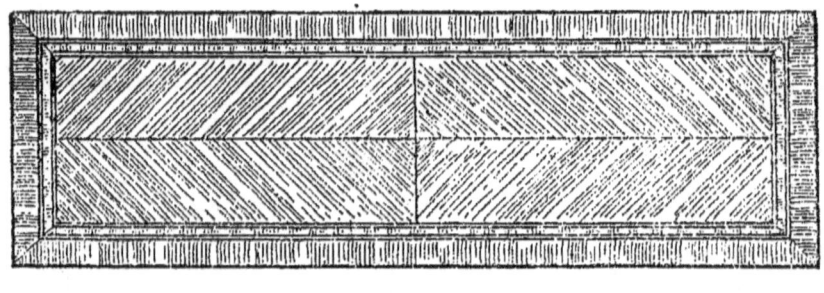

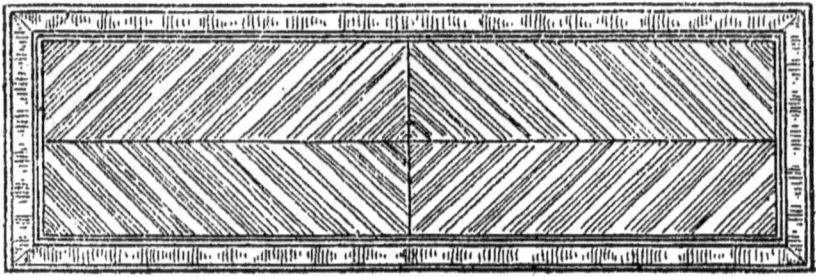

Fig. 153.—Quartered Veneer Fronts.

a lessened effect in oak. It is best retained where satinwood is in use.

Many beautiful effects are obtainable by the use of figured woods such as maple, Circassian ash, burr walnut, etc., either with moulded or inlaid surrounds.

Drawers in a Corner Cabinet.— It sometimes happens that a drawer has to be fitted to a corner cabinet. It is obviously impossible for it to occupy the

How to Make Drawers

full width of the job owing to the backs of the job converging. Fig. 154 shows how this difficulty is overcome.

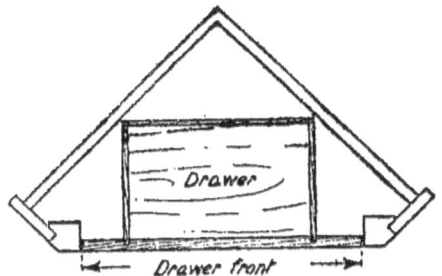

FIG. 154.—HOW DRAWER IS FITTED IN CORNER CABINET.

The drawer sides stand in considerably and are slot dovetailed into the front.

DRAWER RAILS AND RUNNERS

A WELL-FITTING drawer is one of the signs of a careful worker, and the drop-in and fall-out type of article that shoots right away at the first unwary tilt of the drawer case will not occur in a specimen piece of work. At the same time, a carefully made drawer will not prove a success if the rail and runners upon which it is to travel are not level and smooth. As we have just dealt fully with drawer *making*, the important question of drawer *running* may well be considered now.

A drawer should pull easily forward, tightening slightly in its progress towards the end. Using picked stuff, well-seasoned and dry, this is achievable to a nicety so that, when a drawer is drawn out a portion of its length, the compression of air within caused by pushing it back will propel the adjacent drawer slightly forward. Incidentally it may here be mentioned that the best position for a piece of furniture containing drawers is not near a window, or in a damp room, as the moisture in time is pretty sure to affect the drawer sides (especially if these are of deal or other soft wood) with unsatisfactory results. For this reason, in all best work, mahogany sides, back and bottom are preferable as being less susceptible to atmospheric conditions.

Jewel Drawers.—As these drawers usually run on the floor or bottom of the case constructed previously for them, runner slips are not required and little else than accurate fitting is needed. Fig. 155 indicates a method of putting the parts together, looking from the *back* of case. The top and sides can be of $\frac{5}{8}$ in. thickness, dovetail-grooved together as shown. As the top projects at front it will not be necessary to notch the dove-

Drawer Rails and Runners

tail back the usual $\frac{3}{8}$ in. to conceal the joint A, this being only necessary when the edges of the parts finish flush. The dovetail groove is stopped to just receive the dovetail flush home. The bottom can be of $\frac{1}{2}$ in. or $\frac{3}{8}$ in.

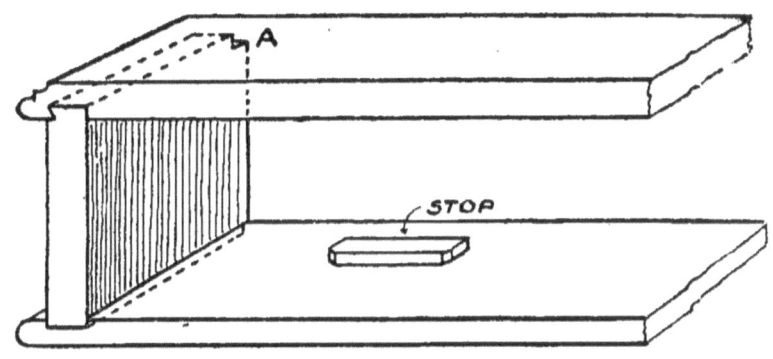

FIG. 155.—CASE FOR JEWEL DRAWER, AS SEEN FROM THE BACK.

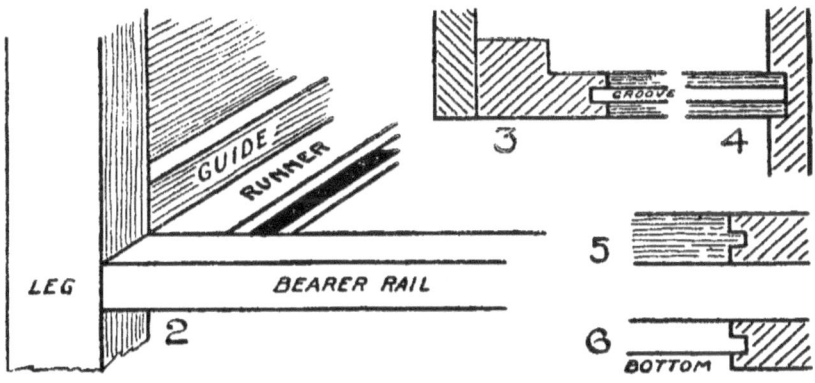

FIG. 156.—SHOWING BEARER RAILS AND RUNNERS OF A WRITING-TABLE.

thickness, grooved to receive the sides which are screwed through up from the under side. A couple of stops can be glued and pinned on to engage the inner edge of drawer front, so that it is kept flush with front

Cabinet Construction

edge of case sides. A thin back can be screwed or nailed to each case, or (preferably in a dressing table) the case sides may be screwed to a back rail if there happens to be one extending the full width above the table top.

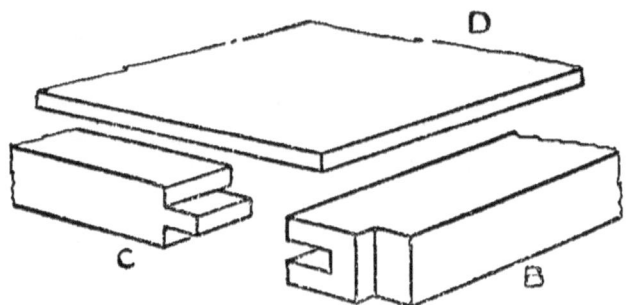

Fig. 157.—B, Bearer Rail; C. Runner; D, Dustboard.

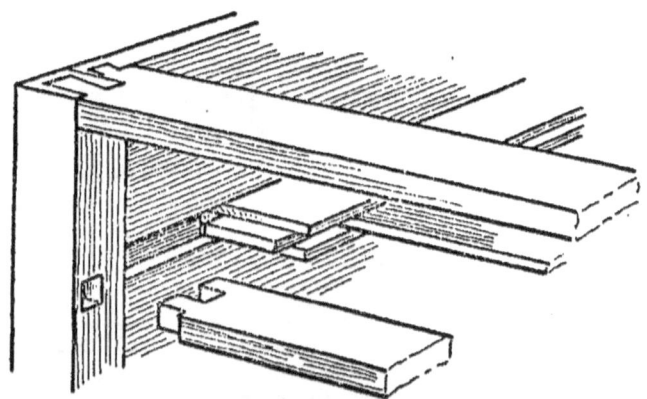

Fig. 158.—Bearer Rail, Runner and Dustboard in Position.

Writing-Table Drawers.—Fig. 156 indicates the usual running arrangement in a small writing-table, the parts being marked for reference. The bottom edge of drawer sides travels over the drawer or bearer rail and along the runner slips, being kept from working right and left by the guides which should finish flush with

Drawer Rails and Runners

the inner sides of legs. As shown in the section at Fig. 156 (3), both guide and runner may be in one piece, rebated in the manner shown, to be glued and screwed or nailed to the table sides.

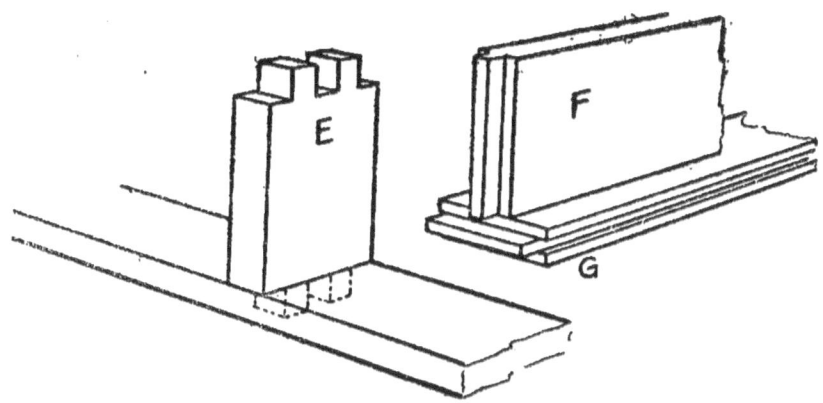

Fig. 159.—E, Vertical Rail ; F, Continuation Piece ; G, Runners.

The mouldings which form the chief decorative motif are worked separately.

If a bottom is to be fitted the runner should be grooved to receive it, and the bottom itself may be either a thin dustboard (say ¼ in. or thicker) as suggested by Fig. 156 (5 and 6). The runners do not always extend from front rail to back, but if so they can be notched as Fig. 156 (4) into the back or nailed to it. The guide portion, however, is frequently made as a separate slip, glued and nailed into position. Fig. 157 shows bearer rail (B), runner (C), and dustboard (D). The runner enters the bearer as indicated and both are grooved to receive the dustboard. Fig. 158 shows these parts inserted into the carcase and pushed home. The bearer rail is tenoned to the legs and the runner housed into the carcase sides with dustboard inserted in its groove to be pushed home

Cabinet Construction

from the back. The dustboard is cut with the grain running from runner to runner, as indicated.

In many instances two smaller drawers are required instead of one long one, as in a chest of drawers or 3 ft. 6 in. writing-table, and this necessitates a partition between the two. In this case a vertical rail (E, Fig. 159) is tenoned to rails above and below, and grooved for the continuation piece (F) to enter. To the under

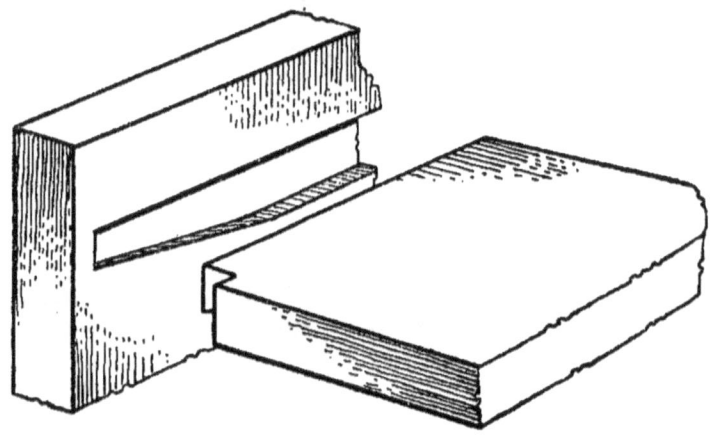

Fig. 160.—Showing Dovetailing as in Larger Carcase Work.

edge of F the drawer runners (G) will be screwed. For the purpose a piece sufficiently wide to allow 1 in. for running at each side of the continuation rail should be prepared. They are grooved each side for dustboards, and stubbed to enter the bearer rail. The piece F also serves as a guide, but it is often replaced by a slip of the same thickness by 1 in. high when economising stuff.

In Larger Carcase Work, such as pedestal writing-tables, sideboards, stationery presses, wardrobes, etc., where the sides and divisions may be of the same thick-

Drawer Rails and Runners

ness throughout, divisions upon which drawers are required to run may be dovetail-grooved to the carcase sides. The dovetail may be cut the whole width of the division or shelf, to enter corresponding grooves in the sides; or, as is often done, the forepart of the division edge is cut, for 4 to 5 ins., with a diminishing or tapered dovetail, the remainder of the edge being kept square. As indicated at Fig. 160 the sides are grooved across the grain to receive the shelf, but stopped; and the forepart

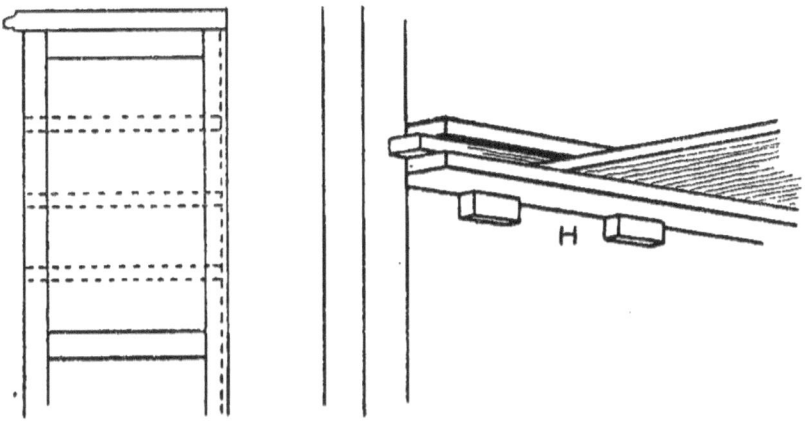

FIG. 161.—FITTING RUNNERS TO NEST OF DRAWERS WITH PANELLED ENDS. RUNNERS ARE NOTCHED TO UPRIGHTS, AND BLOCKS (H) GLUED AS SHOWN.

is slotted with the chisel to receive the tapered dovetail, the joint being stopped back $\frac{1}{2}$ in.

Sometimes it occurs that a nest of drawers has panelled ends, and a drawer runner requires fitting across the panels as well as across the rails. The little proposition can be met by notching the runner into the uprights, and fitting a couple of glued blocks to runner and panels as at H, Fig. 161, by way of suggestion. Such blocks must finish flush with the posts or thicknessed sides (whichever they happen to be), so that no projec-

Cabinet Construction

tion interferes with the passing of the drawer. In large work the latter is often left somewhat full in size at the back and a shave taken off the runners at back. In addition to this the carcase itself may be made a shade wider at the back.

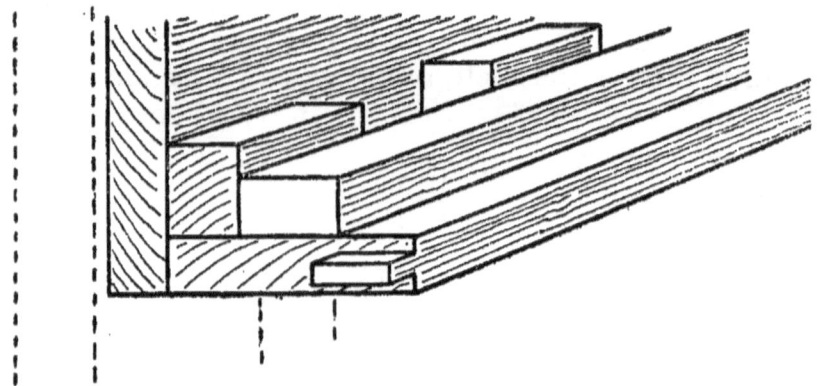

FIG. 162.—RUNNER FOR KITCHEN TABLE, WITH GUIDE SLIP BLOCKED FLUSH WITH INNER SIDE OF LEG.

Fig. 162 shows a kitchen table runner as a hint how the guide slip can be blocked out flush with the inner side of leg when this is 3½ ins. or 4 ins. square.

HOW TO FIT CORNICES AND CAPPINGS

WHEN setting out an article which is about to be constructed some special regard may well be paid to the importance and finish that a suitable capping or cornice is capable of imparting to the assembled effect. Too frequently one sees any available section that may be ready to hand worked in without the slightest attention extended to the surrounding detail or to its suitability for the purpose. The various moulds and methods instanced here may therefore prove of service to the less experienced worker when dealing with this portion of his work.

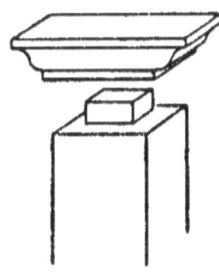
FIG. 163.
POST CAPPING.

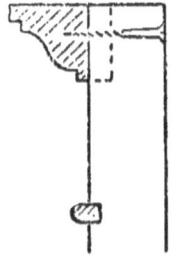
FIG. 164.
CAPPING SCREWED.

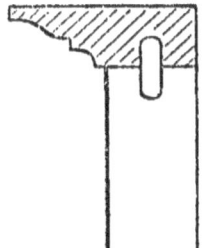
FIG. 165.
CAPPING DOWELLED.

CAPPINGS.

In Fitting Cappings, these may be finished with plain square edges, or the edges may be rounded, nosed, or thumb-moulded; or, again, the edges may be beaded or have a bevel taken off the upper or lower edge according as this is below or above the eye when fixed in position. Generally speaking, however, a three or more membered mould will give a distinctly enhanced effect

Cabinet Construction

to a portion of the work that cannot well be dispensed with. The simplest form of capping is that used as a terminal finish for posts and frequently employed

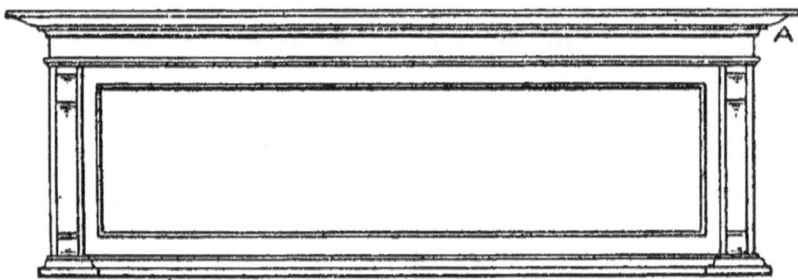

FIG. 166.—CAPPING ON WASHSTAND BACK.

in the construction of bedstead ends. As indicated at Fig. 163, the caps on a 2 ins. by 2 ins. post finish about 4 ins. by 4 ins. square by ⅞ in. thick with a flat top. This portion is improved by a raised and rounded finish,

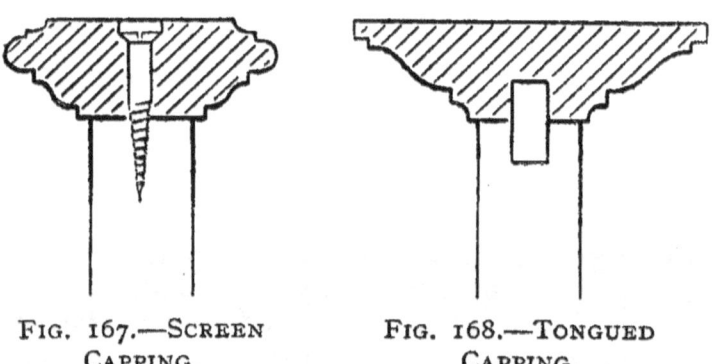

FIG. 167.—SCREEN CAPPING.

FIG. 168.—TONGUED CAPPING.

for which purpose a 4 ins. by 4 ins. square of ¼ in. thickness is glued on to the flat, or the detail can be finished from stuff 1⅛ in. thick net. These cappings are best fixed with a stub-tenon cut on top of post to enter

Cornices and Cappings

a corresponding mortise in capping, but three small dowels can be utilised instead. One dowel is a mistake, as, sooner or later, the capping will be found to have twisted out of the square.

Back Cappings.—The capping mould often seen at the back of a hall table or dinner wagon or on the top of a washing-stand back, as Fig. 166 at A, is sometimes fixed to the face of the rail, and in other instances (when

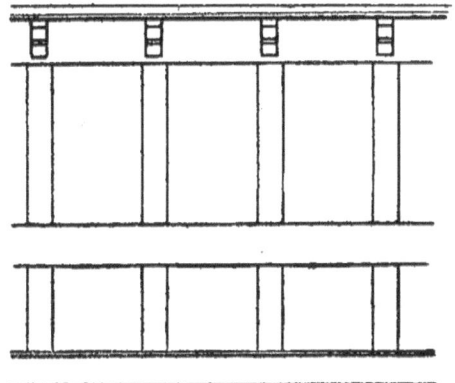

FIG. 169.—OFFICE SCREEN FITMENT.

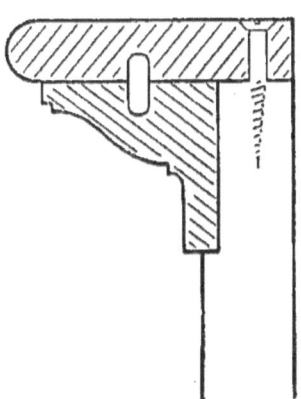

FIG. 170.—BRACKETED CAPPING.

below the level of the eye) is fitted to the top edge of rail. In the former case it may be glued and pinned into position, but is preferably screwed from the back (Fig. 164) and either mitred or returned on itself at ends with the chisel.

Better work may have the section rebated into the face of rail, as indicated by dotted line. In the latter case, the capping is dowelled on as Fig. 165 to finish flush at back, and with a projection of $\frac{3}{4}$ in. or $\frac{7}{8}$ in. at front, according to the section in use. The bead grooved in below the capping mould in Fig. 164 is often added when

Cabinet Construction

a shelf is not provided above the tiles or marble panel of a washstand back. If well above the eye the capping (Fig. 165) may be screwed instead of being dowelled into position.

The Cappings on Screens and partitions erected to divide or enclose a portion of an office or other large room often project on both sides of the framework. They

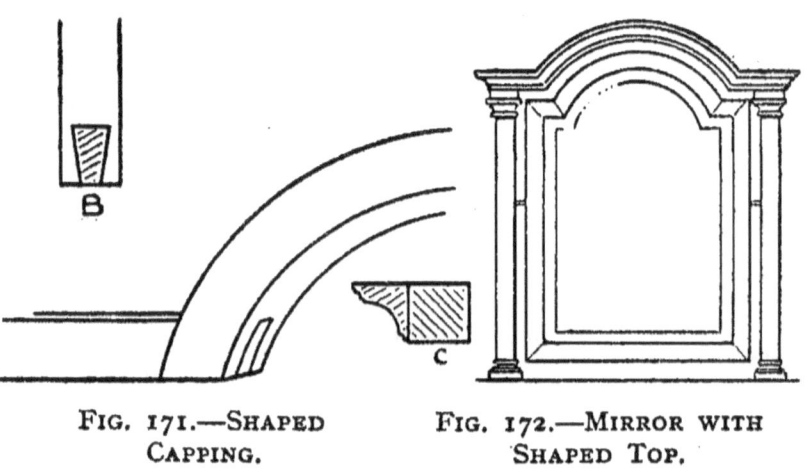

FIG. 171.—SHAPED CAPPING.

FIG. 172.—MIRROR WITH SHAPED TOP.

are generally about 3 ins. wide by ⅞ in. or 1⅛ in. high and are screwed into position from above as Fig. 167. At times, however, they may be dowelled on or may be grooved for tongueing (Fig. 168). It is, of course, always preferable to use a well-greased screw where the question of portability or extension has to be considered, as often happens in the case of an office fitting such as shown at Fig. 169.

As a further suggestion this is instanced with a bracketed capping which may work out in detail as Fig. 170, the capping being screwed down on to the framework with the shaped brackets screwed or dowelled to it under, in addition to being grooved into the frame-

Cornices and Cappings

work to afford a bearing. The method indicated at Fig. 164 would also apply.

Shaped Cappings are sometimes fitted to follow the line of a curved break or heading and occasionally in the case of a swing mirror, after the manner instanced in Fig. 172. The portion to be moulded here would be

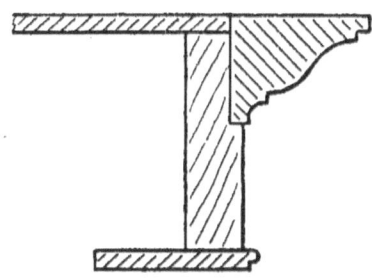

Fig. 173.—Cornice Rebated to Frieze Rail.

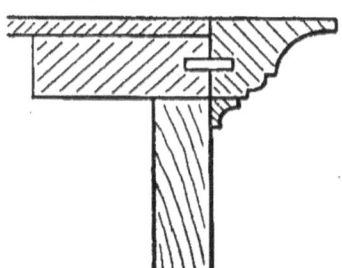

Fig. 174.—Cornice Tongued, and with Dustboard.

built up upon a bed or base of the required shape, the horizontal ends being dowelled, bridle-jointed, or halved and screwed to the central rise, or preferably dovetailed to it in the manner indicated at B, Fig. 171. A section of the part is given at C, the whole thing being tenoned to the supporting columns upon which the mirror frame pivots.

CORNICES.

The Cornice mould of a well-made article of minor dimensions would probably be worked on the edges of a solid top of ¾ in. or ⅞ in. thickness, whilst in common, hastily constructed work it is often merely glued on or pinned on. A neat method is that indicated in the section (Fig. 173). The mould is let into the frieze rail about

Cabinet Construction

¼ in., and a ⅜-in. top fitted into the rebate formed by the rise of the mould beyond the top edge of rail. Another method is shown at Fig. 174, the mould being tongued to a lining slip behind it to form a rebate for dustboard to drop in and be screwed. Either of these methods could be applied to a wall cabinet as well as to cupboards of larger size.

Built up Cornices.—In some forms of cabinet work the cornice and frieze may be built up in the manner indicated at Fig. 175, the top being housed into the frieze rail, and the frieze mould mitred at corners out of slips about 2¼ ins. by ¼ in. glued to under edge of frame.

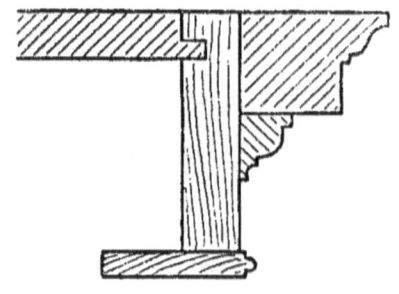

FIG. 175.—BUILT-UP CORNICE.

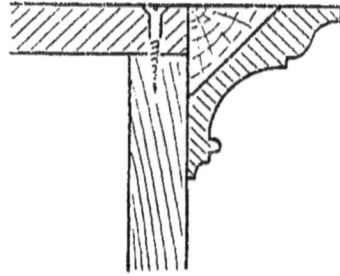

FIG. 176.—USE OF A STOCK CORNICE.

Stock moulds may be obtained from the furnishing wood yards, the whole section of which (as at Fig. 176) is cut out of 1-in. stuff, or less, to be glued into position on the cornice framing. Such a section is sometimes completed by glueing a lining slip behind in the angle formed by the pitch of the mould; in other instances it will be held by angle blocks at intervals of 9 ins. or so apart.

The top is shown as screwed down to the framing, and the method with lining slip is suitable for an article

Cornices and Cappings

such as Fig. 177—a china cabinet about 5 ft. 9 ins. to 6 ft. high. Below eye level a solid ⅜-in. or ½-in. top to

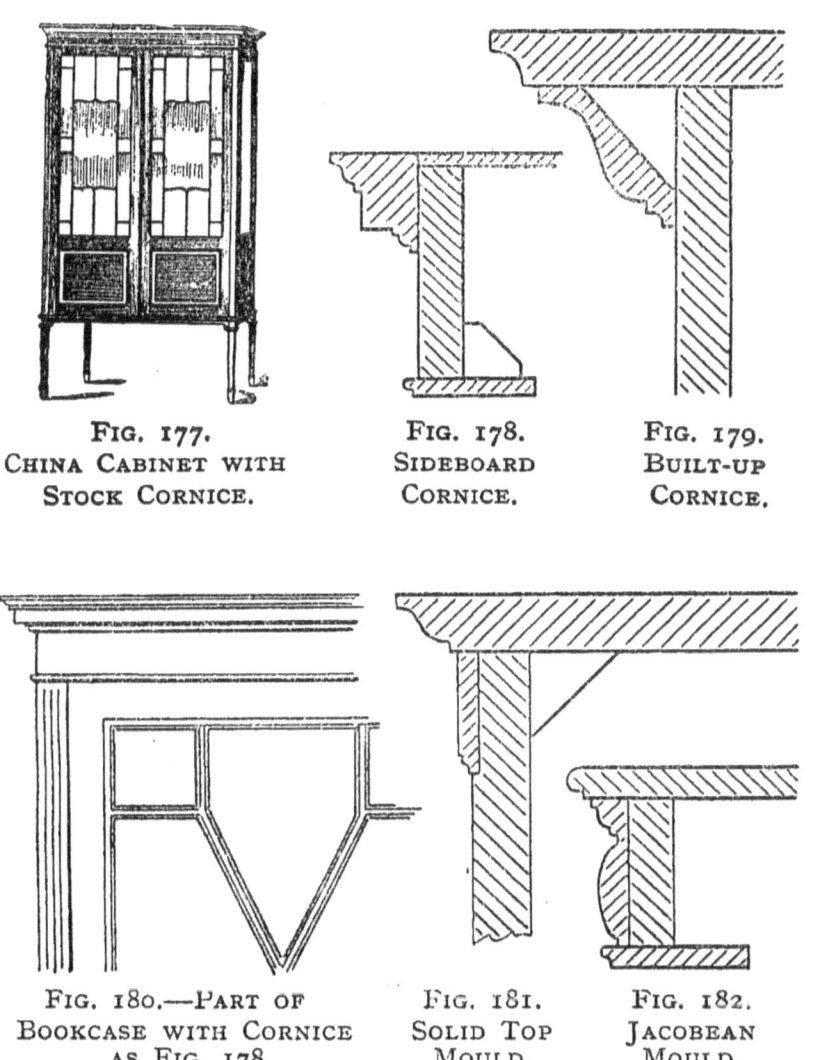

Fig. 177.
China Cabinet with Stock Cornice.

Fig. 178.
Sideboard Cornice.

Fig. 179.
Built-up Cornice.

Fig. 180.—Part of Bookcase with Cornice as Fig. 178.

Fig. 181.
Solid Top Mould.

Fig. 182.
Jacobean Mould.

overlap had best be provided, to be glue-blocked under into position. The entry holes of screws are unsightly

Cabinet Construction

and, even when well stopped, tend to show through the surface finish owing to shrinkage of the wood in course of wear.

Another fixing for the upper mould is that given at Fig. 179, the top being made to project beyond the carcase sufficiently to cover the pitch of the section

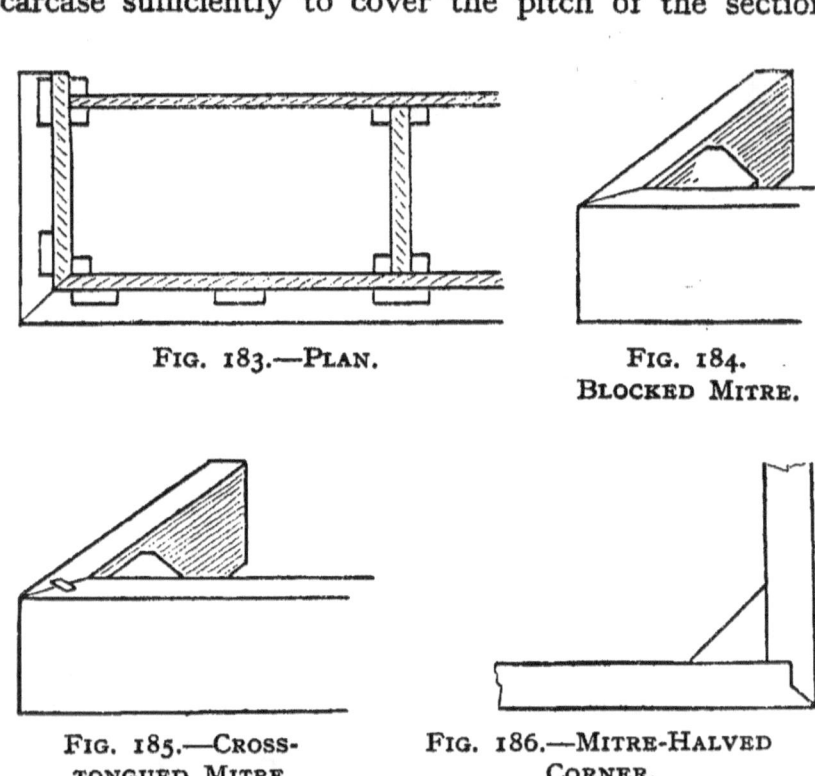

Fig. 183.—Plan.

Fig. 184.
Blocked Mitre.

Fig. 185.—Cross-Tongued Mitre.

Fig. 186.—Mitre-Halved Corner.

Methods of Fitting Loose Cornices.

below it, which is glued into position above and below. Such a section would be suitable for a dwarf linen cupboard of Jacobean type, or could be adopted in the construction of a mantel.

A Useful Section suitable for a sideboard which has the top enclosed by cupboards, or for a bookcase or

Cornices and Cappings

cabinet worked out on the lines of Fig. 180, is that given at Fig. 178. The dustboard is dropped in above and the frieze mould glue-blocked to framing behind.

Solid Top Mould.—An instance of a solid top moulded is given at Fig. 181, the rail under being rebated to receive a lining flat of ⅜-in. stuff or so, thus extending the mould with a sort of frieze effect. Framing and top are glue-blocked behind and the section is very suitable for an oak cupboard. In the section at Fig. 182 this method is developed, the arrangement being useful where it is desired to achieve a carved frieze effect after the Jacobean style.

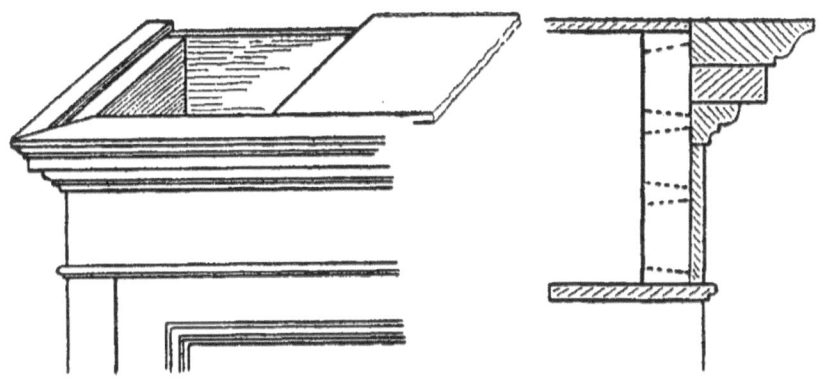

FIG. 187.—LOOSE WARDROBE CORNICE IN POSITION.   FIG. 188.—DOVETAILING OF CORNICE.

Loose Cornices, separately made to be easily detachable from bulky pieces of furniture (such as a wardrobe), are usually fixed into position by means of glued blocks on the upper part of carcase. Cornice and frieze moulds are mounted upon a separate framing, and the arrangement is most convenient for portability. In cheap work the framing may be found to be merely mitred and nailed together at front and sides, with a glued block in the

Cabinet Construction

inner angle. A back rail is nailed and glue-blocked at back to hold the whole thing square, a stretcher rail being also similarly fitted in centre. The cornice mould is glue-blocked into position and nailed, and a dust-board is usually omitted, as indicated in the part plan, Fig. 183.

An enlargement of the blocked mitre is shown at Fig. 184, which may be turned into a strong joint if cross-tongued as an additional hold and blocked as at Fig. 185. Another method is to mitre-halve the front and side rails together as at Fig. 186.

A more workmanlike method of putting the framework together is by dovetailing, which is generally done in the best class of work.

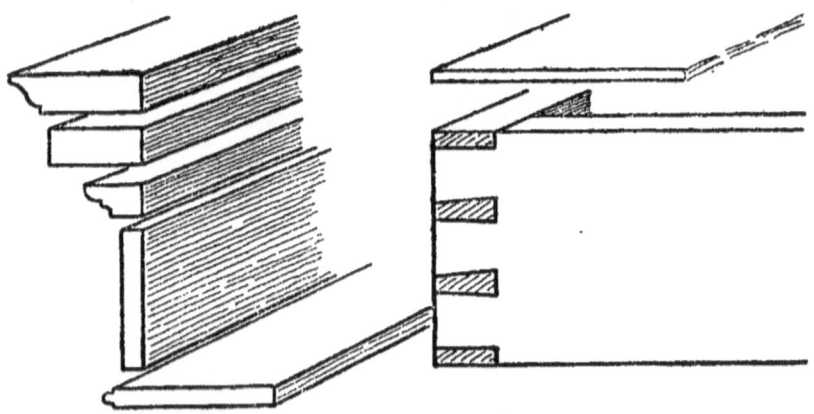

Fig. 189.—Detail of Loose Wardrobe Cornice Moulding in Three Parts.

A Sketch of a Loose Cornice is given at Fig. 187, showing it in position on wardrobe carcase as viewed from above. Height over all may work out at 4½ ins. to 6 ins. according to detail. The method of dovetailing front and side rails of framing is given at Fig. 188, and from this it will be seen that the mould is mounted

Cornices and Cappings

higher than the front and side rails to form a rebate for the dustboard top. The side rails have the back rail fixed to them by means of a housed dovetail as shown in Fig. 190, and the stretcher rail between front and back rails by means of a dovetail into each as Fig. 192.

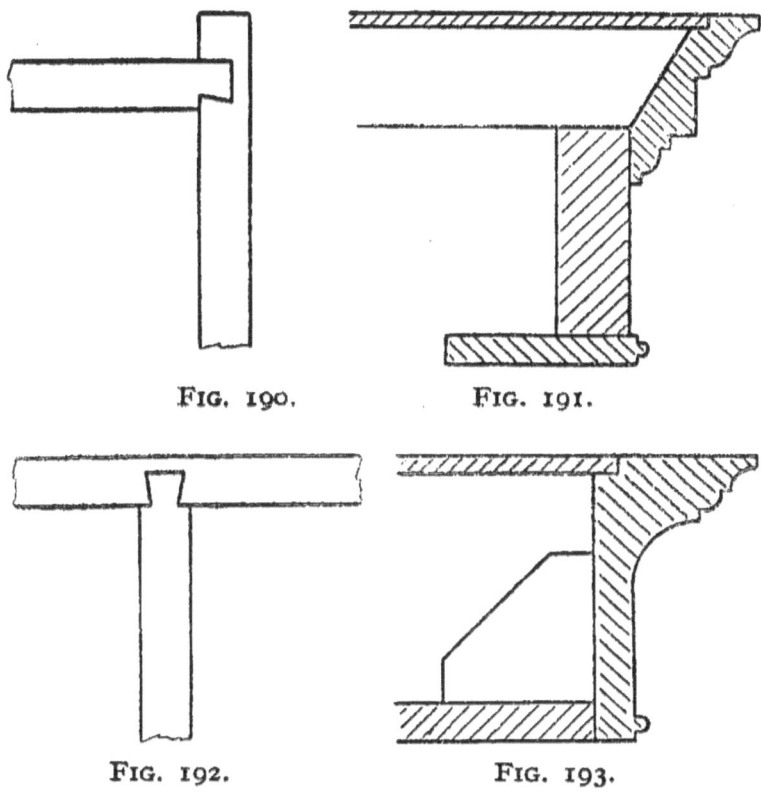

FIG. 190.   FIG. 191.

FIG. 192.   FIG. 193.

ADDITIONAL DETAILS OF LOOSE WARDROBE CORNICE.

If properly done the whole thing should be as firm as a rock when glued up. The through-dovetailing is masked by means of facing slips of the hardwood in use ($\frac{1}{4}$ in. thick or so), glued on after mitreing at corners. The width of these slips is determined by the height of the cornice mould which beds upon the top edge.

Cabinet Construction

Instead of being in one piece the cornice mould may be built up of three parts as shown. A sketch of the front and side rails dovetailed together, frieze facing and mould, cornice mould in parts and dustboard, is outlined at Fig. 189, which should make the construction clear.

A section (Fig. 191) showing the cornice mould pitched high and rebated to receive dustboard will be found to work out very effectively, and an alternative section (Fig. 193) giving the cornice and frieze in one piece, to be glued to the front and sides of carcase top and glue-blocked in the angles behind, is a simple and direct treatment affording a neat result.

When Fixing a Cornice Mould, in cramping up after glueing, it will be necessary to use a suitable block to fill the space caused by the pitch or projection of the members between the jaws of the hand screw. Where the flat member, often dentilled, exists, a square slip of necessary size will suffice, but in other cases it may be essential to scribe the block to prevent it slipping when pressure is applied. It may be found that use can be made of a spare cut of the mould in hand for the purpose, possibly with a layer of felt between to avoid bruising any points of contact.

The Receding Cornice.—Varieties in section, of the receding type of cornice are given in Fig. 194. When setting out the section, it should be borne in mind that it must not slope backwards at too acute an angle, for this would make it invisible. The best plan is to draw a line at 45 degrees and place the top member at least no further back than the line. The actual contour depends in a great measure upon the wood used and the style, although on the latter score one does not discriminate too finely, for the receding cornice cannot be said to follow any of the classic styles. A point to bear in mind is the actual position in which the moulding will be

Cornices and Cappings

fixed. As a rule, it is advisable to allow the lowest member to overhang slightly to give a sense of definition to the job. Occasionally, however, the whole can be set back slightly as at C.

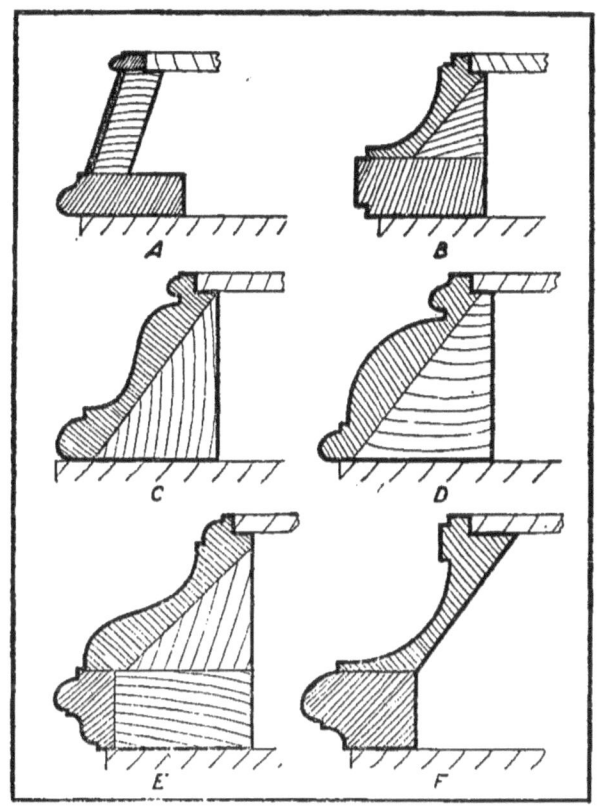

FIG. 194.—EXAMPLES OF RECEDING CORNICES. A, MAHOGANY WITH VENEERED FACE. B, PLAIN SECTION. C, OAK CORNICE. D, BOLD OAK SECTION. E, LARGE WALNUT MOULDING. F, MAHOGANY CORNICE.

Glancing at Fig. 194, it will be noticed that some are receding mouldings pure and simple, whilst others are more or less of a compromise. At E and F, for example, the moulding projects at the bottom before it begins to

Cabinet Construction

slope backwards. This, in the writer's opinion, is the most successful type for it preserves (to a minor extent) the interesting shadows of the overhanging cornice. It is really an exaggeration of the type at A, B and D, in which the lower member overhangs. Another feature of interest is that four of the six sections have a small projecting member at the top (A, C, D and F). The reader will probably feel that this gives a more definite finish to the top.

Probably, the chief point in favour of the receding cornice is that it catches the light more than the overhanging type and helps to take away any suggestion of heaviness.

SHAPINGS IN CABINET WORK

THE character and successful effect of a piece of cabinet work is considerably affected by the shapings introduced. In a severe type of design, such as might be worked out in fumed oak, these may be restricted almost to the mere rounding of angles as the construction suggests. In mahogany, walnut, satinwood, satin walnut, basswood stained and

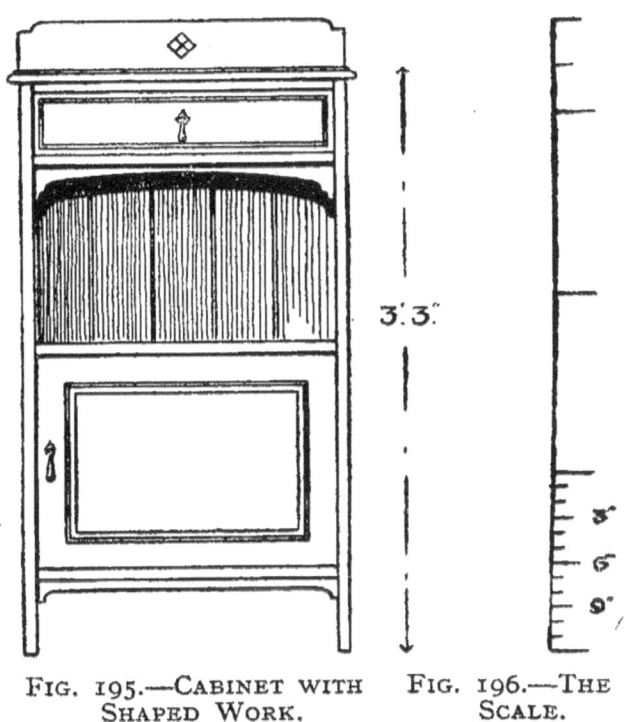

Fig. 195.—Cabinet with Shaped Work. Fig. 196.—The Scale.

polished (or the last-named white enamelled), a greater diversity of curve may be looked for. It is, however, very easy to run riot in the matter of shaping with a

Cabinet Construction

consequent suggestion of "snakes" rather than of a quiet easing of squareness, so that, generally speaking, it will be on the safer side to set out any curve with an initial idea of restraint, correcting the line till a sense of balance is felt.

Setting Out from Scale Drawings.—In setting out from a scale drawing, the most convenient method will probably be found to make a neat tracing with a fine pen on tracing-paper. Then fasten this with a piece of white card under to the drawing-board. Assuming that Fig. 195 is the article traced, and the height to table top being given as 3 ft. 3 ins., divide with the compasses this height into thirteen parts, representing thirteen times 3 ins. (equals 3 ft. 3 ins.), and mark off the scale as indicated at Fig. 196. With the dividers and this scale any portion of the tracing can be

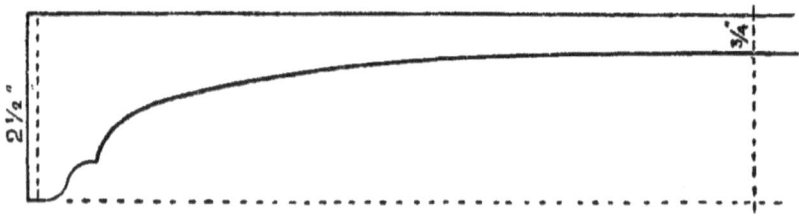

Fig. 197.—Enlarged Detail of Shaped Rail.

accurately measured, and it will be a simple matter to set out as Fig. 197 from the dimensions thus obtained. This will answer for simple outline, but where proportions and other details may be involved it will be preferable to take the extra trouble of ruling the tracing with vertical and horizontal lines, one (scale) inch apart as Fig. 198, so that the proportion can be transferred to a full size squaring as indicated at Fig. 199.

Shapings

Transferring to Wood.—Tracing paper, or the semi-transparent detail paper sold at artists' colourmen's, is suitable for the setting out, if enough confidence is not felt to pencil in the outlines direct on the wood,

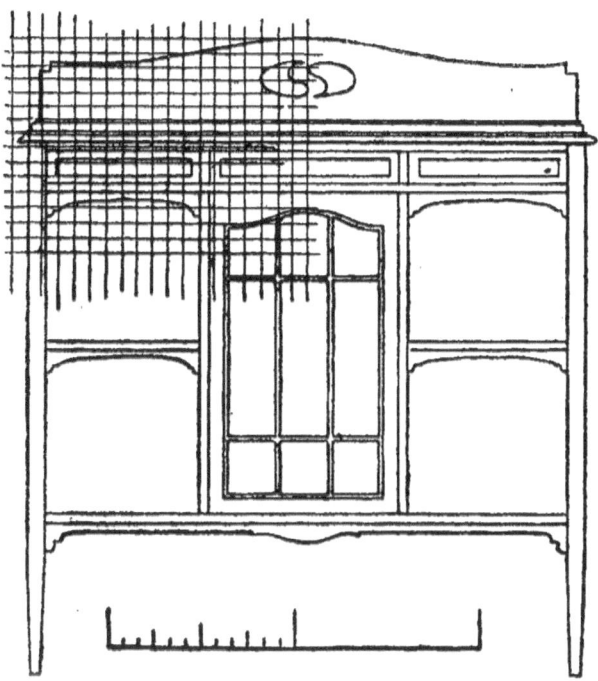

FIG. 198.—SCALE DIAGRAM PARTLY PLOTTED OUT.

measuring as you go. The set-out can be transferred by tracing to the wood after interposing a sheet of carbon paper between, or even by rubbing the back of the set out with a BB pencil, afterwards going over the transfer with a harder pencil to fix it on the wood.

How to Set Out Direct on Wood.—Apron pieces, which go between the uprights and head the openings of the framework, are the most likely pieces to want cutting, and a series of these will all play upon the simple line as seen at Fig. 200. The first one (A) can

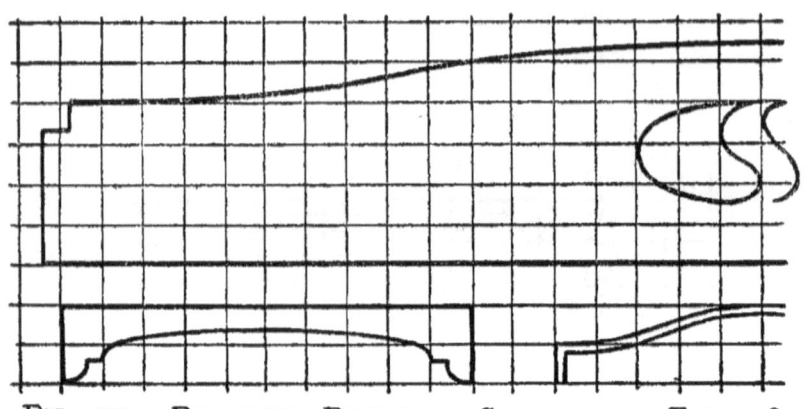

FIG. 199.—ENLARGED DETAIL OF SHAPINGS ON FIG. 198.

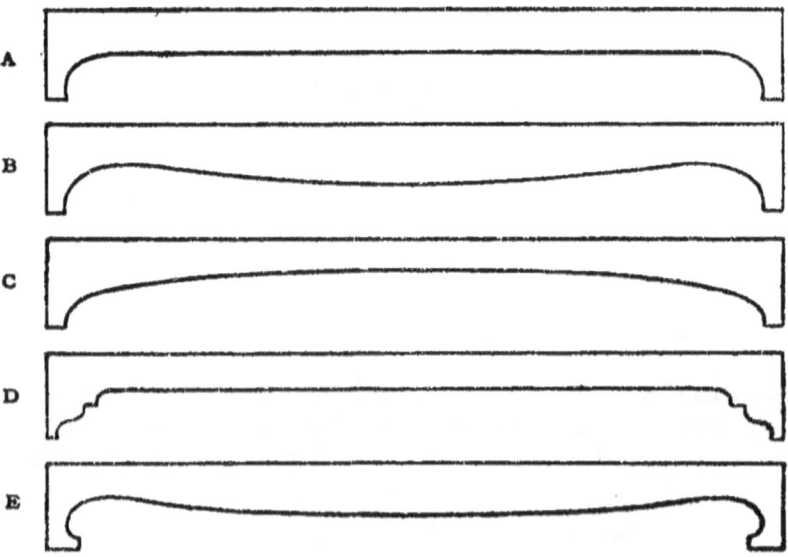

FIG. 200.—EXAMPLES OF SHAPED RAILS.

be cut from a piece 2¼ ins. wide by ½ in. thick. It is shaped back to 1 in. wide. The end curves of A and B

Shapings

may be struck with compasses, but it is preferable when possible to get a nice freehand line. The curves of B, C and E are set out freehand. Shapings have changed considerably in character within recent years, the curves being ellipitical rather than circular. The heavier type of apron piece is now rarely seen, simpler forms taking their place. In setting out such lines as Figs. 201 (F and H) the quickest and simplest method is to draw

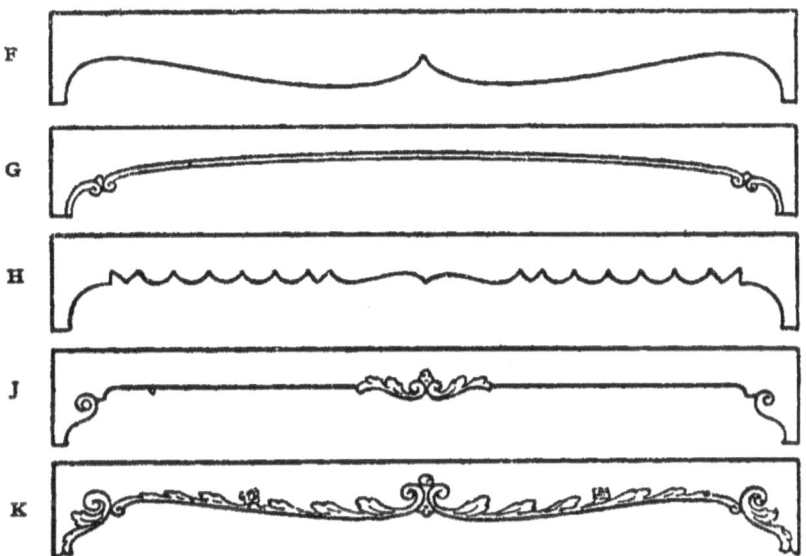

FIG. 201.—EXAMPLES OF SHAPED RAILS OR APRON-PIECES.

one half on paper and trace over, which will permit of the shaping being set in freehand by the beginner without loss of time in measuring the counterpart. G, J and K are indicated as carved, a fret-cut thicknessing of ¼-in. stuff being applied to the edge and touched up with the chisel. G can alternatively be treated with a scratched bead and finished at intersections with the chisel.

In the way of pediments the three shapings, Fig. 202,

Cabinet Construction

are suitable for plain or fumed oak, either with or without the central fret-cut openings. Such centre effects, by the way, look very dainty if inlaid with polished pewter, outlined black, in place of fret-cutting. If the white portion is grounded in and oiled, and molten lead poured in, to be smoothed off flush before polishing, a quick effect is obtainable.

Various hints are also offered for shelf brackets at Fig. 203.

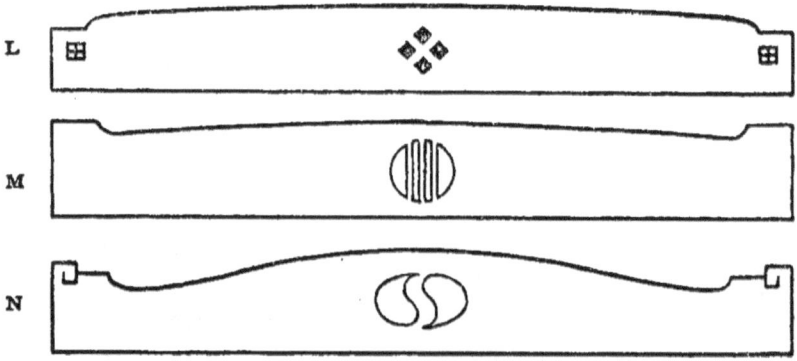

Fig. 202.—Examples of Shaped Pediments.

How to Cut Shapings.—For the purpose of cutting out the bow saw will be useful. The required shapings should be plainly marked, and every endeavour made to keep to the line when cutting; this will save a considerable amount of time and labour in trying to make good what might have been done at first. The wood should be firmly gripped in the vice between two spare pieces, to avoid bruising; and the angle at which it is held should be convenient for the saw to travel along the particular pitch of the shaping, for which purpose it may require shifting once or twice, as the cut proceeds. A set of compass saws and keyhole saw will also come in handy, together with a rasp, paring chisel and glass-paper.

Shapings

How to Finish.—In finishing it may be necessary to use the paring chisel in curves and small angles,

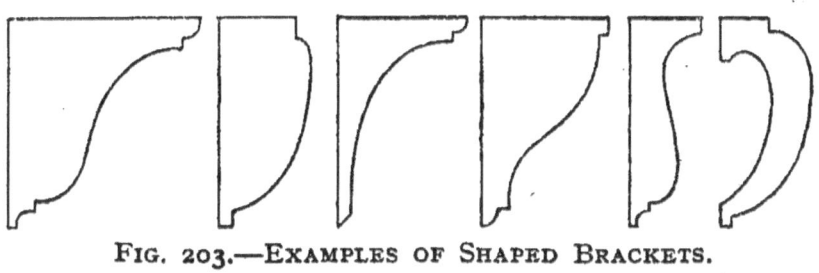

Fig. 203.—Examples of Shaped Brackets.

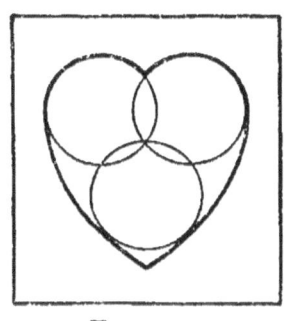

Fig. 204.

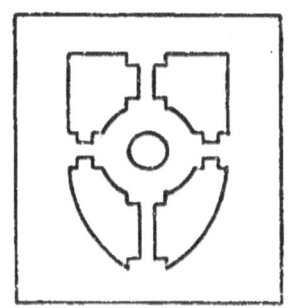

Fig. 205.

Fig. 206.
Examples of Fret-cut Openings.

taking out any splintered waste by cuts, both horizontally and vertically. A touch up of the spokeshave (or,

Cabinet Construction

occasionally, the rasp) may be required where curves have a tendency to waver, but the glass-paper and block should be sparingly used, as it has a rounding tendency on edges. When the edges are clean the face sides of the wood should be glasspapered.

To Cut Fret-cut Openings.—In cutting, say, a heart shape as Fig. 204, the waste may be quickly got away with a brace and twist, but inserted in the

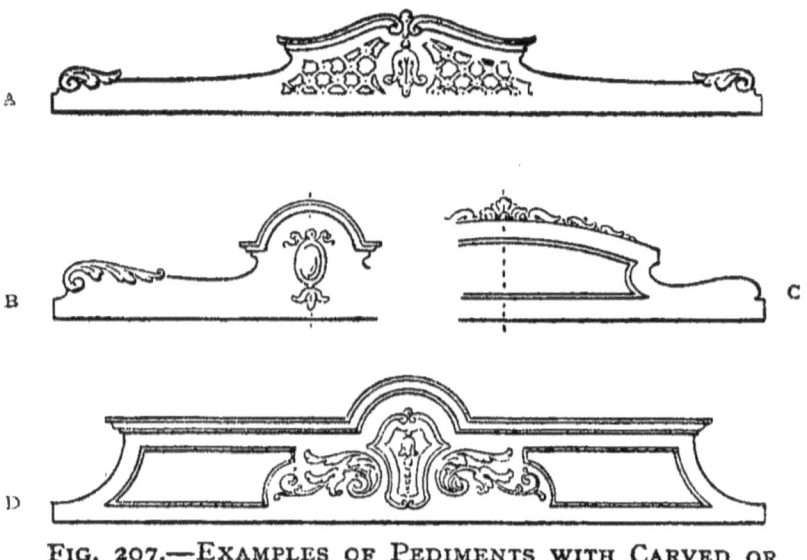

Fig. 207.—Examples of Pediments with Carved or Inlaid Decoration.

centres as indicated. For a shaping such as Fig. 205 some of the waste can be removed in the same manner, the keyhole saw then coming into play with good result.

An alternative opening is offered at Fig. 206 to a larger scale, which will afford a pleasing centre effect. The line of the oval will require carefully preserving, and should be cut sharp up to the leaves.

Shapings

Pediments.—Where a cabinet finishes on a level with the eye a more elaborate treatment of the pediment or upper back shaping often spells success. In such cases the four pediments (Fig. 207) may prove serviceable. A has applied scroll shapings to centre with terminal scrolls carved up. The

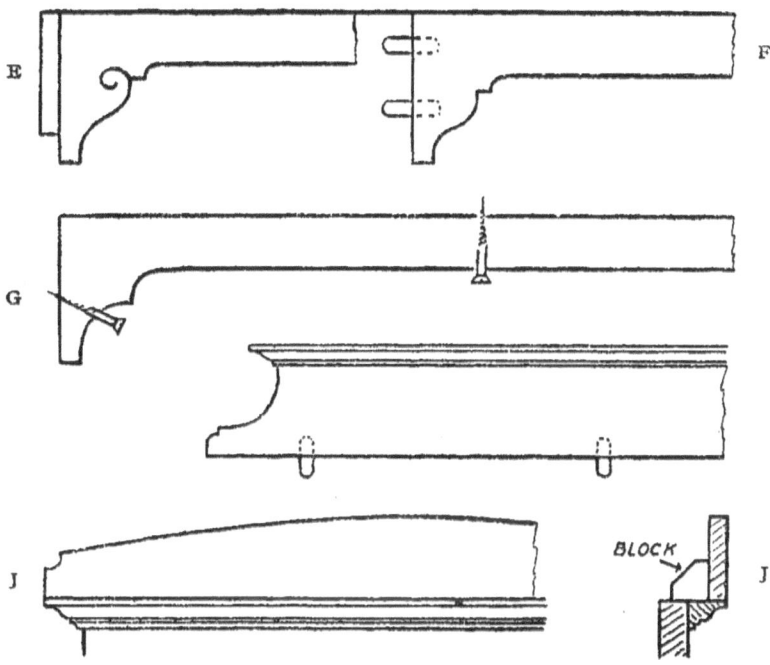

FIG. 208.—FITTING SHAPED WORK.

centre of this pediment has also an applied husk pendent from the scroll, and the scroll fretted on either side.

B has a moulded heading with applied carving.

C is a plain shaping with inlaid panel-outlined banding very suitable for mahogany or rosewood, with carved ribbon and husks, which can be fret-cut and applied. The lower panelled pediment carries a capping mould

Cabinet Construction

mitred up, and is carved with foliated scrolls, the centre being emphasised by an applied fret-cut and carved shield.

Fitting Shaped Work.—In fitting parts such as those being dealt with, the apron-pieces may be tenoned or tongued into grooves in the uprights between which they occur, as in Fig. 208 (E).

Alternatively, a deeper shaping may be fitted with a couple of suitable dowels as at F.

Shapings similar to G offer an opportunity of fixing by a thin screw in the manner indicated, and the same applies to small shapings forming spandrils, although a dowel at side and a screw at top are more often used.

Pediments can be fixed by dowelling, a dowel being inserted at intervals of about 12 ins. In boring for dowels to enter, the usual method is to place both pieces in the vice with their meeting edges level and side by side as they will come together. Lines at intervals are then squared across and the centre of thickness gauged across these, the intersection of the lines giving the centre for inserting a suitable twist bit. This should be inserted about 1 in. deep, the regulation of the depth being obtained by noting the number of twists of the brace. The edges of the holes should be very slightly countersunk and the end of the dowel tapped round with the hammer. The dowel in addition should be roughened and slightly channelled so that excess glue may squeeze out. The length of the dowel can be 2 ins., *i.e.*, 1 in. to enter above and 1 in. below.

In glue-blocking a pediment or apron-piece the blocks should be of sound and dry pine and cut to fit well up to their work. They should be cut with the grain to agree with that of the pieces they hold, and may have the outer corner or arris taken off with the

Shapings

plane as a finishing touch. In some instances a screw may be used in conjunction with glue, and in others screws only. In the latter case, if the wood is thick enough, the part can be fixed by screwing through pockets.

FACING, LINING AND LIPPING

FACING up is often necessary from many points of view. It is generally the most expeditious, economical and in some circumstances the most practical and only method to adopt. Let us suppose that we have some finely figured mahogany, satinwood, rosewood, or Italian walnut in thin stuff—say, $\frac{1}{4}$-in. or $\frac{3}{16}$-in. boards—and we want to make a mirror or door frame with it. The best thing to do is to make an under frame, either tenoned or lapped together, and " face " the front up with our finely figured stuff. It can be done as shown in Fig. 209, where the facing hangs over to form the rebate, or as in Fig. 210, where it stands back to form a recess for a moulding to be planted on. This method is often adopted in the best kind of work. Wood for the ground depends entirely on the job, but in all cases it should be dry and straight grained, or the frame will be likely to cast. Cornice and plinth frames are faced up in this way where it is not more advisable to make them in the solid.

Lining Up or Thicknessing is a different process. In a sideboard or table top, where it is necessary to have a thick outside moulding, the edges are lined up on the under side, as seen in Fig. 211, the grain all round running the same way as the top. In dining-tables this is always done, and often, in the case of chests of drawers and tops of cabinets, etc., a separate frame is made and a piece of solid stuff planted round it, as in Fig. 212.

Lipping is an economical method, and is universally used. Where tops, bottoms, divisions, or shelves only show on the outside edge, a lip or strip of solid stuff is jointed on the front, as Fig. 213. If the job is in

Facing, Lining and Lipping

mahogany, the inside may be of good pine or bay wood, and if of Italian walnut it may be of mahogany or American walnut. In rarer woods it would be very costly and unwise to make a job solid throughout. In the case of a writing-table top, which is to be lined with leather or cloth, the edges are lipped with solid stuff,

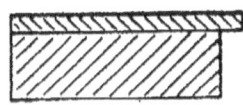

Fig. 209.—Facing a Mirror or Door Frame.

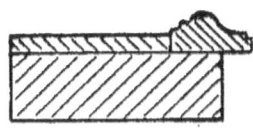

Fig. 210.—Facing behind a Planted-on Mould.

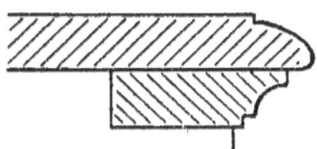

Fig. 211.—Lining up a Sideboard Top.

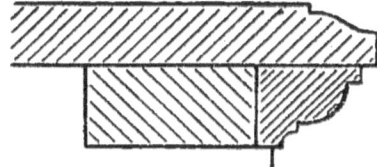

Fig. 212.—Lined-up Cabinet-Top.

Fig. 213.—Lipping for Tops or Shelves.

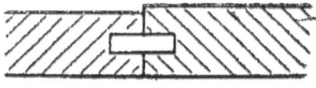

Fig. 214.—Lipping a Writing-Table Top.

which is allowed to stand above the inside surface just the thickness of the leather (see Fig. 214). In the old Queen Anne furniture the tops were lipped like this and then veneered, and all three methods are recognised in the workshops and are not necessarily associated with cheap work.

Cabinet Construction

Loose Chair Seats.—Although a little removed from the subject of facing, a sketch may be given here of the loose chair seat. When constructing a chair the simplest form of upholstering the seat is to fit a " pin-cushion " stuffing. This form of seating has the merit of being loose, being made up on a separate framing to drop into the recessed seat frame prepared for it, an arrangement which affords the opportunity of easily repairing or re-stuffing the upholstered portion. The frame can be made from stuff 2 ins. × $\frac{7}{8}$ in. or $\frac{3}{4}$ in., put together to

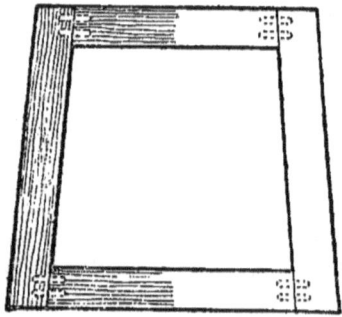

FIG. 215.—LOOSE SEAT FRAME FOR PIN-CUSHION STUFFING.

fit the chair seat framing, but to finish to such a size as will allow $\frac{1}{8}$ in. clearance all round from the rebate or recess into which it drops, this being necessary as an allowance for the thickness of any overlapping stuffing, in addition to the thickness of the material used for final covering. When completed the seat should press tightly home into position. The rails forming the frame will be dowelled together, with the side rails, outside front and back rails in the manner indicated in Fig. 215. If preferred, the frame may be mortised and tenoned together, or it could be halved and screwed, or bridle-jointed and pegged like a school slate frame.

RULE JOINT FOR DROP LEAVES

THE rule joint is a great improvement on the square joint for such articles as table and drop leaves, etc., showing as it does a neat closed joint instead of an ugly open one when the leaf is down.

In Figs. 216 and 217 are shown the finished joint, hinged, both up and down. In Figs. 219 and 220 are given the two parts set out ready for making the joint, the surplus being rebated away in the former.

The Circles.—It will be noticed that the circles which form the joint are not struck from the bottom of the table top and leaf, but from where the cross marks are made. The reason for this is that, when the hinge is let in flush with the wood, the centre of the pin on which the parts are pivoted will come to this point. Consequently this must be the point of the quarter circle on the table. The hollow on the leaf, being struck in the same way, and from the same centre, will, when hinged, touch at all parts as in Fig. 216, and never bind at any part whilst raising or lowering.

Special planes are made to work these joints, but it will hardly pay to buy these to make one or two joints only, and they can be made equally well with the ordinary hollows and rounds. Where care has to be taken is to set out the circles as above, to work to the lines, and to make the joints straight.

Hinges.—Figs. 221 and 222 show the two parts ready for hingeing, and Fig. 218 shows the special hinges used for these (called table joint hinges). These are let into the under side of the table top first, keeping the centre of the knuckle or pin perfectly square with the top at A, and letting it in far enough to bring the centre to the

Cabinet Construction

point from which the curve was struck. When the first part of the hinge (which must in all cases be the shortest part) is let in and screwed, it is easy to put the leaf in

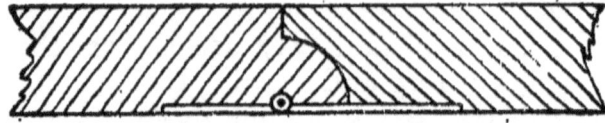

Fig. 216.—Rule Joint with Leaf up.

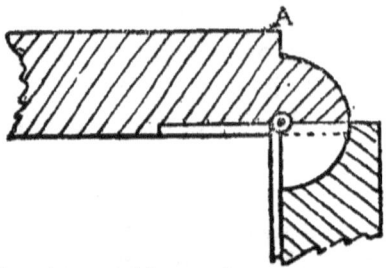

Fig. 217.—Rule Joint with Leaf down.

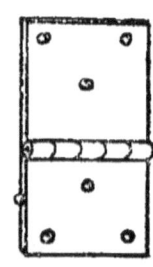

Fig. 218.—Table Joint Hinge.

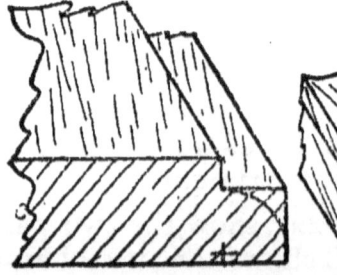

Fig. 219.—Round Part of Joint Set Out and Rebated.

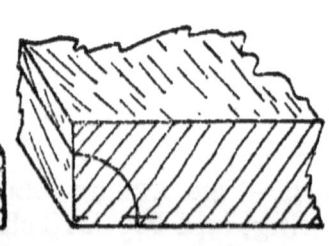

Fig. 220.—Hollow Part of Joint Set Out.

position and mark round the hinges, then cut out the marks and screw in as before.

If the whole has been done as described, the leaf will now open smoothly and easily, without friction, but

The Rule Joint

without any space showing between the two at any part of the opening. This is assuming the setting out and the making of the joint to have been done correctly; if not correctly done at the start it is practically impossible to put it right later with any certainty of success.

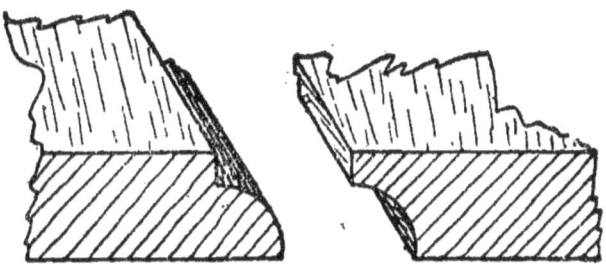

FIG. 221.—ROUND PART OF JOINT FINISHED READY FOR HINGEING.

FIG. 222.—HOLLOW PART OF JOINT READY FOR HINGEING.

Error to Guard Against.—Now, to show where the mistake is often made. Figs. 223 and 224 show what at first sight seems to be the same as Figs. 221 and 222, but the difference lies in the centre of the quarter circle, the former being struck from the bottom of the table top and leaf, instead of allowing for the thickness of the hinge as in the latter; the consequence is that, when hinged as in Fig. 225, they are quite right until the leaf is lowered. When this is done, however, the top part of the latter binds more and more as it goes down, until there is a risk of splitting off some part of the round.

The remedy for this is obvious. The leaf is taken off and a few shavings removed from the bottom part of the round, or out of the top part of the hollow, or both, as shown by the dotted lines. On replacing the leaf, it opens right enough, but does not fit the round as it should do, except when quite down, and when up the joint appears as at B, Fig. 225. This, of course, is not a correct rule joint, the real article appearing as Fig. 216;

FIG. 223.   FIG. 224.
ROUND AND HOLLOW PARTS OF JOINT MADE BY WRONG METHOD.

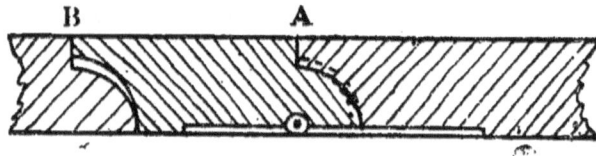

FIG. 225.—SHOWING JOINT WRONGLY MADE WITH THE RESULT OF "EASING" TO MAKE IT WORK.

and when we consider how little difference there is in making the proper joint and the false one it is to be hoped that the former will at least be tried.

HOW TO WORK MOULDINGS WITH PLANES

PREVIOUS to the introduction of wood-working machinery all the decoration on woodwork which took the form of mouldings was worked (or "stuck," as the old craftsman called it) by the aid of hollow and round planes, the plough plane, the rebate plane, and assorted sizes of gouges. There are many amateurs who never attempt any decorative effect, with perhaps the exception of a bevel or a chamfer, simply because they have not had the opportunity of seeing to what good use a few hollow and round planes can be put if manipulated by capable hands.

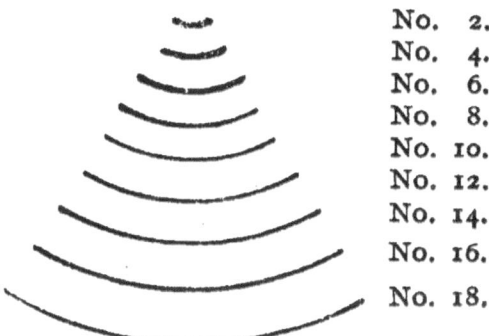

No. 2.
No. 4.
No. 6.
No. 8.
No. 10.
No. 12.
No. 14.
No. 16.
No. 18.

FIG. 226.—SHOWING FULL-SIZE PITCH OF HOLLOW AND ROUND PLANES NUMBERED (FROM CENTRE) 2, 4, 6, 8, 10, 12, 14, 16 AND 18.

A pair of No. 4 and a pair of No. 6 hollow and round planes can be put to great advantage and will cover the bulk of the work likely to be attempted by an amateur.

Cabinet Construction

Hollow and Round Planes are made in two distinct types: (*a*) planes having square mouths, and (*b*) planes having skew mouths. The square-mouthed planes are probably the best for an amateur, because they are

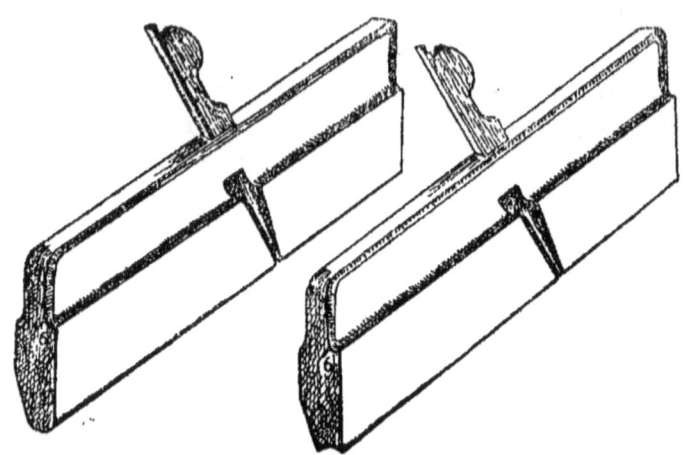

FIG. 227.—ROUND PLANE.   FIG. 228.—HOLLOW PLANE.

easier to sharpen and less liable to choke up at the mouth. The skew-mouthed planes, however, give a finer finish to the work, and are exceptionally fine tools if used by patient workers.

Working a Small Hollow or Scotia.—We will take as our example the working of a small hollow—or scotia moulding, as it is also called. It is required to work the moulding on the edge of a shelf and in the direction of the grain of the wood. Take a cutting gauge and lightly strike a line on the face and edge of the timber; then, with a pencil and a piece of cardboard, cut to the desired shape and mark out the hollow at each end of the wood, as Fig. 229. Next take a jack plane and proceed to plane away the surplus material until the bevelling

Mouldings

almost touches the two gauged lines, Fig. 230. The next operation is shown at Fig. 231, and consists of

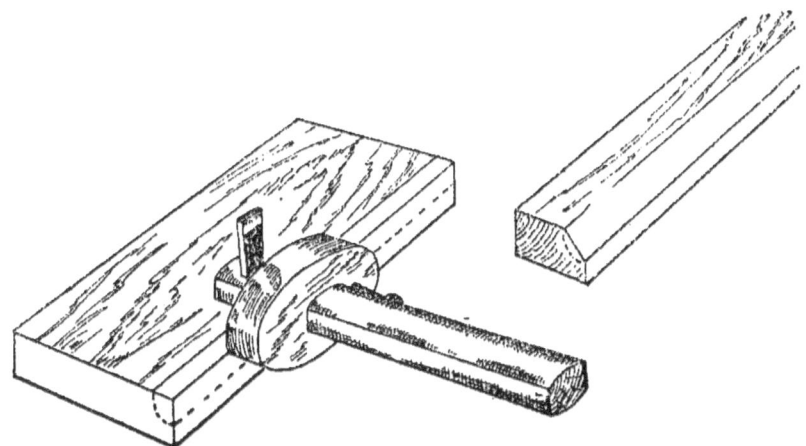

Fig. 229.—Gauging for a Small Hollow.

Fig. 230.—Bevelling for a Small Hollow.

roughly cutting the hollow with a suitably shaped gouge; the object of this operation is to form a rough channel in which to start the plane.

Method of Using Plane.—The plane is now grasped as at Fig. 233, and it is important that *the long finger of the left hand should be used as a guide,* touching as it does with the tip of the finger both the lower edge of the plane and the edge of the shelf. The planing is continued until the gauge lines are reached, and then the work is glasspapered up by using a cork rubber of suitable size around which the glasspaper has been wrapped, as Fig. 232. The plane must be finely set so as to take off very thin shavings.

To work a hollow across the end way of the grain the same procedure is followed with the exception that, previous to the use of glasspaper, it may be necessary to run a round rat-tailed file along the hollow.

Cabinet Construction

Working an Ovolo Moulding.—For our next example we will take the working of an ovolo moulding. There are, of course, special ovolo moulding planes made purposely for this operation, but we shall concern ourselves with working up an ovolo moulding by using a hollow plane, because by using the hollow we can work several sizes of moulding with one plane, whereas with a ⅜-in. ovolo plane we are confined to the working of

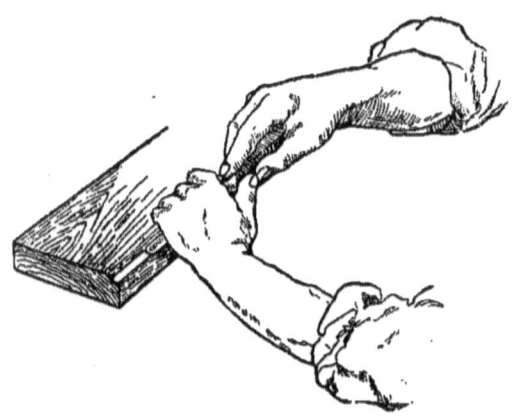

Fig. 231.—Cutting Hollow with Gouge.

Fig.—232.—Finishing a Mould with Glasspaper.

a ⅜-in. ovolo. Strike a line up the face and edge of the wood with a cutting gauge, and mark out the ovolo mould at each end of the timber. Take a ¾-in. or 1-in. sharp chisel and pare away a small channel, as shown at Fig. 234; now turn your wood on its edge, and cut a similar channel along the other gauge mark; bevel away the wood with a jack plane, as far as it is possible to do so, and take care not to plane below your marked moulding. Now take your hollow plane as shown at Fig. 236, and proceed to round over your work. The pitch or inclination of the plane will have to be altered as you plane your wood away, so that the contour of the

Mouldings

moulding is a clean sweep, *i.e.*, free from any small facets. A hollow plane (No. 6) would in this manner work or round up a curvature even double the size of its own face width; see Fig. 235, which shows a large ovolo worked by altering the inclination of the plane from B to A.

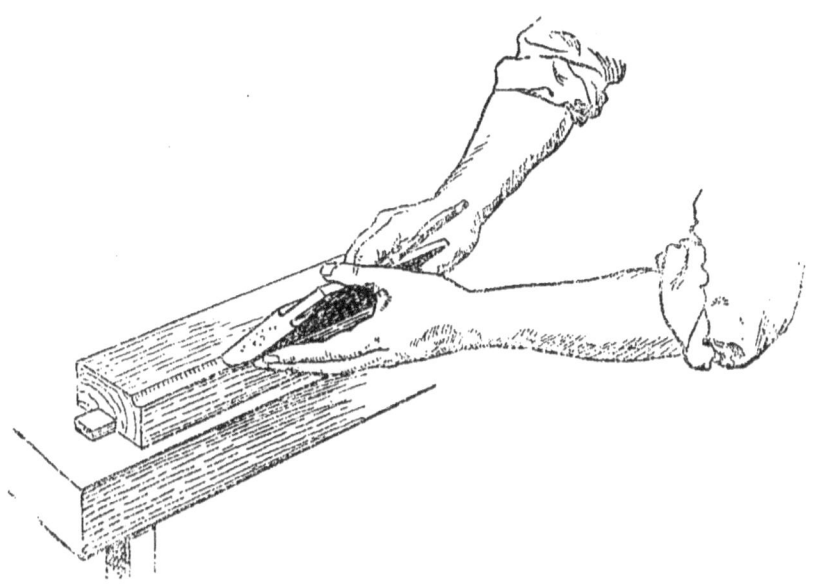

FIG. 233.—PLANING A SMALL HOLLOW.

Working Mouldings with many Members.— Fig. 237 illustrates the plough, rebate, hollow, round and bead planes for the working of a complicated 4-in. architrave moulding, such as is used round a door or window casing. The plough is first used to make grooves at 1, 2 and 3; this will cut away piece 4 entirely, thus saving a bead which can be used to advantage upon some other work. The plough plane may then be readjusted to plough away piece 5; or, considering that the width of piece 5 is only approximately $\frac{3}{8}$ in., it may be cut down with a chisel and worked away with a rebate plane. The portion marked 7 would now be roughly cut with a

Cabinet Construction

gouge and a suitable-sized round plane would be used to work it up to a finish. The small bead and quirk (the quirk is shown at B, Fig. 238) could be worked at one

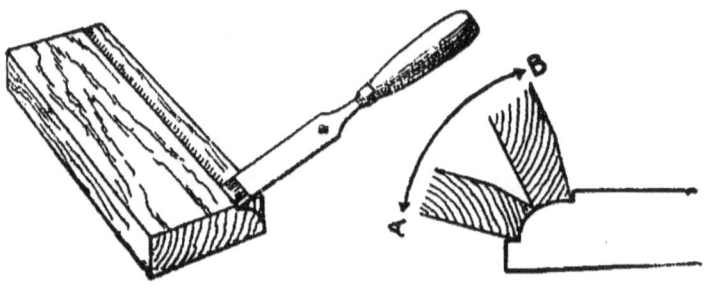

Fig. 234.—Chiselling for an Ovolo.

Fig. 235.—Inclination of Planes for Large Ovolo.

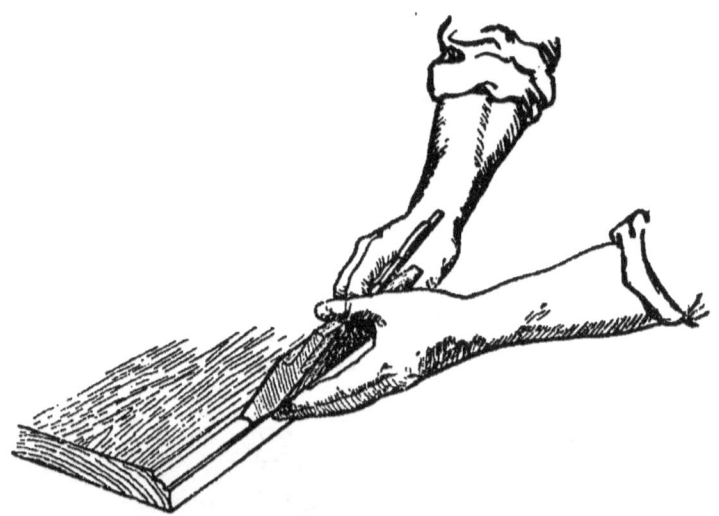

Fig. 236.—Planing an Ovolo.

operation with a ⅜-in. bead plane, or failing a bead plane, the quirk could be worked with a scratch stock, and the bead part worked over with the hollow plane. A gauge line would be marked at 8, and by using a rebate plane

Mouldings

in a tilted position as indicated the portion 8 would be gradually worked away. Part 9 would be similarly treated, and 10 would be bevelled away with the jack

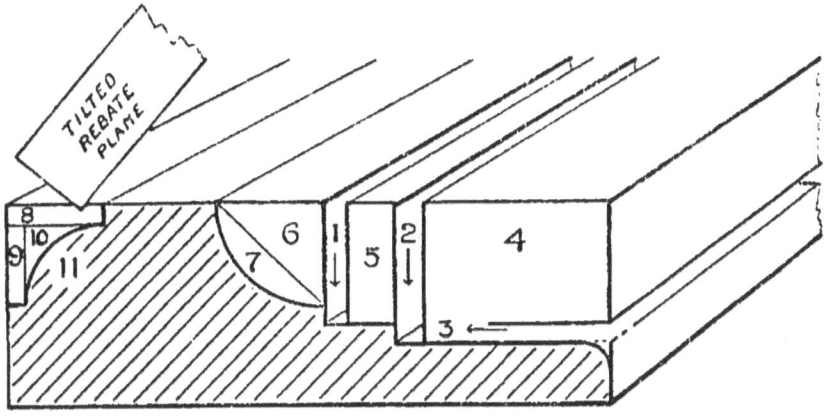

Fig. 237.—Working an Architrave Moulding.

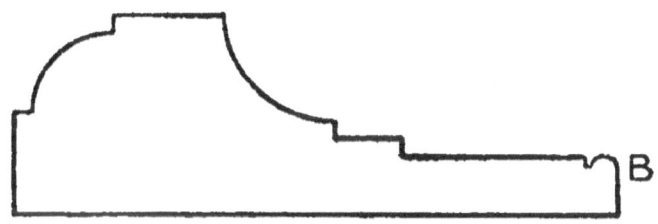

Fig. 238.—Section of Architrave Mould.

plane. A hollow plane would now be used to merge 8, 9, and 10 into a completed ovolo.

Fig. 238 shows an end section of the finished moulding.

INLAID STRINGS AND BANDINGS

THE very considerable improvement that inlaid treatment of a panel with lines or banding is capable of imparting to an otherwise plain piece of wood is so noticeable that the woodworker who neglects this part of his craft is really sacrificing one of his best opportunities of turning out an attractive specimen of work. The process is compelling

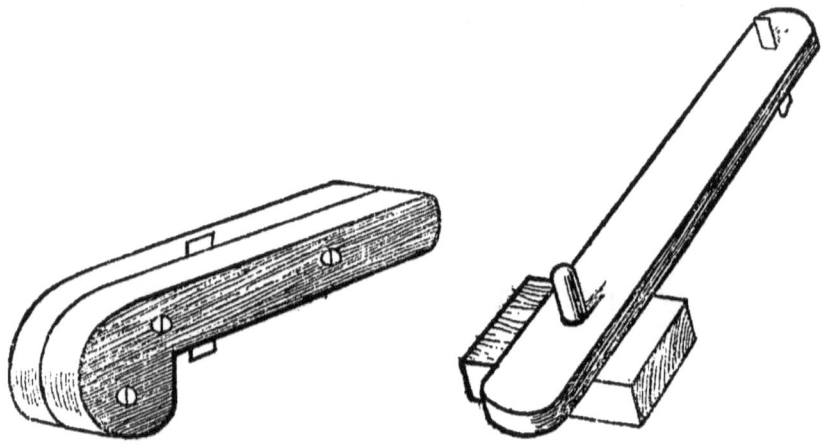

FIG. 239.—CUTTER OR ROUTER FOR CHANNELLING.

FIG. 240.—SCRIBER FOR CUTTING CIRCLES.

in its interest, and in the simple stages involves little difficulties that a watchful eye and careful hand will not readily surmount; whilst, as experience comes, the more intricate cutting will prove as absorbing a challenge to one's ingenuity as the extra knowledge of figured grain and texture is interesting.

Stringings and Bandings

Tools.—In the way of tools, little but what is probably already possessed will be necessary, and a lot can be done with a straight-edge, template and well-sharpened penknife. A fine dovetail saw, marking and cutting gauges, a hammer, some sharp chisels, a marker and a mallet should also be at hand. A few hand-screws will be useful, but in small work the domestic flat-iron and a lead weight or two, used on a zinc sheet or stout and true board, will often do all that is required.

Cutters.—The little pistol-shaped cutter, Fig. 239, is an item that any worker can quickly make for himself. It should be of oak, mahogany or other hard wood, and consists of two pieces screwed tightly together to form a grip for the cutter which is of thin steel. The edge should be kept square, and a little practice in its use will soon make it evident that, to get a good result, it is necessary to grip it firmly with both hands and work as close as possible up to the panel edge. The tool is constantly useful for routing out the core for lines and bandings.

Scribers.—Another simple and handy device is the scriber indicated at Fig. 240, which is readily knocked up from a spare block and length of stout lath or fillet. A screw or dowel is entered to form a pivot for the holed lath, which has a cutter tightly inserted at the other end as shown. The tool will cut a circle or any segment of it, as required; the method of using it being to glue the block to the panel in a centred position as at Fig. 241, press on the dowel end with the left hand and work the cutter with the right. To facilitate removal, paper should be glued with weak glue between the block and panel surface. A panel such as that indicated, with circle centre in box line and an edge of banded satinwood, has a very neat effect.

Front of Lady's Workbox, with Inlaid Band and Inlaid Ornament in Centre.

Stringings and Bandings

STRINGINGS.

Stringing or Lining.—The strings for inlaying are sold by marquetry cutters in bundles of about 3 ft. long, but it is possible to purchase a few lengths only, as required, the size varying from the very finest to about ⅛ in. square. Ebony and box lines are most generally in use, but dyed stringings offer a fairly wide range of colour. Being thin and quite pliable they can usually

FIG. 241.—USING THE SCRIBER.

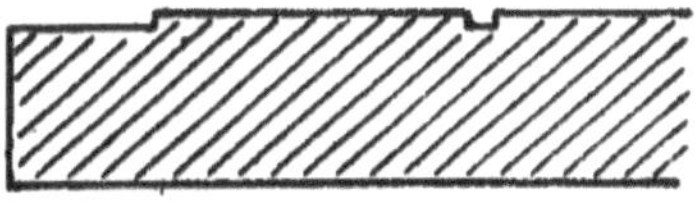

FIG. 242.—SECTION OF EDGE OF FIG. 241.

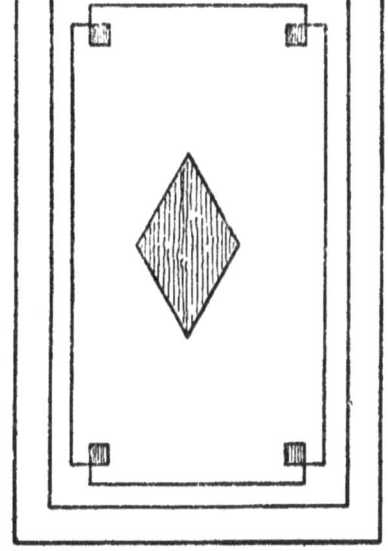

FIG. 243.—LINE-INLAYING DESIGN.

be sprung to a simple curving, failing which they can be bent by steaming or be cramped. The sinking or channel can be cut with a marking gauge, sharp bradawl, or spike end of a chisel, taking care to keep on the narrow side or width, so that the string fits tight when glued in.

Cabinet Construction

Use the hammer head for pressing in, and do not seek to hurry the work. If more than one string is to be laid in the same channel, finish one first and let it dry before doing the next.

Instead of purchasing his strings the worker may cut his own from a sheet of veneer by the aid of a fine toothed saw and straight-edge, but, being so cheap, there is little economy in it either as regards time or money.

If a string rises after glueing, this may be due to its being cut a shade too long for its groove, but a touch of glue inserted underneath with a warm penknife blade and a weight on top will generally put matters right. Let the string get thoroughly dry and set before cleaning off, to allow for the moisture evaporating from the glue with a corresponding contraction.

Line-inlaying Design.—For the benefit of the beginner, a suggestion for simple line inlaying is offered at Fig. 243, which should be useful for the door of a smoker's cabinet or medicine cupboard. In setting out the design the face of the panel may be chalked over so that the pencilled lines show clearly. Each angle should be cleanly cut, and stopped by working away from it before finishing the cutting of the channel between. The diamond centre can be worked round the edges of a template with awl or file end, taking care to centre the template before cutting.

BANDINGS.

Bandings.—These are very varied in pattern and are obtainable from $\frac{1}{4}$ in. to about 1 in. in width. Fig. 244 shows a "herring-bone" design with purplewood and box centre, edged with ebony and box lines. Fig. 245 is a satinwood banding, edged with ebony and box; Figs. 246 and 247 are chequered patterns. Both Figs.

Stringings and Bandings

249 and 250, about $\frac{5}{16}$ in. wide, are very useful and quaint in effect for drawer fronts or panels. Fig. 251 indicates a greywood and chequered combination which is very successful on a Sheraton mahogany finish.

FIG. 244.—HERRING-BONE BANDING.

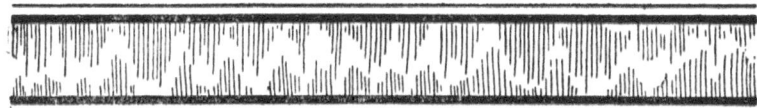

FIG. 245.—SATINWOOD BANDING WITH EBONY AND BOXWOOD EDGE.

FIG. 246.—CHEQUERED PATTERN.

FIG. 247.—ANOTHER CHEQUERED DESIGN.

A Home-made Chequered Pattern can be got by carefully glueing up slips of cross-grained ebony and satinwood or boxwood alternately with veneered edging top and bottom. Strips cut off the end with

Cabinet Construction

tenon saw and straight-edge, when all is thoroughly dry, will supply the banding required. See Fig. 248.

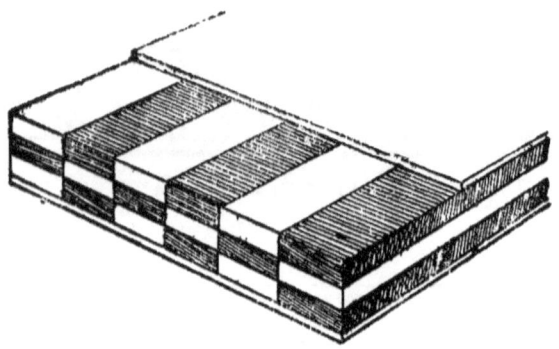

FIG. 248.—METHOD OF MAKING A CHEQUERED BANDING.

FIGS. 249 AND 250.—NARROW BANDINGS FOR DRAWER FRONTS.

FIG. 251.—GREYWOOD AND CHEQUERED COMBINATION FOR SHERATON MAHOGANY FURNITURE.

The Channel or sinking for the banding should be cut with a gauge having two cutters so that, when set to width, both edges of channel can be cut under one operation. Cut in the corners at the start to ensure their being clean. The core or waste can then be

Stringings and Bandings

removed with the router or scratch tool (Fig. 239) or with the chisel to the required depth. The ground should be pricked up slightly or holed with a steel point to give the glue an extra grip.

The best Scotch glue only should be used, and it should be rather thin. The tendency of the banding being to sink in its channel as the glue sets, no cleaning should be done till all is dry and hard.

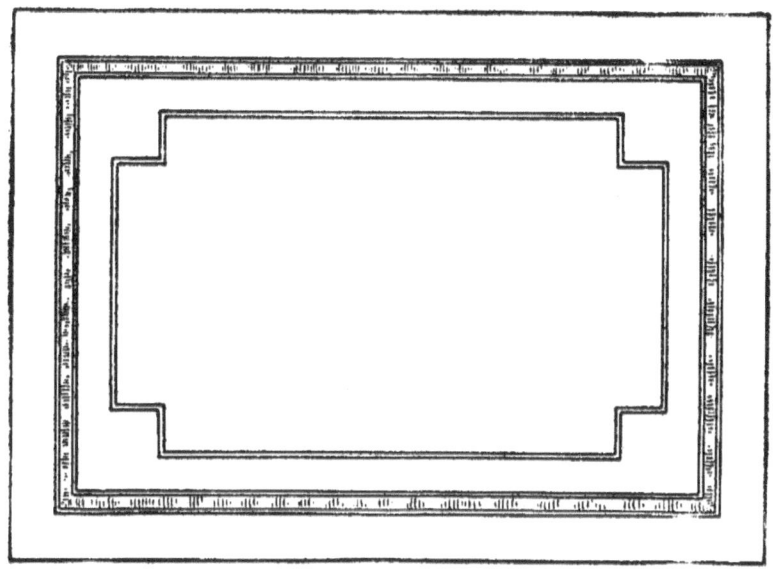

FIG. 252.—BANDED PANEL WITH INNER STRING LINE.

Inlaying the Binding, glue the groove and the underside of the banding; then place one end of the banding in the groove, and with the hammer head press all along till the full length is in position. Cover with paper and a caul, and hand-screw down, or the banding can be held in position with strappings of tape bound over it. Take care that no grit gets into the glue, and apply it sparingly.

Cabinet Construction

For light woods, such as satinwood, box, holly, oak, etc., it is best to mix flake white with the glue to prevent it showing at the edges as a hair line. Should the banding blister or not lie flat, apply a moderately hot strip of ⅛-in. zinc. and place a weight over. Zinc cauls are preferable, as they hold heat longer than wood.

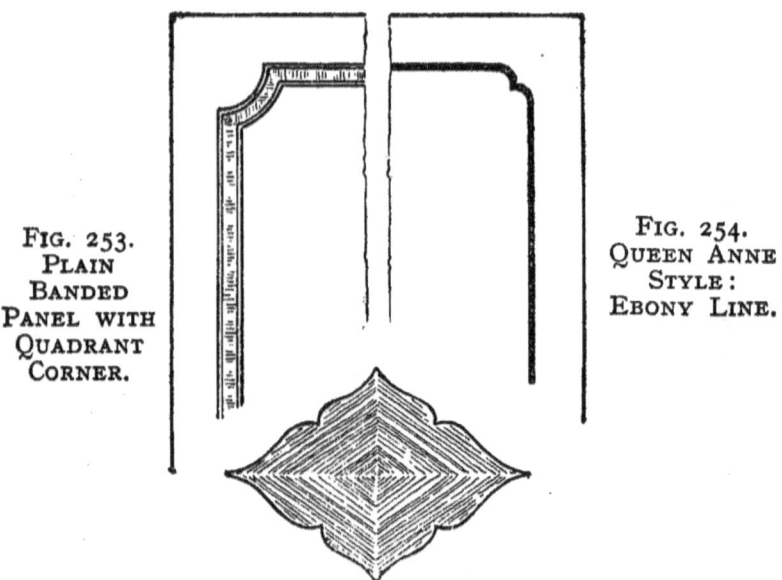

FIG. 253. PLAIN BANDED PANEL WITH QUADRANT CORNER.

FIG. 254. QUEEN ANNE STYLE: EBONY LINE.

FIG. 255.—QUEEN ANNE PANEL CENTRE.

SOME PATTERNS.

Fig. 252 gives an example of a banded panel with interior line and broken corners. Purplewood and ebony go well with oak and satinwood, or greywood with box line on mahogany. Fig. 253 shows a plain banded panel with quadrant corner, the shaping of which can be cut to line round a template with a sharp penknife. The

Stringings and Bandings

cross-grain may present a little difficulty at first glance, but, if cut in centre and mitred up at angles as indicated, the result will be right. Fig. 254 is a Queen Anne line in frequent use and can be in ebony, cut round a template. It is often seen in conjunction with quartered mahogany panels.

Fig. 255 is of similar character and has a good effect used as a panel centre. It can be built up and laid on cartridge paper, or the channel for the stringing can be cut round a template. The design may be elongated for an oblong panel centre, if desired, with or without quartering. The core can be removed from centre with a chisel, carefully avoiding all cutting into the outline. Roughen and hole the ground slightly, glue the back of inlay and ground just sufficiently, lay the inlay in, cover with paper and a small caul, and handscrew down. Clean off with the toothing plane and hammer.

Fig. 256 is a design suitable for a workbox or small cabinet door. It will be found very interesting to cut, and is a type of border banding that is not seen so often as it might be nowadays. It will be seen that the outline is in repeats, so that, if one half of top and side is set out on paper, the design can be carefully traced over as a short cut to getting it exact. Paste the pattern on the veneer and cut out with a fretsaw. Then mitre up the lengths and lay in position, so that it can be marked round with a hard and sharp pencil and the outline be cut in with suitable gouges and chisels. It is, however, preferable to spend a little extra time over the work and make a template of wood, cutting in the outline with the sharp penknife, which can be quickly edged on a strip of fine emery cloth kept at hand for frequent use. Take out the core with chisels, cutting cautiously up to line ; keep the ground flat and bevel off with the router. See that the glue is clear before applying to the rebate and edging ; then rub in and caul or tape

Cabinet Construction

over. The edging is also suitable for cutting in brass or other metal, which should be scored with a graving tool or the tang of a file. Mix a little gold size with the glue, and when cleaning off use hot water.

Fig. 256.—Design for Workbox Top or Small Cabinet Door.

Fig. 257 could be inlaid in ebony with chequered extremities. The design is also suitable for stringing in brass or pewter, the edging being rebated and mitred.

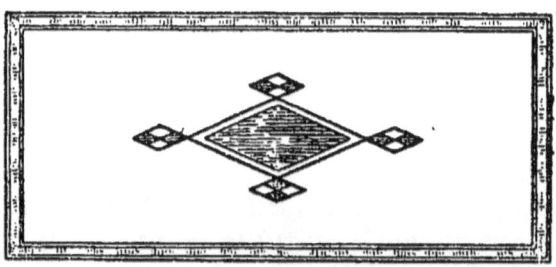

Fig. 257.—Centre Ornament in Ebony and with Chequered Extremities.

Fig. 259 shows a panel suitable for the door of a mahogany sideboard or dinner-wagon, and may be treated as a raised panel. Set the cutting gauge carefully to inner and outer lines, so that the banding will

Stringings and Bandings

fit easily and enter with a little pressure. Cut and enter the corner squares first, and, when set, cut the bandings to butt full tight up to the squares. Caul one side at a time and do not rush the work if a good result is sought. Any cutting of channels should be done before the edge is bevelled.

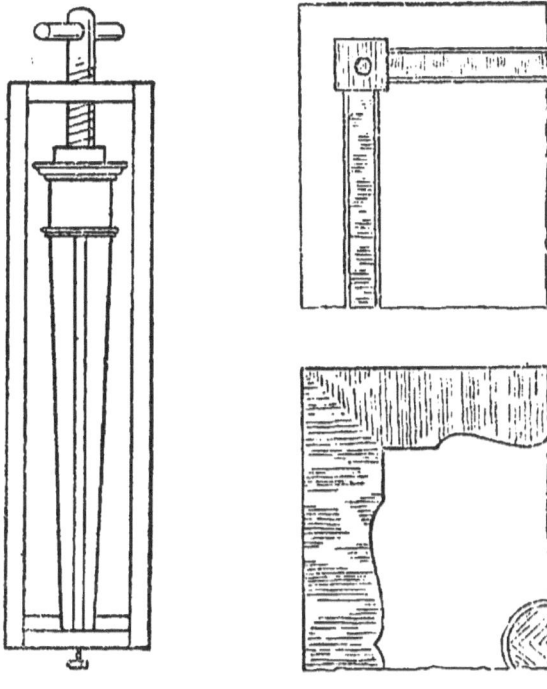

FIG. 258.—HOLDING TAPERED LEGS.

FIGS. 259 AND 260. SUGGESTIONS FOR DOOR PANELS.

Fig. 260 makes a successful panel when complete and is suitable for the doors of a mahogany or walnut china cabinet.

Tapered Legs with a banding down centre (Fig. 258) may present some difficulty owing to the absence of a parallel edge to work the cutting upon. This may be

Cabinet Construction

got over by making a box of stuff sufficiently stout to stand the strain (a cube sugar box has served the purpose before now) with a wood screw entered at top for adjustment, and an ordinary screw at the bottom to hold the extremity of the column or leg. Any play can be corrected by blocking.

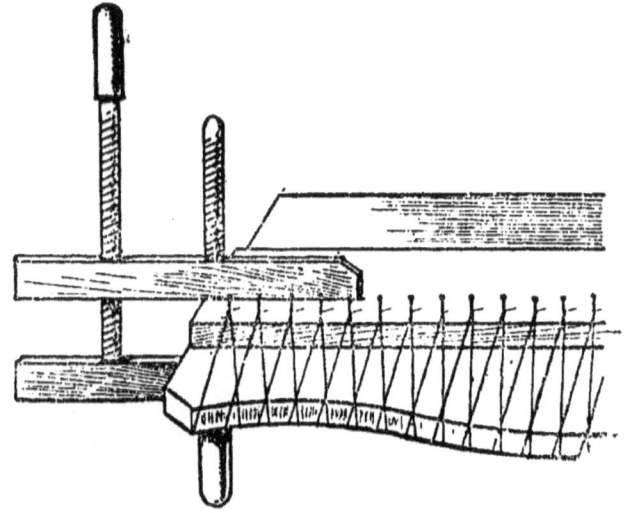

FIG. 261.—METHOD OF TAPING BANDINGS GLUED TO A SHAPED EDGE.

Taping.—Straight edges are easily taped, but it is not quite so simple to bind a square line or banding in position on a shaped edge after glueing. Fig. 261 is a suggestion as to how the little problem may be dealt with by handscrewing a board above and another below the surface to be treated. Nails or screws are inserted at close intervals into each board as winding stays for the tapes, which can be laced round them.

METAL FITTINGS ON FURNITURE

THE metal furnishings of any piece of cabinet work are capable of greatly enhancing the artistic effect, whilst the accurate fitting of such details as hinges, locks, catches, etc., so that they work freely, bears testimony to the thinking capacity of the worker, who should use no tool on his work till he can clearly see what are his limitations.

HINGES.

Butt Hinges.—Even the innocent-looking butt hinge (Fig. 262) is ripe for trouble if the niceties of the fitting are not observed, and a hinge-bound door or lid is the result. At the outset, the closed hinge should be carefully gauged, the marking point being central on the pivot pin of the hinge, with the sliding head of the gauge set against the edge of the flanges. This distance is then gauged on to the edge to be hinged from the outer or face side of the part. Next transfer the thickness of the flange, a shade under than over, to allow for the tool when cutting to line. The limit of the waste is then carefully cut at ends with tenon saw and pared out with chisel, V-cuts being taken out along the gauged line to prevent overshooting the mark. Should it happen that the resulting recess is a trifle too deep, it can be packed with brown paper under the flange.

Special attention must be paid in fitting two or more hinges to the necessity of getting the centre pivots of the hinges exactly in line. If this is not done the door or lid cannot work smoothly, and will crackle and bind if force is used. If finished a trifle thicker than necessary

Cabinet Construction

it will generally bind upon the stops behind it, in which case the door should be planed a shade thinner; or the trouble may be met by slightly easing the edge of the door.

Frequently a door is screw-bound by reason of the heads of the screws being too large to go flush into the countersunk holes of the flange. The remedy is to enlarge the holes with a rose-bit if the right size screws are not at hand.

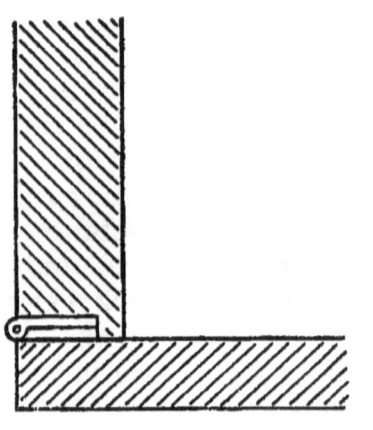

FIG. 262.—BUTT HINGE.
(Both flanges let into Door.)

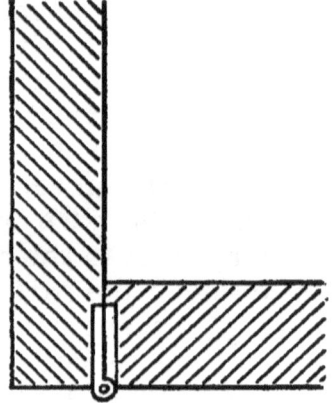

FIG. 263.—BUTT HINGE.
(One flange into Door, the other into Carcase End.)

With regard to the position of the hinge on the door, this is generally fitted so that it clears the joint of the cross-rail nicely—a third hinge (as in a wardrobe door) being midway between the two.

Butt hinges are always let into the edges of frame or door, and at times into both of these. At Fig. 262 a butt hinge is shown in the position it would occupy if let into door to its whole thickness and screwed on to end, a method frequently adopted in hasty work.

Metal Fittings

Fig. 263 shows one flange of butt let into door and the other into end, and is a more satisfactory method. It is adopted when the door opens and shuts upon the carcase end, from which it swings clear to the extent of a semicircle.

Fig. 264 shows another method often used. The hinge has its full thickness cut into the door at the knuckle end, with the cuts slanting so that the edges of the flanges lie one in the door and one in the end flush.

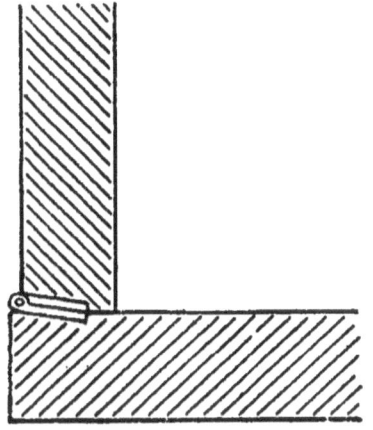

Fig. 264.—Butt Hinge.
(Let in slantwise.)

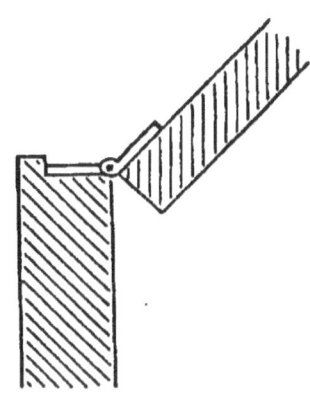

Fig. 265.—Box Lid Hinge.
(Note bed for Flange.)

Box Lid Hinges (Fig. 265).—In cases such as hingeing the lid of a box, both flanges may be recessed into the edge of the box side if this will take the screw length better than with one flange in box and one flange in lid. In this instance the centre of knuckle-pin is in line with the outer face of parts to which the hinge is screwed —as also at Fig. 262.

At times it is desired to stop the hinged part that opens to a right angle, as may happen in the case of a workbox. The hinge is then recessed *within* the outer edges

Cabinet Construction

of the hinged parts, as at Fig. 266, the angles of both edges being equally planed off to an angle of 45 degrees, so that when open they meet at a mitre as in Fig. 267.

The above hints will cover most needs of door hanging in cabinet work, but little points outside them often give rise to temporary trouble that will require close observation to overcome. It is, therefore, advisable to have a trial fit-up with one screw only in the butt when screwing on the door.

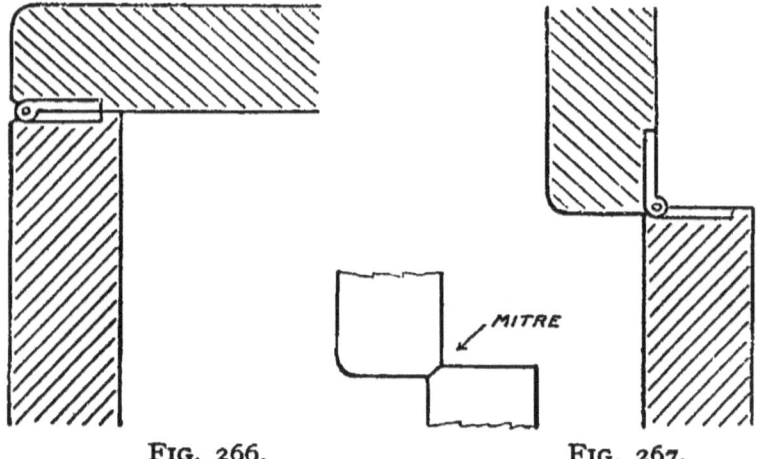

FIG. 266.   FIG. 267.
BOX HINGES FITTED FOR LID TO OPEN AT RIGHT ANGLE.

Stopped Butt Hinges.—Apart from the ordinary butt hinge (Fig. 268) various types are made for special purposes, one being the stopped butt—so-called because it opens and stops at a right-angle, and can in consequence be used instead of proceeding as Figs. 266 and 267.

A Back Flap Hinge, used for fixing fall-down flaps, is shown at Fig. 269. The fixing is of the simplest, requiring merely to be held in position and screwed on.

Metal Fittings

Strap Work Hinge.—In furniture of a Gothic or Renaissance character strap-work hinges are frequently fitted outside, and in some cases are very ornate in detail. Such hinges require the knuckle to be centred carefully over the meeting edges of the parts to which they are screwed.

A Rising Butt Hinge, which allows of a door fitted with same being readily lifted off from position, is

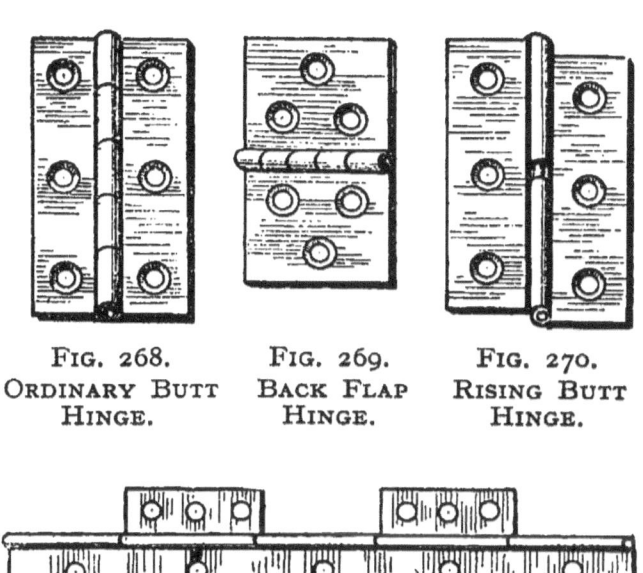

FIG. 268. ORDINARY BUTT HINGE. FIG. 269. BACK FLAP HINGE. FIG. 270. RISING BUTT HINGE.

FIG. 271.—PIANO HINGE.

shown at Fig. 270. It is often useful where wide panelled doors are required to swing open in a limited gangway.

Piano Hinge.—Fig. 271 shows a section of piano hinge which can be obtained in length up to several feet, and is serviceable and neat for hingeing the lid to a lengthy box.

Cabinet Construction

Cross Garnet and H-Hinges are fitted by screwing on the front, the H-hinges of antique pattern being very effective on oak, fumigated or stained to a Jacobean colour and polished.

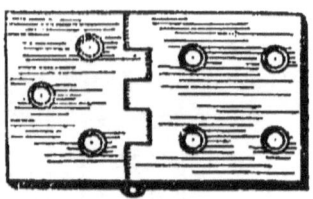

Fig. 272.—Table Rule Joint Hinge.

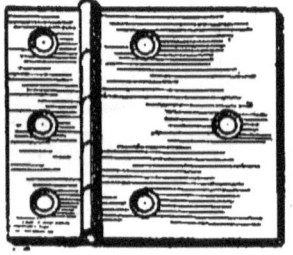

Fig. 273.—Wardrobe Door Hinge.

Fig. 274. Knobbed Butt Hinge.

A Table Rule Joint Hinge (Fig. 272) requires the knuckle to be let into the wood in fitting, and consequently has the screw holes countersunk on the reverse side to the knuckle. It is very neat in appearance, but difficult to fit accurately. (See page 113.)

Knobbed Butt Hinge.—Fig. 273 is a hinge specially made for wardrobe doors, and Fig. 274 is a "knobbed butt" hinge for the same purpose with a neater and more pleasing finish.

Metal Fittings

Fig. 275.—Card Table Hinge.

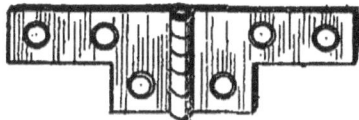

Fig. 276.—Card Table Strap Hinge.

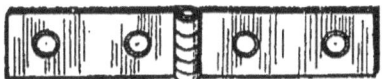

Fig. 277.—Strap Hinge.

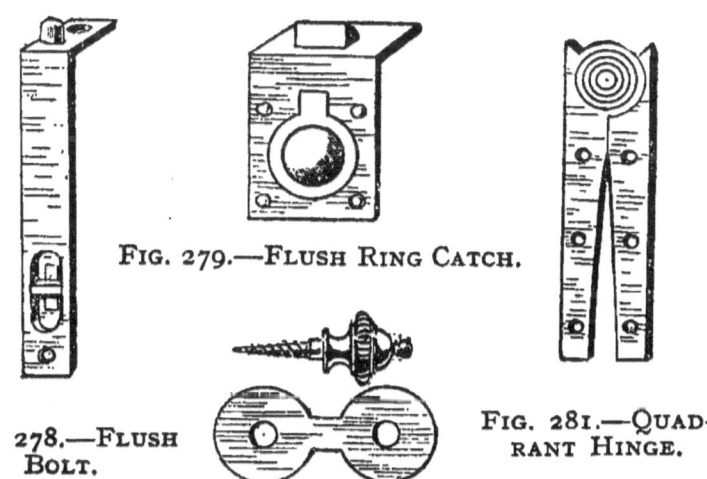

Fig. 279.—Flush Ring Catch.

Fig. 278.—Flush Bolt.

Fig. 280.—Screw and Plate for Rod Screen.

Fig. 281.—Quadrant Hinge.

Cabinet Construction

A Card Table Hinge, which requires to be cut flush into the parts to be connected, is shown at Fig. 275.

Where the fixing space is on the narrow side, strap hinges (Figs. 276 and 277) are serviceable types to use and will need to be bedded flush in a similar manner.

Centre Hinges are another type used for fitting to top and bottom of a door. They are in two parts, the one with a holed plate which fits to the carcase, and the other with a projecting pin in the plate to correspond with the hole. This is screwed on to the door, every precaution being taken to secure alignment of the centres.

A Quadrant Hinge (Fig. 281) is used for fitting to secretaire flaps.

Of Screen Hinges there is the patent reversible, which has double knuckles and flanges and allows the screen folds to close left or right. There is also the non-reversible hinge-knuckle joint screen hinges found on screens with draught-proof joints, and a simple arrangement of screws and plates to fit top and bottom of rod screens, as Fig. 280.

Of Spring Catches there are several kinds. The bullet catch is very suitable for small doors such as those on medicine cupboards, smoking cabinets, pedestals, etc. The French spring catch is another type for the same purpose, and Fig. 279 shows a flush ring catch. There are also thumb catches for flaps of secretaires.

Bolts.—Brass bolts used to fasten doors top and bottom may be had either open or flush. The former have the barrel exposed to view, and are fitted to inside of door and are classed as either straight or necked. A flush bolt of the type shown at Fig. 278 is cut into the edge of door and the bolt shot by the thumb up into the framing.

Metal Fittings

Handles.—Of handles a wide choice, ranging from the simplest to the more ornate, is readily accessible, and designs should therefore only be selected which will duly emphasise and harmoniously enhance the character of the piece to be mounted. For instance, where oak is in use, wrought-iron handles and escutcheons to the keyholes would be most suitable to work of Gothic or Jacobean feeling; whilst, with walnut or mahogany, the metal work would be more suitable if of oxydised or nickel finish or of brass. It should be remembered that an ornate mounting is not necessarily in the best taste. Also, as the shape and character of the mountings have varied with the various periods of furniture, care should be exercised to secure handles, etc., in keeping with the style of work in hand. (See Plates pages 206 to 211.)

In fixing, the plate may either be screwed to the drawer front, or handles of the drop or knob variety may be fitted by means of spindles which pass right through the door or drawer front and are fastened inside by a nut.

Cup Handles or Drawer Pulls are screwed on to the face of drawers. Sunk or flush handles are let into face of drawers, the handle lying flush within its own plate, and are usually fitted in cases where drawers are enclosed by a door, as in a wardrobe.

Keyhole Plates or Escutcheons are either pinned or screwed on or sunk in flush on face, for which purpose the keyhole may require a slight easing.

Castors.—Turned legs are fitted with round socket castors, holed to be screwed into position through the socket. The socket, however, is often replaced by a plate and ring or a screw and screw-plate, whilst dining table castors may have a centre pin to enter leg and a screwplate for fixing. Square taper legs are filled with square socket castors.

Cabinet Construction

LOCKS.

The Straight Cupboard Lock is the simplest to fix, as it is merely screwed on and needs no cutting in. It is made to shoot right or left, but lacks the neatness in appearance of the flush inserted lock. The principal thing requiring attention is to cut the keyhole in the right place. The latter can be obtained by careful measurement, but another method is to hold the lock in position on the inside of door and set back a shade from its edge, and (pressing smartly) indent the door stile with the projecting top of the pin upon which the key barrel pivots. This indentation will be the centre for boring the keyhole head with a suitable twist bit, a hole marking the bottom of keyhole being also bored at a distance below the upper hole that will allow the key barrel and ward to pass freely. The hole can then be cut to shape with a pad-saw, care being taken to make it no larger than necessary. Fig. 282 shows a straight lock in position on the door stile.

Cut Cupboard Lock.—In order to fit a cut cupboard lock it is necessary to cut away the wood of the door to receive it. When procuring, it will be necessary to know beforehand whether a right or left-handed lock is wanted. As before the keyhole will demand care and its position must be exactly ascertained. Measure from the centre of key pin to front of plate, and transfer this distance to the inside of door stile. Then across this square a line indicating top of keyhole head. Bore top and bottom holes as before. Then hold the lock close up and insert the key from front of stile, afterwards marking round the outline of the box.

When let in, round the plates of the lock with a pointed pencil or awl. If the key happens to be short, hold the lock close up so that the lock keyhole coincides

Metal Fittings

with the holes just bored. If satisfactory, the keyhole may then be completed with a sharp chisel or pad-saw. Cut away the waste from inside of stile so that the box is well home and the plates bedded in. Every care must be taken not to remove more wood than is necessary to receive the lock properly, and both keyholes must be in line before cutting. Keep the keyhole as small as possible, consistent with the easy entry, turning and

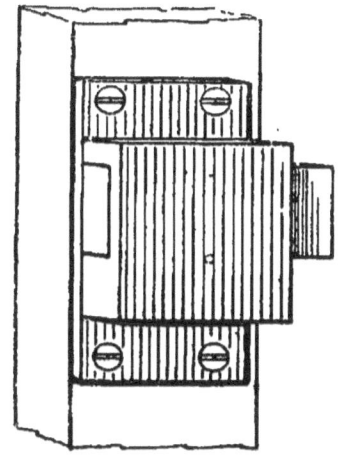

FIG. 282.—STRAIGHT LOCK IN POSITION.

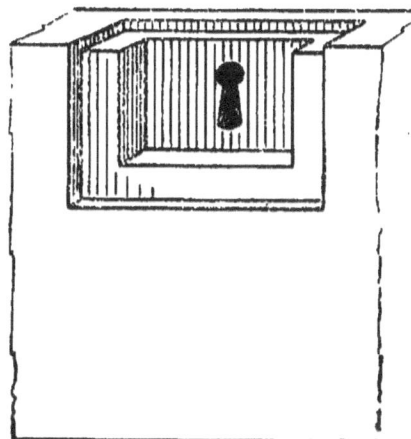

FIG. 283.—DRAWER OR TILL LOCK.

withdrawal of the key. This settled, the lock can be screwed on straight away. A portion of the framework will also require cutting out to allow the bolt to pass.

A quick way of ascertaining the position of this is to smear the end of the bolt with tallow and blacklead, or scrapings from the oil stone, and turn the bolt on to a piece of paper gummed over the approximate position of the part to be cut away, the resulting black mark defining the limits of the waste to be taken out.

Cabinet Construction

Drawer or Till Lock.—Fig. 283 gives a view of the waste taken out of a drawer front to receive the lock, and this will apply to most locks in general use. In the present case the bolt of the lock will shoot upwards into the drawer rail immediately above it. The first proceeding is to mark off the centre of the drawer front by a vertical line, and on this box the keyhole in its exact position to agree with the lock when cut in and screwed home. The correct position of the slot in the rail, into which the bolt enters, can be marked as before with black lead and tallow, or the bolt can be shot and the drawer closed as far as possible so that a mark can be made each side of bolt with the awl. The depth to which the slot has to be set in must be gauged on the under side of rail from the front. A special tool is made for cutting the slot (called a drawer lock chisel), and this is serviceable in the case of shallow drawers where the clearance is limited. Where a deep drawer is concerned however, the slot is quite easily taken out with a narrow chisel.

The Box Lock and pedestal lock with link plates differ in the placing of the keyhole, but otherwise the fitting is similar to the foregoing instruction; and the same applies to the sliding door lock, except that the catch plate into which the bolt shoots will require careful marking for position before screwing on.

Wardrobe Locks.—Such locks as are fitted to wardrobes have a key for shooting the bolt and a handle which operates a spring catch. Cupboards may have a cupboard turn or a simple turn-buckle only. Some variation of the ordinary treatment may be made by fitting special beaten copper or oxydised handles in addition to a lock.

CABINET BACKS AND BACK FRAMING

IN many instances, whilst every care is lavished on the general construction of a piece of work in hand, it is noticeable that the back of the job receives but scant attention and is frequently finished in a very indifferent manner indeed. Those of us who occasionally buy furniture know too well how often we are disappointed with the careless lack of finish on the back. No doubt

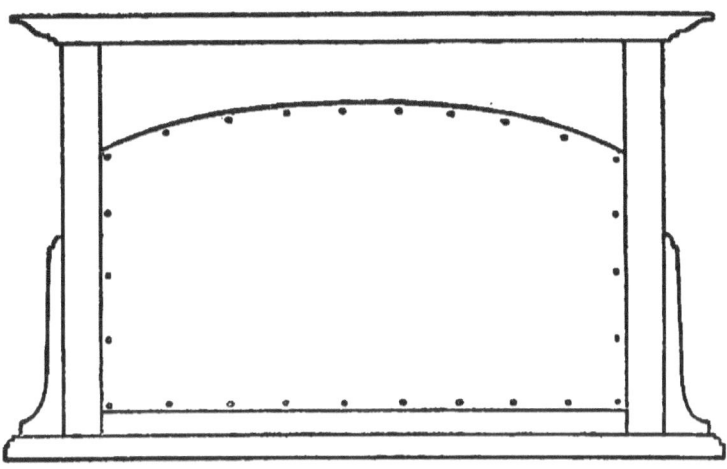

FIG. 284.—THREE-PLY OVERMANTEL BACK.

the home worker feels that there may be some excuse for hurrying this portion of the work, inasmuch as the back is generally placed against a wall and is thus screened from view for the best part of its existence ; but such hurry makes for neither thoroughness nor durability, and it indicates a lack of interest that may prove to be the thin edge of the wedge that divides good work from

Cabinet Construction

bad. Nothing makes a more favourable impression on handling a specimen of the worker's craft than to discover a well-finished back, whilst for the article that is required to stand in the open this feature becomes a necessity.

Three-ply Backs.—When arriving at this stage of the work, it may be as well to give just a little consideration to the kind of back to be fitted. There is the three-ply back, which generally takes the vote by reason of its covering the required space at a minimum of cost, and with at least an easily achieved and clean effect.

FIG. 285.—CHEST OF DRAWERS WITH ¼-IN. BACK.

This method is at its best for small work, using $\frac{5}{16}$ in. or stout three-ply, but the article must subsequently be placed in a dry position. When used for larger surfaces, the ultimate result may possibly be disastrous if dampness is present, a risk that is frequently run when fires are not regularly lighted in a spare room. The

Back Framing

action of dampness is to impoverish the glue between the layers of wood, which thereupon part company, warp, and often split up badly. But as the backing for, say, an overmantel, the material should prove successful; or for picture frames, hanging cabinets, mirrors, small nests of drawers and other items of lighter construction, three-ply is a useful backing where the air is reasonably dry.

In fitting a Three-ply Back the stuff is usually cut to overlap the opening about ½ in. or so all round, and is then fixed with panel pins or small round-headed brass screws. Sometimes the stuff is cut to fit into an

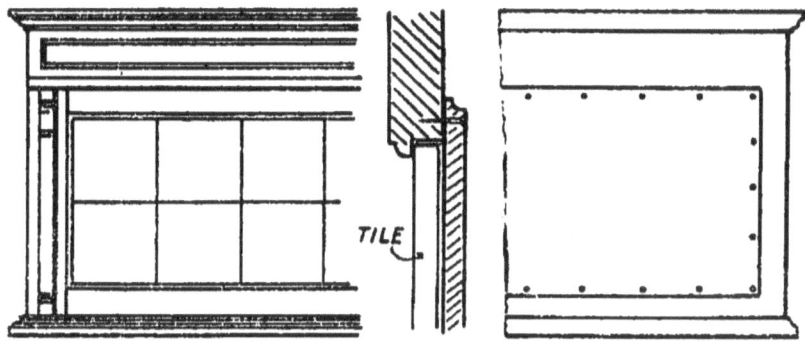

Fig. 286.—Back for Tiled Washstand
(showing Front, Section and Back).

existing rebate. In cases where the heading is finished with a sweep, or other shaping, the back may be put on as a rectangle, but the effect is improved by cutting the back to the line of the given shaping, as indicated in Fig. 284.

Thin or ¼-in. Backing.—Where it is desired to make up the back of ⅜-in. stuff, using lengths of board, 5 ins. to 9 ins. wide, these may be grooved and tongued or rebated together (as an alternative to the square edges

Cabinet Construction

being glued up) to the required size. If put together dry, that is, without glueing, the plain edges are pretty sure to gape or open in course of use, and this does not make for the exclusion of dust. It then becomes a good plan to paste strips of brown paper over the meeting edges and angles formed by the back, sides, top and bottom.

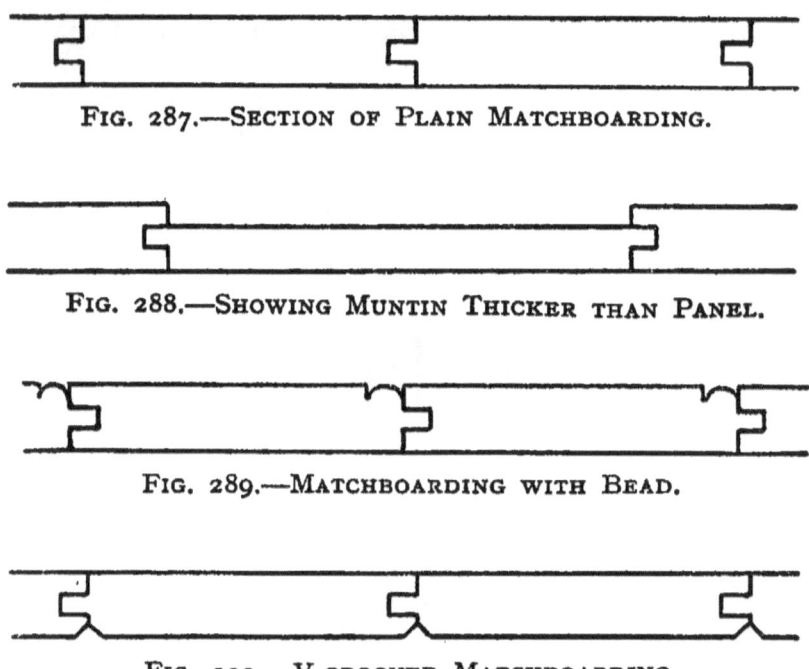

Fig. 287.—Section of Plain Matchboarding.

Fig. 288.—Showing Muntin Thicker than Panel.

Fig. 289.—Matchboarding with Bead.

Fig. 290.—V-grooved Matchboarding.

Stuff, ½-in. thick, is best glued up. The boards, being fitted as Fig. 285, with the grain running horizontally, will have the end grain edges lying flush in a rebate cut for them in the back edge of carcase sides and be screwed. For such a back as that of a tiled washstand, Fig. 286, stuff of ¼ in. thickness is often used; the edges are rounded off or worked with a small hollow by way of

Back Framing

finish, the back overlapping the opening and being screwed on. It should be noted that, for screwing oak, brass screws are preferable, as an acid secretion is present in this wood and causes the ordinary steel screw to rust.

Matched Backs.—These afford a clean and neat effect and can be quickly fitted. A matched back indicates what one may term a medium finish, and is

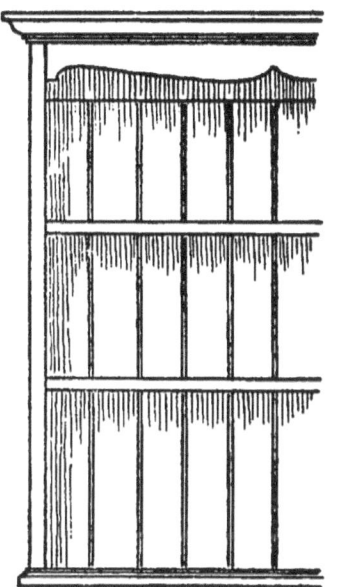 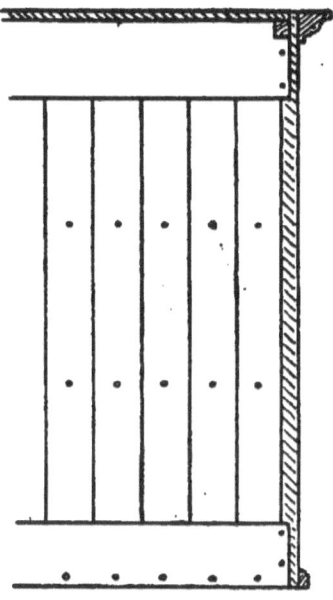

FIG. 291.—MATCHED BACK FOR DRESSER.

FIG. 292.—BACK VIEW OF FIG. 291 (GROOVED).

suitable for most furniture of intermediate size, especially for the backing of such pieces as dressers or high-back settees or hall seats, where a considerable portion of the back surface is exposed to view.

Matching varies slightly in detail, there being the plain, the beaded, and the V-type in general use. Sections of each are indicated (Fig. 287 to 290). In the plain

Cabinet Construction

matching the tongue in each case is worked on the solid board (Fig. 287), the only difference between this and the tongued joint proper being that the latter has the tongue separately or loosely inserted.

In the beaded matching the effect is enhanced by the working of a bead upon the board carrying the tongue as Fig. 289, and this is the kind of backing most frequently met with in furniture.

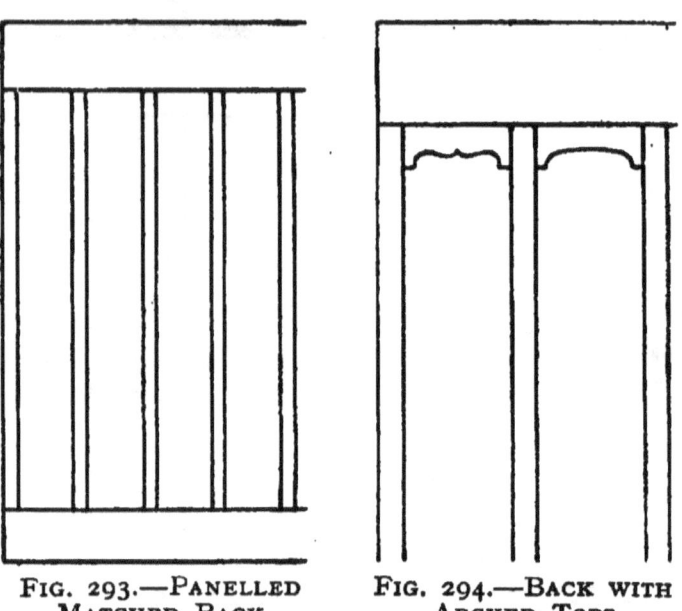

Fig. 293.—Panelled Matched Back.   Fig. 294.—Back with Arched Tops.

The V-matching, however, has a neat effect, the bead being replaced by a bevel or chamfer taken off each of the meeting edges of the boards, as at Fig. 290, thus forming a V-groove. Fig. 291 shows the front of a dresser back with bead or V-matching. This may be screwed to a top and bottom rail and to the back edges of shelves; or, alternatively, the matching may be grooved into the rails as the back view, Fig. 292. If the matching is screwed to the back of upper and lower

Back Framing

rails, or rebated into them to give a recessed effect, an opportunity arises for a pleasing elaboration by glueing slips about ⅜ in. wide over the front meeting edges. This gives a series of long vertical panels (Fig. 293), between which, as an additional feature, shaped headings or arches may be butted after the manner indicated in Fig. 294. The result obtained is a quiet and quaint effect, and very suitable for treatment in brown oak

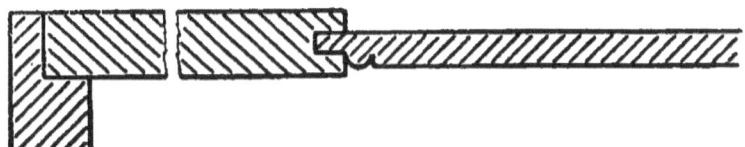

Fig. 295.—Muntin Back with Bead Finish.

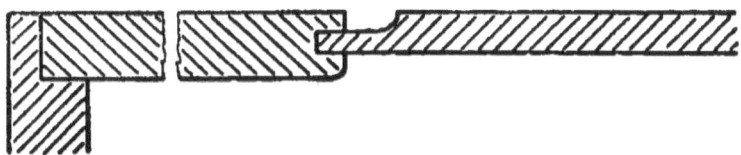

Fig. 296.—Muntin with Rounded Corner.

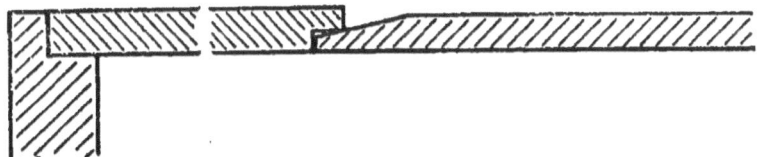

Fig. 297.—Section for Light Wardrobe Back.

colour. In other instances, the back may be tongued together as in the section Fig. 288, where the panel is not equal in thickness to the muntin.

The Bead and Groove Joint with a barefaced tongue is the one mostly met with in munted backs where it is

Cabinet Construction

desired to break away from a very plain finish, the panel often being a trifle thinner than the muntin. Fig. 296 gives a plain section with the corner of the muntin rounded off, which well repays the little extra trouble involved. Fig. 295 shows a beaded finish where thin

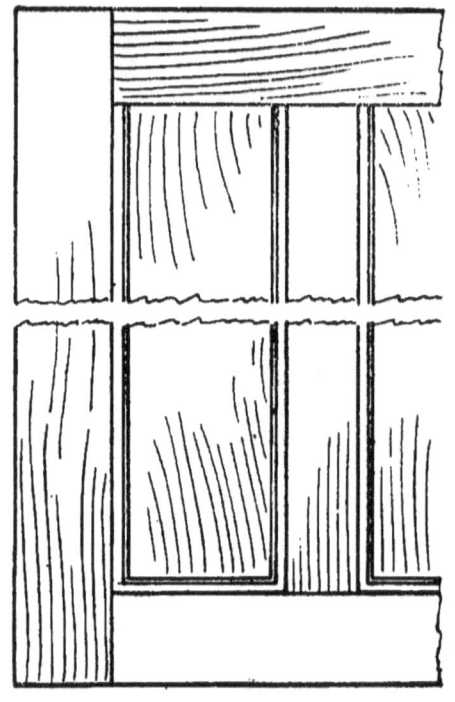

Fig. 298.—Back with Muntins.

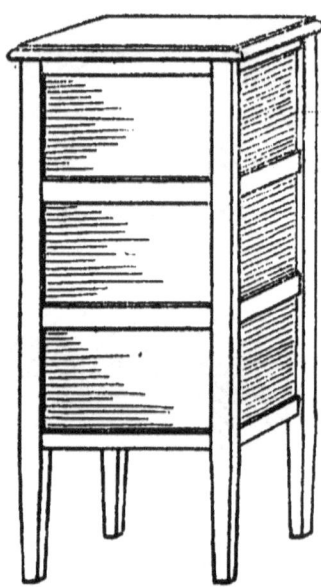

Fig. 299.—Back and Side of Cabinet Nest of Drawers, the Back Panelled in same way as Sides.

narrow panels are in use, as often happens when stuff in hand has to be used up. Usually the bead finishes by butting against the top and bottom rails of back, as Fig. 298 (upper half of sketch). This abrupt finish is much improved by either working a return bead across the grain above and below, or by rebating these edges

156

Back Framing

away and inserting slips of mould mitred up at ends. Fig. 298 (lower half) gives an explanation of this. The section, Fig. 295, also shows the back rebated into the back edge of carcase sides. The back should finish flush with edges of carcase sides for neatness ; and, if it projects slightly when in position, it can have the excess planed to bevel away.

Fig. 300.—Matched Cupboard Back.

Fig. 301.—Panelled Wardrobe Back.

Framed Sides.—Such an article as a cabinet nest of drawers, often machine made, frequently has the sides panelled instead of being plain, and the back may then be carried out to match. Fig. 299 gives an instance of this (showing back and side), the uprights being 1½ ins. square, the rails 3 ins. by ¾ in., and the panels ⅝ in. or

Cabinet Construction

⅜ in., or ply-wood, grooved in. In an inferior way the skeleton framing formed by the rails and uprights could have the back of ¼ in. thickness or three-ply screwed or panel-pinned to it, inside or out as preferred.

Bookcases, both dwarf and tall, frequently have the back omitted when used as a fitment in a recess, the wall being made to serve the purpose. The ordinary bookcase also often has the upper covered-in back omitted, this being replaced by a mere rail behind each shelf, usually dovetailed to back edges of bookcase sides and screwed. The shelves are then stiffened by screwing through these rails, which also serve as stops for the books to keep them in line. Either matched or panelled backs are otherwise provided.

Wardrobe Backs again, vary according to the class of work, those of cheaper construction often being fitted in the manner indicated at Fig. 297. This may have an outer stile or muntin, 6 ins. wide by ⅝ in. or ½ in. thick, and the others, 4 ins. wide with panels between 10½ ins. wide by ¼ in. or ⅜ in. thick. The muntins are rebated; the panels have the edges bevelled away, and are kept in position by nailing up the back edges of carcase top and bottom flush within the sides. It is, of course, preferable to groove the panels in, so that the completed back appears as elevation sketch and section, Fig. 300, and much medium-class work is backed in this way. It is not usual to fit a matched back to a wardrobe of good quality, although it may be found in pieces such as hall cupboards.

Panelled Backs.—A panelled back has a much improved appearance, and would be looked for in the best class work. Fig. 301 gives a sketch of a panelled back, as fitted to a 3 ft. 6 ins. or 4 ft. wardrobe. The stiles of the

Back Framing

framing would be about 4½ ins. wide by ⅝ in. thick, and the top rail 3½ ins. to 4 ins. by ⅝ in. The bottom rail, probably backing a drawer or well in the wardrobe, would be 10 ins. to 12½ ins. wide. Both the muntin and cross rail are 3 ins. wide and the ½-in. panels grooved in; in some cases ⅜-in. stuff only is used for the panel. The

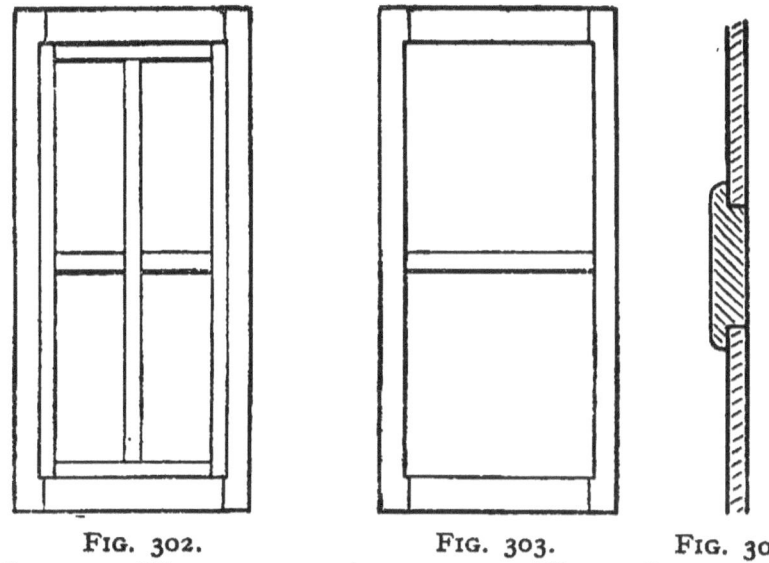

FIG. 302. BACK FOR WARDROBE MIRRORED DOOR.

FIG. 303. ALTERNATIVE WARDROBE DOOR BACK.

FIG. 304. SECTION OF FIG. 303.

frame can be mortised and tenoned or dowelled together in the usual way, and the whole screwed into the rebated sides. Where a wardrobe is in two parts the bottom carcase portion has a separate panelled back, in some instances being merely plain boarded.

Carcase Backs.—Most carcase ends are rebated at the back to hold the back. When the latter is quite thin the simple square rebate is satisfactory. For a thick

Cabinet Construction

FIG. 305.
FIG. 306.
SHOWING SHAPED BACK FOR MIRROR DOOR.

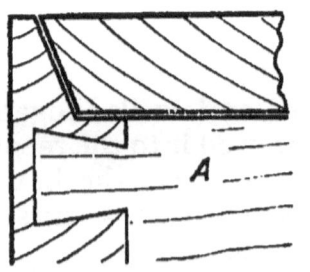
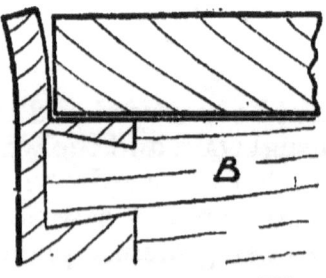

FIG. 307, A.—BEVELLED REBATE FOR BACK.

FIG. 308, B,—ORDINARY REBATE, RESULTING IN CURLING.

Back Framing

back, however, a slanting rebate such as that at A, Fig. 307, is better because it allows a greater inner thickness, thus preventing any tendency for the wood to curl outwards. Fig. 308, B, shows this defect, often found in large pieces of furniture with thick backs.

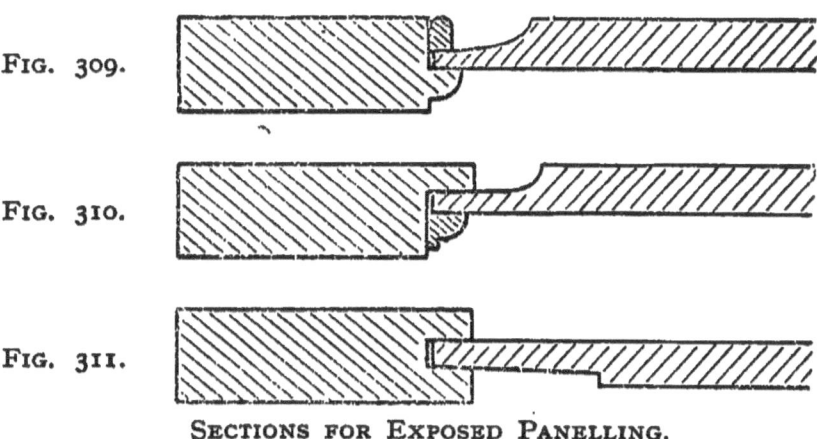

Fig. 309.

Fig. 310.

Fig. 311.

SECTIONS FOR EXPOSED PANELLING.

Backs to Mirrored Doors.—In the cheapest form these may consist of $\frac{1}{4}$ in. stuff, screwed over the door frame opening. In a long door, such as that of a wardrobe, a light framed back is fitted in good class work in the manner indicated at Fig. 302, the stiles and rails being $2\frac{1}{2}$ ins. by $\frac{3}{8}$ in. thick, and the muntin and cross rail 2 ins. by $\frac{3}{8}$ in., halved together and stubbed into the framing, in addition to being rebated to receive the panels, which are of $\frac{1}{4}$-in. stuff, say, $\frac{3}{16}$ in. net. A simpler form of back, and more often met with, is that at Fig. 303. This consists of two panels of $\frac{1}{4}$-in. stuff with a rebated cross rail in centre, the detail finish of the section being as shown at Fig. 304. The back is usually secured over the opening of door framing with panel pins or round-headed brass screws.

Cabinet Construction

Frequently a mirrored door has an arched or otherwise shaped heading, as at Fig. 305, and may also be shaped at bottom. In this case the back is made up as Fig. 306, the muntin and cross rail being rebated as before, and the four panels entered and pinned into position or screwed. If well-seasoned stuff is used, this muntin and

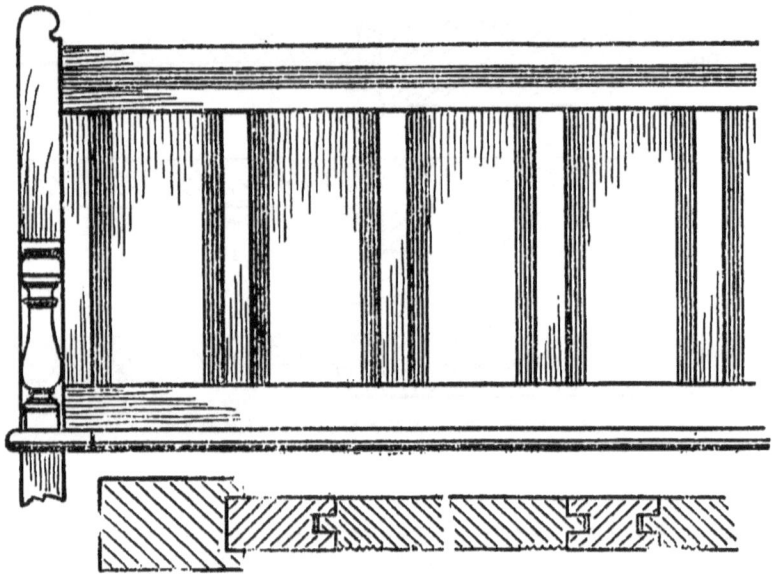

Fig. 312.—Back Framework for Hall Seat.

rail stiffening answers its purpose in all respects, all outside edges being neatly rounded off for finish. Mahogany is the best wood to use, and of course should in all cases be used on articles made in this wood.

The back of a dwarf type china cabinet of the kind standing 5 ft. 9 ins. to 6 ft. high, is often panelled in a similar way to Fig. 301, with two or three muntins, and is polished inside, if not covered with silk, satin, or chintz as a background for the china and glass.

Back Framing

Exposed Panelling.—Occasion arises where the upper part of a cabinet or sideboard has exposed panelling, as at the back of a hall stand or seat. If the panel framing is moulded in the solid the section, Fig. 309, looks very neat, the panel being beaded in from the back, which would have the framing of ⅝ in. thickness and the

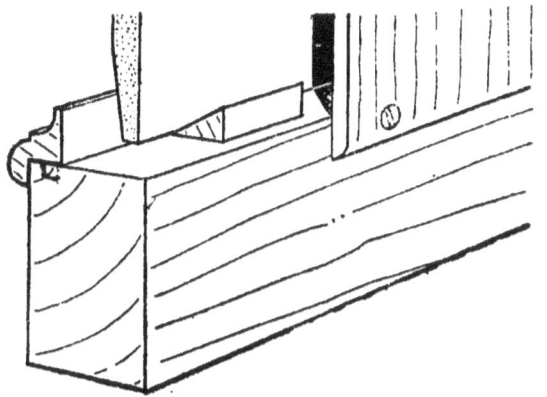

Fig. 313.—Method of Fitting a Mirror.

hollowed edge panels of ¼ in. or ⅜ in. thickness, generally of hardwood. Alternatively the framing may be rebated with the panel fixed in position with loose mould of simple or more elaborate section than Fig. 310. Another method of making the back to different detail is indicated at Figs. 311 and 312, the latter of which applies to a seat such as the illustration indicates.

Wood.—In common grade work the backs are generally found to be of deal, spruce, or other soft wood or three-ply. Basswood is, however, more frequently used in medium work, whilst in the best work hardwood throughout would be desirable.

Fixing Mirrors.—A satisfactory way of fixing a mirror in, say, a rebated door is to lay the frame face

Cabinet Construction

downwards on the bench, insert the mirror and glue a series of wedges *to the rebate* at intervals of 5 or 6 ins., according to the size of the door (Fig. 313). In this way the silver is not touched. A thin back can be fixed over the whole. If the back does not show, a piece of brown paper can be glued over the whole.

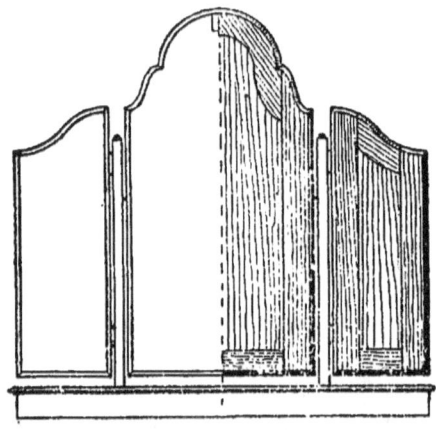

FIG. 314.—BACKS FOR FRAMELESS MIRRORS.

Frameless Mirrors.—Many modern dressing tables and chevals are fitted with frameless mirrors. The mirror, with a bevelled edge about $\frac{3}{4}$ in. wide, is suspended between the supporting standards, and if wing mirrors are present these are treated in the same manner. Although there is no visible framing seen from the front, the mirror itself is backed by a panelled framework to fit the exact outline of the mirror, which in the instance given would be framed up as indicated in Fig. 314. Both stiles and rails for this purpose may vary between $2\frac{1}{2}$ in. to 3 in. wide $\times$ $\frac{7}{8}$ in. thick, the surrounding edge being moulded ogee section to recede. The framework will be mortised and tenoned together in the usual manner, and rebated to receive a panel of $\frac{1}{2}$ in. or $\frac{5}{8}$ in. thickness, which may be of plywood, to finish flush with

Back Framing

the framing so that the whole forms a flat background for the mirror. Attachment is obtained by means of nickelled clips of which either four (*i.e.*, one near each angle top and bottom) or six, in the case of an extra long mirror, are fitted. Alternatively, many mirrors are pierced for attachment to the back by means of glass studs, which can be obtained through the glass factor when procuring the mirror itself. In the case of a small mirror of oval, round, or shield shape, the back may be flat throughout of laminated wood up to about $\frac{3}{4}$ in. thick. The backing, whether panelled or plain, is usually given a full polish to agree with the suite.

It may be added that, if a well constructed back framing is provided, the panelling may be of five-ply, instead of using thicker stuff. The outside edges of the back are usually finished to ogee section, thus practically rendering the part invisible.

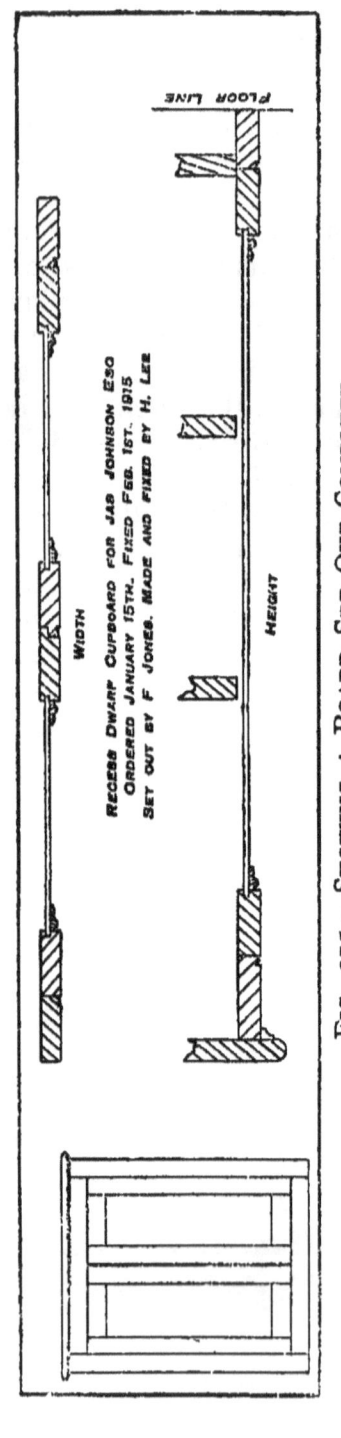

Fig. 315.—Showing a Board Set Out Complete.

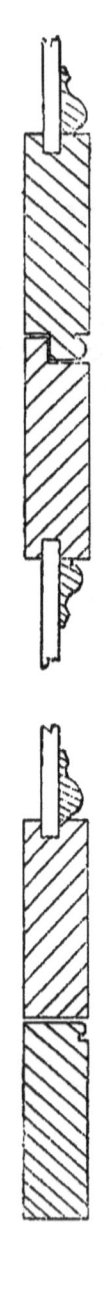

Fig. 316.—Enlarged Detail of Width Section.

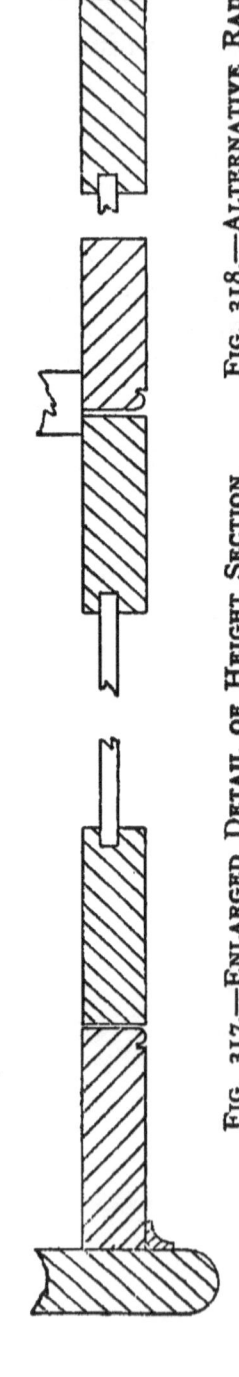

Fig. 317.—Enlarged Detail of Height Section. Fig. 318.—Alternative Rail.

SETTING-OUT BOARDS

IN many cabinet-makers' and joiners' shops in certain parts of the country it is the custom to set out the various jobs on a board instead of an ordinary " rod," such setting out taking the form of full-sized sections of the work in hand, instead of the mortise and shoulder lines used in the latter method. It is needless here to argue as to which may be the better way; each has advantages in practice, and each of course is thought the better by those who have not used the other.

Any one who has had experience will agree that faulty setting out means bad work; and, when one man does the former in a careless manner, it matters little how careful the man who has to do the work may be—he is at a decided disadvantage.

As an illustration of what may be regarded as a correct method of setting out by the " board " system, we may take the case of a small recess cupboard, 3 ft. 3 ins. high under the top, by 3 ft. wide; the depth back to front is immaterial as far as our present work is concerned, a few inches more or less only affecting the shelves and the top.

Fig. 315 shows this cupboard set out on a board as it should be done, and in such a manner that it is practically impossible for a mistake in the making to be made.

The Board shown is 11 ins. wide by 5 ft. long, this allowing plenty of room for the sections and also for an elevation to a small scale as shown towards the left.

The Elevation should be drawn first, as it is then a guide in making the sections. These latter should be drawn so that each member is not the *approximate* size

Cabinet Construction

on the board, but the *actual size* it will be in the finished article; that is, the thickness of the framing of the cupboard and the doors is supposed to be 1 in., but in reality it will only hold up ⅞ in., and it is to this thickness that it should be set out.

Widths.—Important, too, is it to arrange that the width of the various rails, stiles, etc., will cut from a board of stock width without waste. Thus the framing of the cupboard and also the doors is what is called 3 ins. wide; that means that three are to be cut from a 9-in. board. The careless setter-out would mark these 3 ins. wide on the board, trusting to the joiner to use his common sense that this was not intended literally. In some cases the result would be that the material would be sawn out to the full size, and waste would result.

The proper way then is to mark these members to the real size they will finish at; this, with the ordinary width boards, will be 2¾ ins. Exceptions to this are the top rail of the cupboard frame, which should be allowed ⅜ in. wider on account of the small scotia moulding under the top; also the meeting stiles of the doors, which should be the width of the bead extra from the others. This bead will thus be an extra, the four stiles showing equal in width on the plain surface.

Waste can be avoided in both of these cases by making the bottom frame rail less in width by the ⅜ in. which is added to the top, and by reducing the width of the hanging stiles of the doors in the same way. All these little details should be worked out by the setter-out, and nothing left to the maker; the latter has then no excuse in case of a mistake.

Sections.—The vertical and horizontal sections of the cupboard with all members marked to the correct size as above, should be set out on the board, as in the drawing,

Setting-out Boards

and marked plainly " height " and " width " as shown. The positions of the bottom of the cupboard and shelves, as well as the top with the moulding under, should also be marked.

In dealing with the shelves, many cupboards are spoiled through the shelves being placed too far apart—a question of cost in many cases. It will be noticed that in the height section we show three shelves, spaced so as to show equal distances between in the opening. This is as they should be spaced unless there is a special reason against it. In this case it allows 10 ins. between.

It will also be noticed that we show the bottom of the cupboard projecting $\frac{1}{4}$ in. above the bottom rail; this is correct, as a rebate is thus formed for the doors to shut.

In Figs. 316 and 317 we show enlarged sections of the main portions of the width and height sections on the board. These give the detail as it shows on the actual board, and we wish to point out one or two little items of importance which are sometimes overlooked. First, taking Fig. 316, the panels are set well back from the face so that there is room for the moulding to be planted in. Secondly, at the meeting stiles the rebate should be deeper in the left-hand door (which opens last) than the other. If these are made equal, there is a risk of the bead splitting at the quirk.

All these little details should be shown on the board, and the maker should be instructed to follow them out closely.

We may remark that in the case of stock mouldings being used, as round the door panels and under the top, a small piece should be cut off and the actual section marked in on the board.

Sometimes in a cupboard of this description the floor forms the bottom, instead of using a shelf as shown in the drawings. In such a case it is best to have a

Cabinet Construction

shaped bottom rail as in Fig. 318, thus allowing a clear course for brushing out.

The Specifications for this particular job would read as follows :—

> "Dwarf Recess Cupboard for Jas. Johnson, Esq., 3 ft. 4 ins. high, 3 ft. wide, 15 ins. deep. Made in 1 in. yellow deal, 3 ins. framing, ¼ in. three-ply panels, 1 in. moulding planted round, projecting nosing on top, with scotia under. Two shelves and bottom fixed on bearers; doors hung with 2 ins. cast iron butts, and fitted with buttons top and bottom, lock and knob. To be stained and varnished after fixing."

The setting-out boards should always be kept stored away carefully, as it often happens that one can be used from stock for a second job of the same kind; and if they are marked as shown in Fig. 315 and a reference kept, it is easy to look up any particular job, if and when required. If the firm is a large one, the boards should be numbered, and a book kept and indexed specially for this purpose.

Boards set out as described above, although they may take half-an-hour longer to do at the time, will avoid endless mistakes, and save the need of tedious explanations and misunderstandings.

VENEERING

A VOLUME dealing with the details of cabinet construction would be incomplete without a chapter on veneering. The chief test of merit of any given piece of furniture is its suitability for the particular purpose for which it is intended, but there is no reason why a useful piece of work should not possess the further merit of good appearance. Much may be done in this direction by observing elegance in outline and good proportion in the design, but in veneering the craftsman has at his disposal an additional method of beautifying his work which is of the greatest possible value. So many artistic possibilities are open to the process, it is surprising that veneering and inlaying are not more practised. In the making of light articles of furniture perhaps the reader has hitherto confined himself to the use of oak or mahogany. If so, a practical knowledge of veneering may do two things for him. It will, in many cases, enable him to reduce the cost of timber by veneering over less expensive woods, in addition to which he can obtain enriched decorative effects which are impossible with solid woods alone. In short, whilst veneering saves money in woodwork, it throws open opportunities for decorative finish such as may never before have been dreamed of by the worker.

The present chapter describes the actual preparing and laying out of veneers in sheets, as distinct from the running in of bands and simple lines. A knowledge of veneer laying will be invaluable to all woodworkers, as the mosaic pattern plays an important part as decoration in furniture.

Cabinet Construction

TOOLS, ETC.

Many of the tools needed for this work will be found in the usual kit—*e.g.*, two or three chisels, hammer, and an iron smoothing plane for jointing. A good number of hand-screws are also necessary. Three further tools which will be required are a toothing plane for the ground wood, a veneering hammer, and a small hand-saw for cutting veneers. The last two articles can be very easily made by the worker.

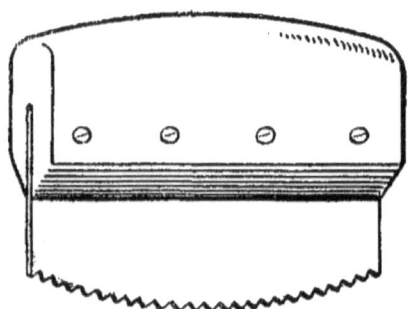

Fig. 319.—Veneer Cutting Saw.

Saw.—As will be seen from Fig. 319, the saw is cut from a convex piece of steel, which is screwed to the handle. The teeth should be cut fairly large, and should not be given too much set. The great advantage of this saw over the ordinary hand-saw is that, being shaped, there are no corners to dig in. Its length should be about 5 ins.

The Veneering Hammer is useful for rubbing down small pieces of veneer by hand, and can be made as shown in Fig. 320. The blade is of zinc, socketed into a wooden head and screwed through. To this head is then affixed a shaft or handle. A convenient size for the blade is $4\frac{1}{2}$ ins. by 3 ins., of $\frac{1}{4}$ in. thickness.

Veneering

Toothing Plane.—This is about the size of a smoothing-plane. It has but one iron, which is fixed with the usual wedge, but in almost an upright position; the back of the iron is grooved, which gives the cutting edge a row of teeth like a saw. When the iron is sharpened in the usual way on the oilstone it must not be rubbed on the back, as other plane-irons are. A rather coarse iron is best for the ground, and a finer one to tooth the veneer, but this latter is only necessary on saw-cut veneers.

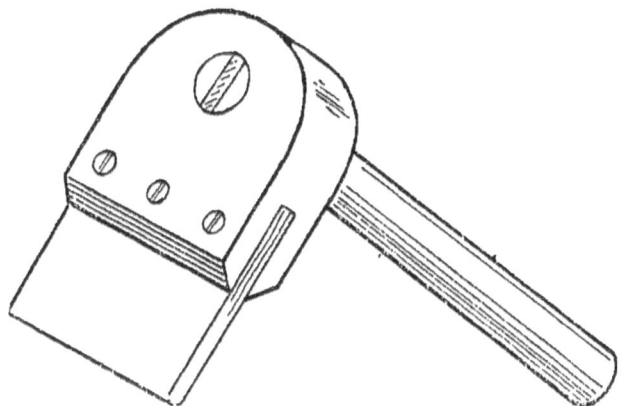

FIG. 320.—VENEERING HAMMER.

Cauls.—To lay veneers, direct even pressure is required, and to do this it is necessary to use a flat press, known as a caul. Cauls can be made from stout pieces of odd boarding, but if made from ⅛-in. zinc they will be found to retain the heat much better. Two or three should be obtained of varying sizes according to the work in hand.

Glue.—As the work will require speedy handling and clean joints, it will be as well to see that the glue is in good condition. Procure good Scotch glue in cakes of a

Cabinet Construction

light colour and break up into the inner pan of a clean glue-pot. Just cover the glue with cold water and allow it to soak overnight. Fill the outer kettle half full of water and bring to the boil in the usual way, constantly stirring the glue. When well mixed, strain through a piece of coarse muslin. White glue should be used if working in light woods.

VENEERS.

Kinds of Veneers.—Coming now to the various veneers, a general survey of those more frequently used and their respective qualities may be of interest. The majority of veneers can be obtained either saw-cut or knife-cut. These names refer to the method by which they are obtained from the log, the saw-cut variety being thicker than veneers stripped with the knife, and bearing the marks of the saw. Apart from their respective thicknesses, which are useful according to varying requirements, neither has any special advantage.

The prices of all veneers increase according to the richness of their grainings, known and spoken of as "figuring," this, in Cuban mahogany and in satinwood, being very rich. Honduras mahogany has a quite straight graining, but lacks figure, and is generally used for plainer work. The different varieties of satinwood always yield a good graining, the straight figuring of the West Indian being especially good for panelling, etc. Walnut, rosewood, and oak veneers are very useful, but with the exception of English oak do not offer any great choice of figure. Tulipwood veneer is one of the choicest obtainable, and in its usual form offers great variety of colours. All the above can be laid in a simple direct manner.

Such woods as bird's-eye maple and the choicer kinds

Veneering

of burr veneers (woods with very twisted grainings, such as burr walnut), need special attention when laying, as they are very fragile, being made up of so many loose fragments. In the maple, for instance, the eyes are slightly wider on one side than on the other. They narrow inwards like the head of a screw; consequently the veneer should be laid with the widest end of the eyes downwards; otherwise they will pull out. Boxwood veneer is well known, and is often used in small quantities. It has a close grain and is free from any figuring.

How Veneer is Made.—The manufacture of veneer is a process of which little is known to the uninitiated. A good deal of it is made in America, and after a tree has been cut in the woods and brought to the town on flat cars it is rolled into a pond near the mill. The process through which a log passes from the time it enters the pond and leaves the mill as veneer is one of abundant variety.

Logs are hoisted from the pond to a drag-saw, where they are cut into various lengths. They are then put into a steam box situated directly behind the drag-saw, for at least twelve hours, in order to soften the timber. This steam box is a large box through which passes a 2-in. pipe containing holes by means of which the steam can escape. At the end of the twelve hours the timber is removed from the steam box, and then comes the process called "peeling." With spuds and axes the bark is easily removed, the timber being soft and hot. It is then ready to enter the mill and be cut into veneer.

The peeled log is hoisted on a crane to the veneer lathe, and that is the last one sees of the log. When it once passes this lathe, it comes out on the other side as long, thin sheets of veneer. According to the thicknesses desired, it is cut from $\frac{1}{100}$ in. to $\frac{1}{2}$ in. thick and 64 ins. in length.

Cabinet Construction

As the veneer leaves the machine it slides along 30 ft. in length. Ten feet from the end is a clipper, where it is clipped into different lengths, an inch being allowed for drying. It is now ready to enter the drying process.

The drier is 8 ft. wide and 100 ft. long. It is a chain-driven machine throughout, having four sets of rollers. The temperature must always be from 200° to 250°. Veneer is put into the drier at one end, and slowly propelled through the machine. By the time it reaches the other end it is smooth and dry, but very hot. The men who remove it always wear canvas gloves to prevent their hands from blistering. It takes from fifteen minutes to two hours for veneer to work through this machine.

THE GROUND WOOD.

Woods to Use.—There are only a few woods suitable to veneer upon, and the best are Honduras mahogany, American walnut, and sometimes oak for the best work where hard woods are used, and American yellow pine and whitewood for commoner work. Woods of a resinous nature, such as yellow deal and pitch pine, should never be used. The wood should be well-seasoned, which means dry; it should also be clean, *i.e.*, free from knots and coarse growth and shakes. As a good all-round wood for general work Honduras mahogany cannot be beaten, and all veneers can be safely laid upon it. A hard wood, like ebony or satin-wood, should never be laid on a soft one like pine, as the latter would soak in more than its share of glue.

Keeping the Work Flat.—A common trouble in veneering is to keep the work flat. One way to ensure this is to lay the veneer on the heart side of the wood. As the fibres made up by the annular rings increase at

Veneering

each layer towards the outside, the tendency to go hollow is always away from the heart; so that, if the veneer be laid on the heart side, the pull is fairly equalised. Another method is to cut the board which is to form the ground into narrow widths; the edges are then reversed, and the whole is rejointed so as to get an equalisation of forces. This should always be done where veneer is laid on both sides. When a panel is to be veneered with a pattern and kept flat, it is necessary in addition to the above method to cover it on both sides with thin veneer, laying this across the grain; and, no matter what pattern is afterwards veneered on the front, the panel will keep flat.

Finishing the Ground.—With the wood to the required size, plane and true up in the usual way, finally finishing both its sides with the toothing plane.

Care must be taken to get the surface perfectly flat and true, and if there is a knot in the wood it should be cut out, and a piece of the same stuff fitted and glued in. Any small holes may be filled in with plaster-of-paris. The toothing may be done with and across the grain, and the whole surface should be roughened. Brush the surface with size, or with a weak solution of glue, working it well into the grain and allowing to dry.

In good work veneers are not laid over joints such as dovetails unless very thick veneers are used, otherwise the joints would show through owing to the unequal shrinkage.

CUTTING VENEERS.

The choice of veneer settled, the next step is its preparation for laying. It should first be cut to the size and shape required. All straight lines should be cut by using the veneer-saw and a straight-edge. If shaped pieces are required a wooden template should be made

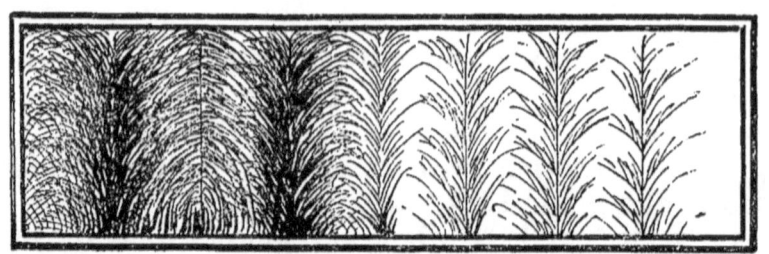

FIG. 321.—DRAWER FRONT WITH FACING OF FIGURED VENEER CUT IN STRIPS. A COCKED BEAD SURROUND IS SHOWN.

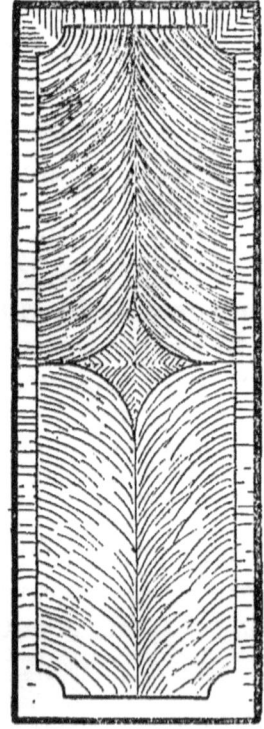 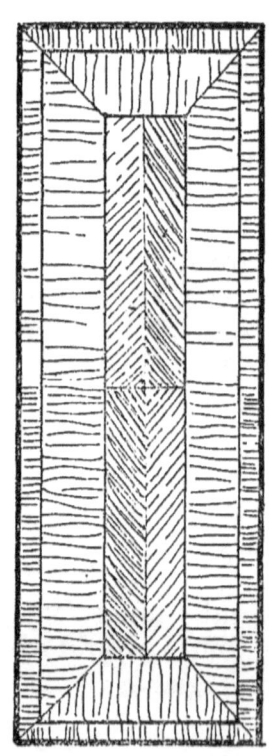

FIG. 322. — CROSS - CUT VENEER WITH QUADRANT CORNERS AND QUARTERED CENTRE.

FIG. 323.—ALTERNATIVE SUGGESTION FOR QUARTERED PANEL.

SUGGESTIONS FOR VENEERED PANELS.

Veneering

and the veneers then cut to it by means of a fine fret-saw. The under sides of all veneers—those sides which will be glued—must be cleaned of all saw marks before laying. Use the scraper and coarse glasspaper for this purpose.

Joints can be shot on an ordinary shooting board, working several veneers at the same time, and keeping them flat by means of a board above. A long Stanley iron plane, well sharpened and with the iron set very fine, is best for this work. If satisfactory when fitted, the edges of all joints can be glued together and a thin strip of linen then pasted over them on the top side to bind them.

Pattern Cutting.—Apart from the general use of veneers as a covering, they can also be used with great advantage for patternings. If several leaves of veneer are procured in the identical order in which they were cut, the figuring in each will be practically facsimile. By cutting the same piece from each veneer in rotation, a number of pieces would be obtained, each bearing a similar figuring. These could then be jointed up into a square or octagon, according to the number and shapes cut, and the result would be a regular pattern. The best method for cutting out such pieces from veneers is to make a cardboard mould, with an aperture of the size and shape required ; this can be laid on each veneer in correct position and the shape marked out and cut.

GLUEING.

When working on a large piece of wood it is necessary to veneer both surfaces, as the board would very quickly be pulled from the true if only one were covered. By laying a second veneer on the under side this tendency is counteracted. The second veneer should be laid

Cabinet Construction

with its grain running in the opposite direction from that of the first, and need not of course be of the best quality.

Both veneers are to be glued down simultaneously. When all is in readiness for laying, the cauls should be placed at the fire to be heated and the glue, cramps, etc., should be at hand. Slightly warm the wood, and brush all dust from its surface.

Rapidly glue over the top surface of the board; using a good-sized brush, and distributing the glue evenly and thinly. Particles of dust will collect, and all should be carefully picked out as those under the veneer would cause trouble.

Lay the veneer in position, press, and tack down with a few small headless pins. These should be driven in half-way and then turned over, without embedding them in the veneer. When this veneer is secure reverse the board, and lay the under veneer in the same way.

Each veneer should then be covered with a sheet of paper to prevent adhesion to the cauls. These, which should contain a good heat, can now be placed on either side of the wood, and the whole quickly cramped together.

Jointing.—Where knife-cut veneer has to be jointed, lay one piece down and partially lay the second, but allow it to lap over the first at the joint; then with straight-edge and chisel or saw—the blade of either just dipped in water—proceed to cut the joint through both veneers. Make sure that the cut goes right through, and when the oddments are cleared away the two veneers should close up in a good joint and the laying may be finished. Glue a strip of paper over the joint, whether large or small, to prevent the air from getting to it.

The Cramps should not be put on at random, but

Veneering

should start from the centre, if possible, in order to expel all surplus glue outwards. In any circumstances the glue must be expelled and pressure should always work from a certain point outwards. Work on this method as the cramping progresses, adding blocks of wood if required under the cramps to maintain the flat pressure. (See Fig. 324.)

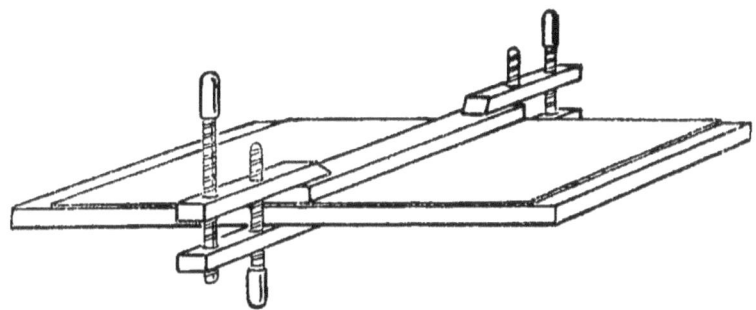

Fig. 324.—Cramping Veneered Work.

It must be borne in mind that it is not the quantity of glue that makes a good joint, but rather the complete expulsion of all the surplus. Only sufficient should be left to enter the grain and to bind the wood.

The importance of ready and systematic cramping will thus be understood, as well as the necessity of heating the cauls to a good heat. Otherwise the glue will be chilled, with a disastrous result. The edges should be watched during the cramping for the expelled glue, as a sign that the veneer is laying well.

Cleaning.—Within a few hours the cramps could be removed, and the paper covering the joints, etc., damped and scraped off. Remove the pins and all surplus glue from the edges, and allow the board to stand for about twenty-four hours. Then clean up the surface, using smoothing plane, scraper, and fine glasspaper. These

Cabinet Construction

must be used with extreme care, as it would be very easy to work through the veneers.

Curved Surfaces.—In this straightforward manner veneers can be laid direct on the flat, but in cases where it is required to veneer surfaces of a shaped character, greater care will need to be exercised. The circumstances decide more or less whether veneers are to be cramped or rubbed down, and on the simpler shaped

FIG. 325.—USING THE VENEERING HAMMER.

sections the latter method is generally employed. In this the veneer is cut to size and prepared in the way described. The surface of the wood should be cleaned up as usual, and the glue laid over it in the same even way. Lay the veneer in position, smooth down and rapidly wet its surface with hot water in order to render it more pliable. Rub down well with the veneering hammer, working from the centre in the same way to expel the glue. (See Fig. 325.)

By passing a hot iron over the surface while damp to heat the glue and by further rubbing with the hammer the veneer will be found to bind well. Attention should be paid to the edges, as these are likely to turn up slightly; they can either be pinned or cramped down.

Acute Shapes.—Special cauls have to be made for

Veneering

cramping down veneers on very acute shapes. These cauls can be made from deal, bass, etc., and should be shaped out to fit the section accurately. If the section is cut out by the band-saw, the waste pieces from the shape would suit very well for this purpose. These cauls should also be shaped to take a cramp without slipping, and the circumstances will decide as to their length. (See Fig. 326.)

Veneers which are to be laid on a quick sweep should first be well damped on their top surface, and then pressed on a hot iron of a similar section to that required. This will draw them in to that shape, and they will remain so. Cramp down with the cauls.

All edges, etc., which are to be covered with end grain veneer should be prepared in the usual way.

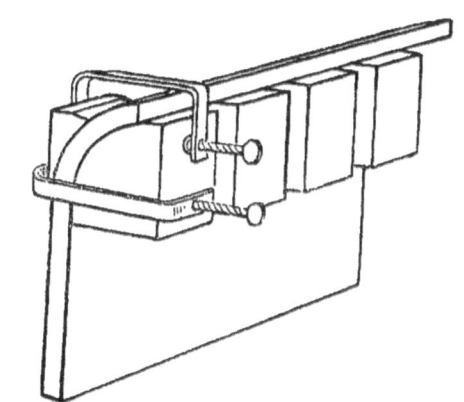

FIG. 326.—CAUL FOR SHAPED WORK.
(For clearness, only two cramps are shown.)

The veneers for these should be cut in strips of the required width, and rubbed down as usual with the veneering hammer. Pass a hot iron once or twice over the surface, which should be well damped to avoid scorching.

Cabinet Construction

Patterns.—Where it is required to lay a made-up pattern on a shaped surface it will be necessary to fit and glue down each division separately. This is advisable when working on an extreme shape, as it ensures good joints and correct shapes. Or the wood should be marked out, the main lines indicating where the joints will fall.

By means of the cardboard mould cut out the veneers to the shape and size required. The first division can then be fitted, trued, and glued into position. Well damp the top side and rub down in the usual way, driving in pins to hold down the corners. Then against this veneer the next can be fitted and glued, rubbing this well up against the first to ensure a good joint. Fit in the remainder in the same way. The first veneer should be laid for preference where it can receive support from the surrounding woodwork or from a cramp, so that the other veneers can be rubbed well up to it or, so to speak, built up against it.

The majority of veneers will rub down well, but care will be necessary with the richer curled veneers when laying them on a shape. Such woods as Cuban mahogany, satinwood, walnut, and the choicer burr woods are extremely fragile, and could be easily broken up. In such cases, when laying these woods on shaped surfaces, cramping down by special cauls should be employed if possible.

DEFECTS IN VENEERING.

Variation in Thickness.—Whenever laying veneers of different woods together to form one pattern, notice should be taken of their respective thicknesses, as these often differ considerably. As far as is possible they should be arranged evenly. Inequalities cannot always

Veneering

be avoided, however, and when such surfaces are cleaned up care must be taken to see that the extra friction needed to reduce the thicker veneers does not scrape through the thinner ones. With ordinary caution this matter should be managed successfully. All freshly-laid joints should be covered with a strip of paper, or preferably linen, in order to bind them.

Blisters, etc.—A common trouble in the best of circumstances is the formation of blisters in the veneer. The cause of these may be due either to an air bubble having formed under the veneer, or to some amount of glue having chilled there and not been properly expelled in the cramping. To remove an air blister, neatly slit it with a sharp tool, insert some hot glue and cramp down with a small heated caul. If the defect is due to congealed glue, the veneer must be slit and well damped, and the glue or dirt expelled through the slit. Use a hot flat-iron over the damped surface to moisten the glue. After this, cramp down with a hot caul.

Pieces of dirt carried in when glueing may also cause considerable trouble at this stage. The surface of the wood should be felt for these defects which it is absolutely necessary to remove. They can easily be detected by the hand, and in the case of an air bubble a slight tapping with a hammer will tell of its extent.

Cracks.—With many of the curl veneers, especially those of the richer satinwoods, it will be noticed that they often contain quite a number of wide cracks. These are not necessarily shakes, but most possibly are caused by shrinkage. They are generally found in the choicest part of the veneer where the grain is very twisted and cross. When the veneer is laid, the glue fills and shows up these cracks as a series of black lines. These must be removed by scraping out the glue from the cracks with a finely-pointed tool and filling up again with a yellow stopping. The best to use for this purpose is litharge, which can be bought in small quantities as a powder at oil and colour depots. Mix a little to a paste with thin glue and work it well into the cracks, when it will set very hard. The surplus can be cleaned off later with a scraper.

Fig. 327.—Quartered Veneer.

Quartered Veneers.—When laying veneer which is quartered, as illustrated at Fig. 327, it must be remembered that quartered veneer pulls away from the edges and also that it has a tendency to make the face of the panel slightly concave. To overcome this difficulty it is usual to lay a common veneer on each side of the panel previous to laying the quartered veneer.

Foundation Veneers.—For instance, take the timber which has to be the foundation of the panel and lay a piece of veneer on each side of it, the grain of the veneer to run across the grain of the foundation board. When this has had sufficient time to harden up (*i.e.*, not less than three days), clean up and tooth the veneer, and then

Veneering

lay the quartering on top of the other veneer. This is the French method of laying veneers, and it counteracts any tendency to warp and twist. All the best work (such as "Boulle" work, consisting of the veneering and inlaying of brass, tortoiseshell, silver, mother-of-pearl, etc.) was laid upon such foundations, with the result that the work still stands good after a lapse of a hundred and fifty years.

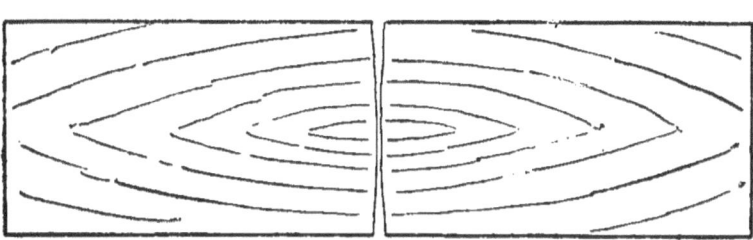

Fig. 328.—Showing Faulty Joint, due to Cutting the Veneer Straight Across.

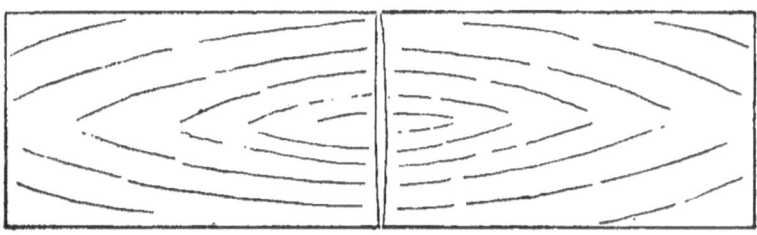

Fig. 329.—Showing how Joint should be made slightly Hollowed.

Curl Veneers.—Another important point is the veneering of mahogany and other curl veneers. Curl veneers, being somewhat large and of wild grain, the timber is of such a nature that some portions will swell more rapidly owing to the moisture contained in the glue. When veneering drawer fronts the veneer is frequently jointed in the centre of a long drawer. If

Cabinet Construction

the veneer be cut and jointed with a perfectly straight joint, the worker is often surprised to find that, when he removes the caul, the joint of the veneer has opened as Fig. 328. This is owing to the difference in the texture of the timber, and the remedy is to make the joint slightly hollow before laying the veneer as at Fig. 329.

Hard Wood Veneers such as satinwood should not be laid upon soft foundations like pine; when laying white or light coloured woods (say, satinwood, holly, boxwood, Hungarian ash, etc.) the glue used should have a little flake white or dry powdered chalk added to it so as to prevent dark hair lines showing at the joints.

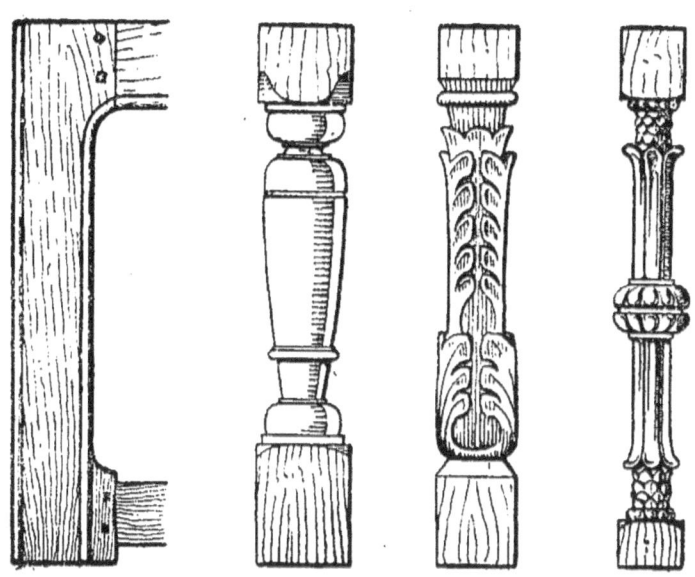

LEGS, PLAIN AND CARVED.

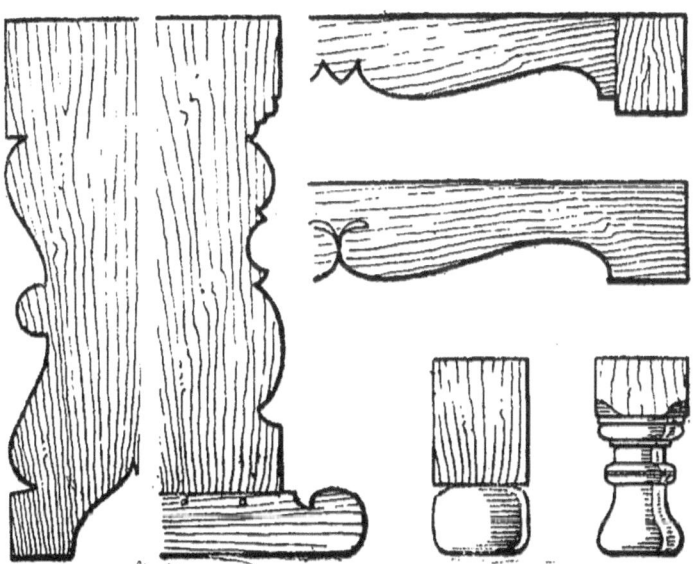

SHAPINGS, SUPPORTS AND FEET.

PLATE II.—DETAILS OF THE TUDOR STYLE.

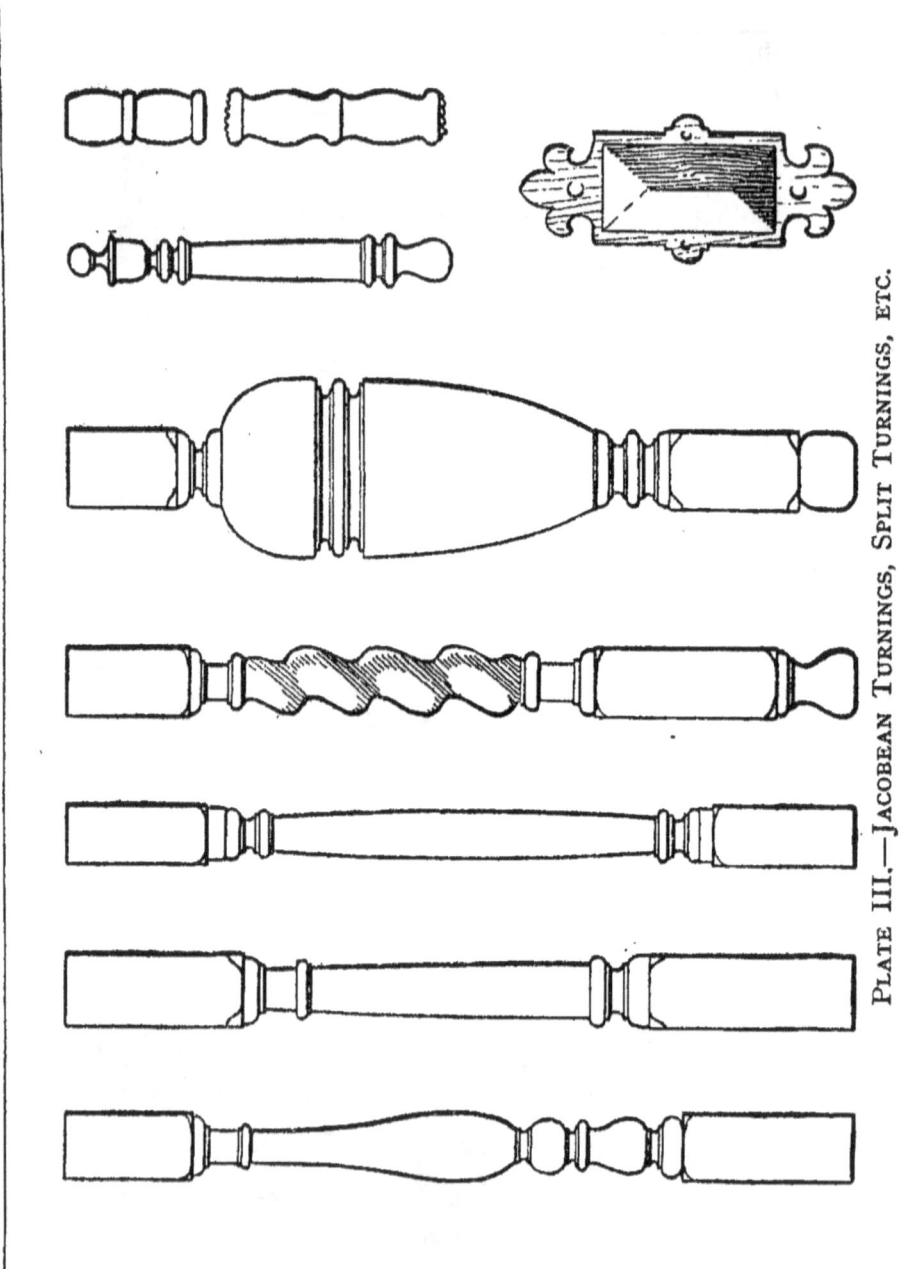

Plate III.—Jacobean Turnings, Split Turnings, etc.

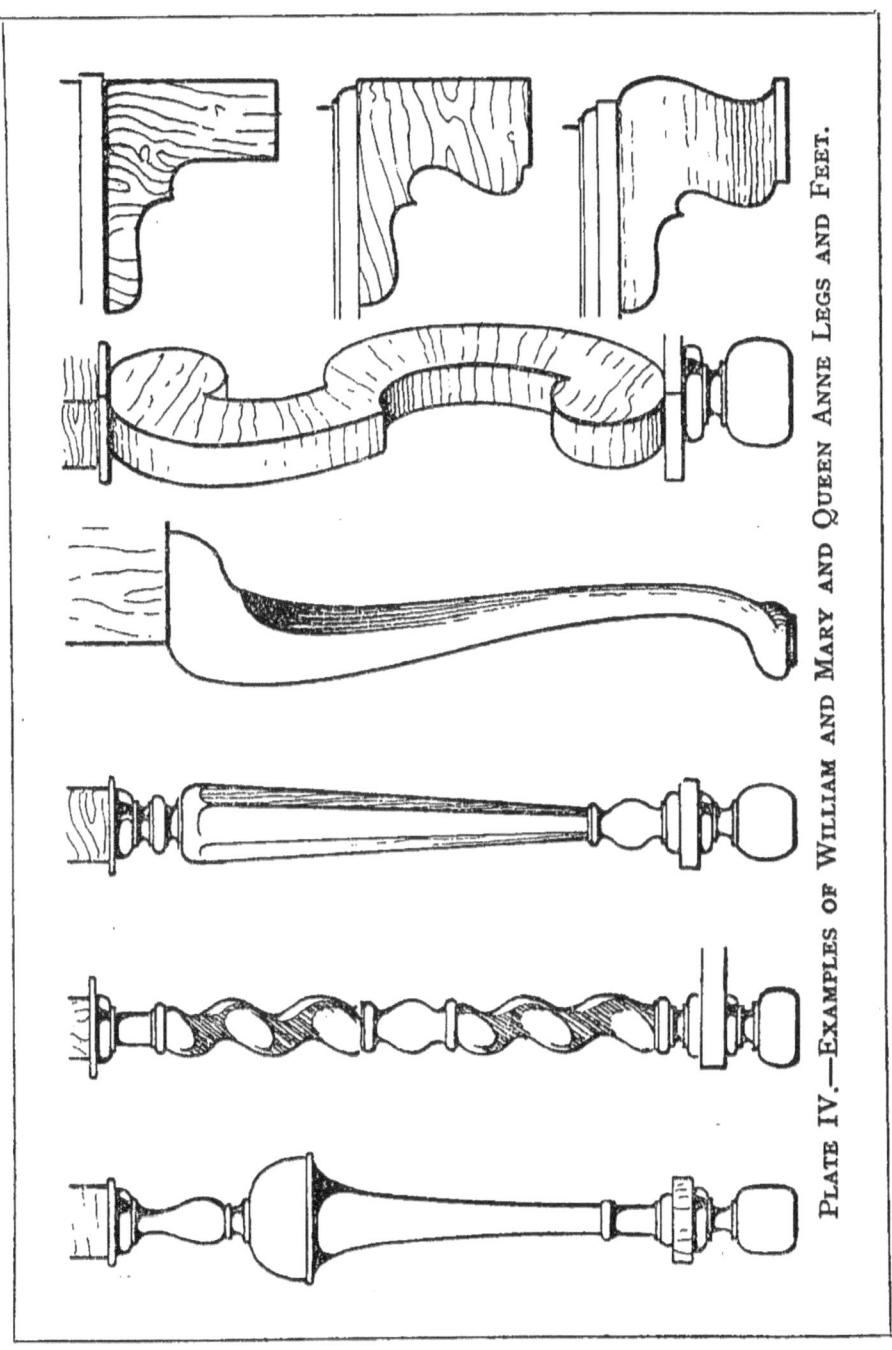

PLATE IV.—EXAMPLES OF WILLIAM AND MARY AND QUEEN ANNE LEGS AND FEET.

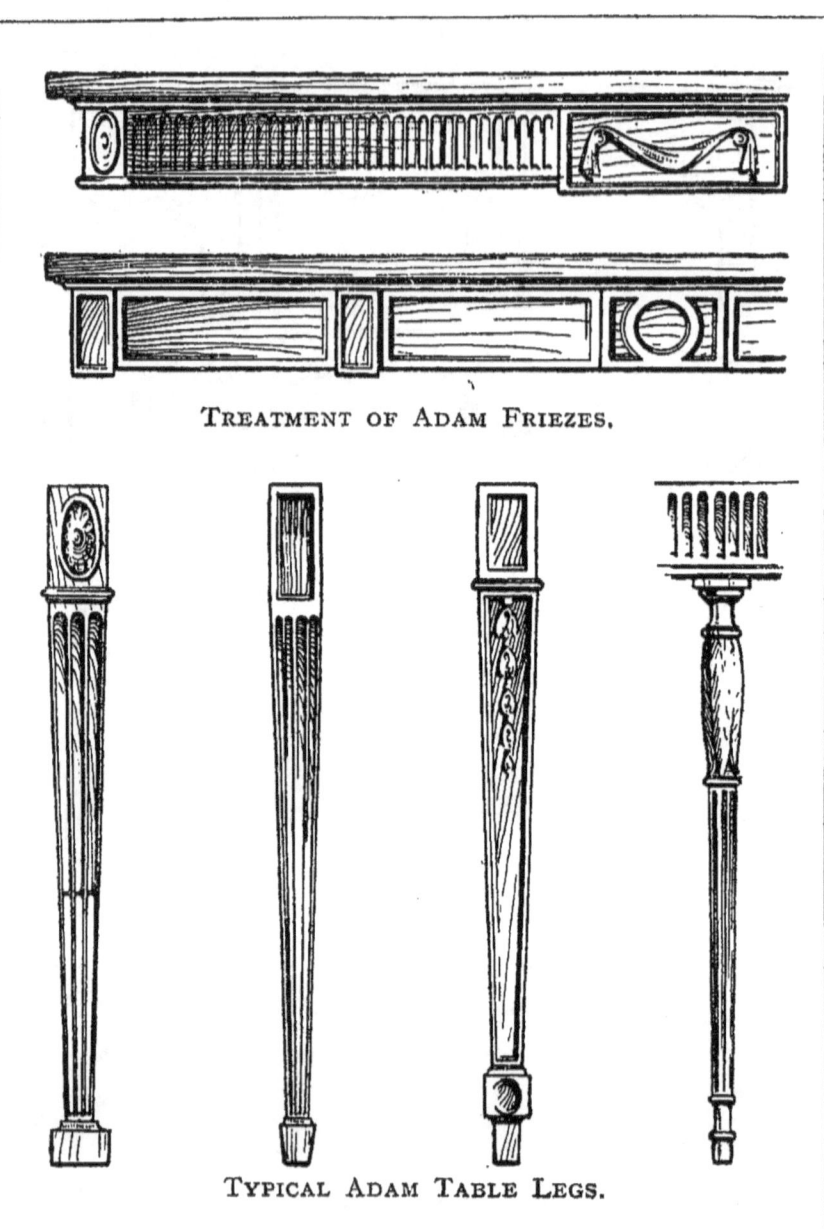

TREATMENT OF ADAM FRIEZES.

TYPICAL ADAM TABLE LEGS.

TREATMENT OF ADAM FRIEZES.

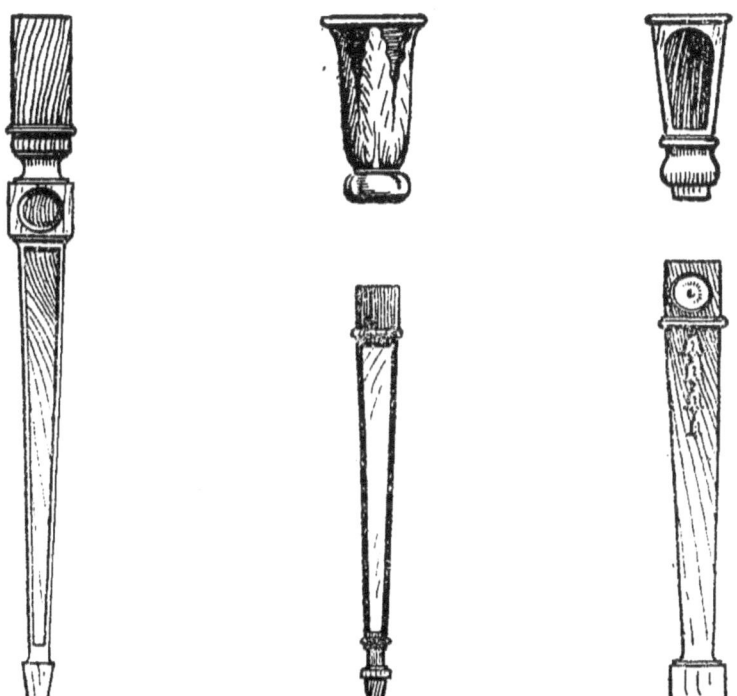

PLATE VI.—EXAMPLES OF ADAM LEGS AND FEET.

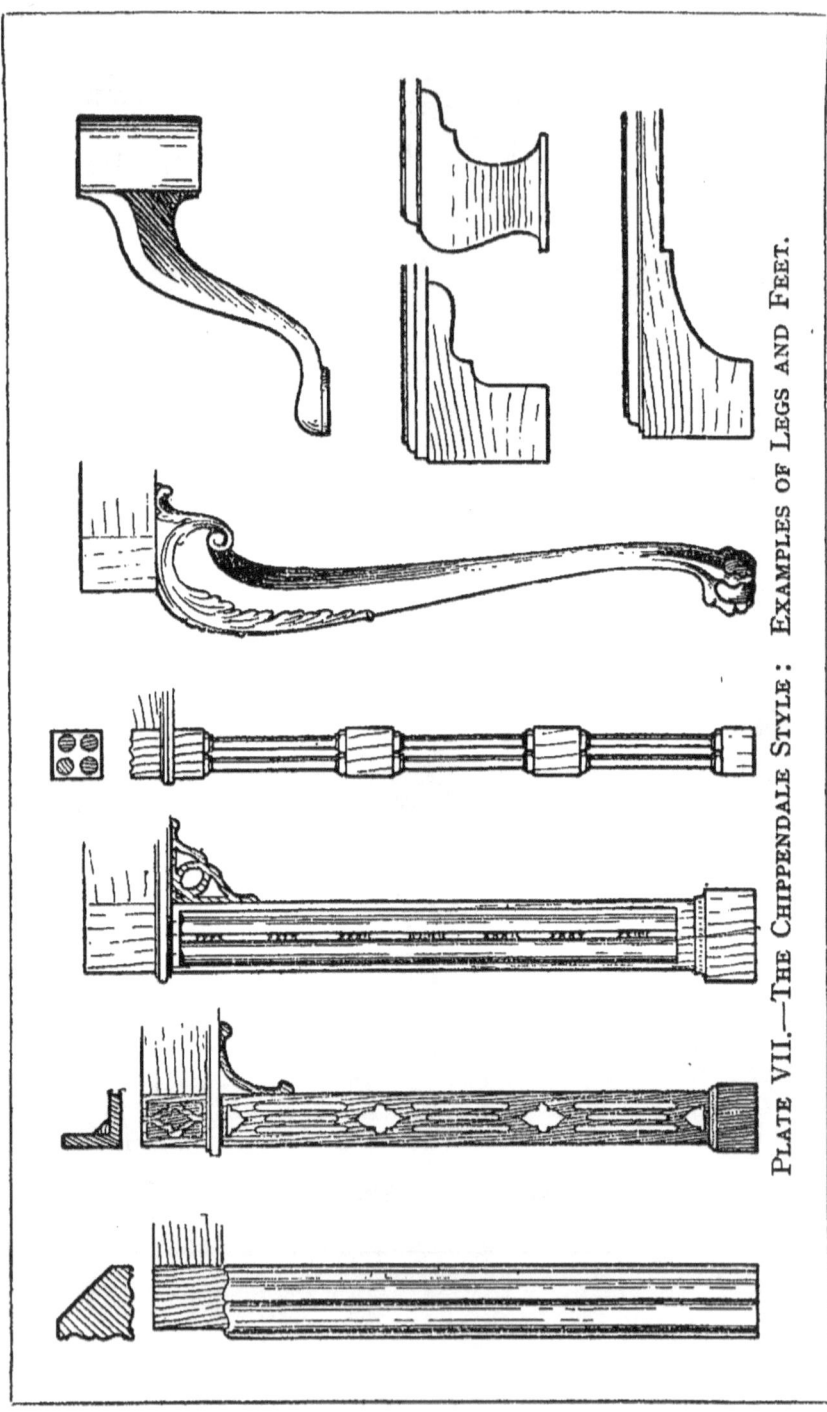

PLATE VII.—THE CHIPPENDALE STYLE: EXAMPLES OF LEGS AND FEET.

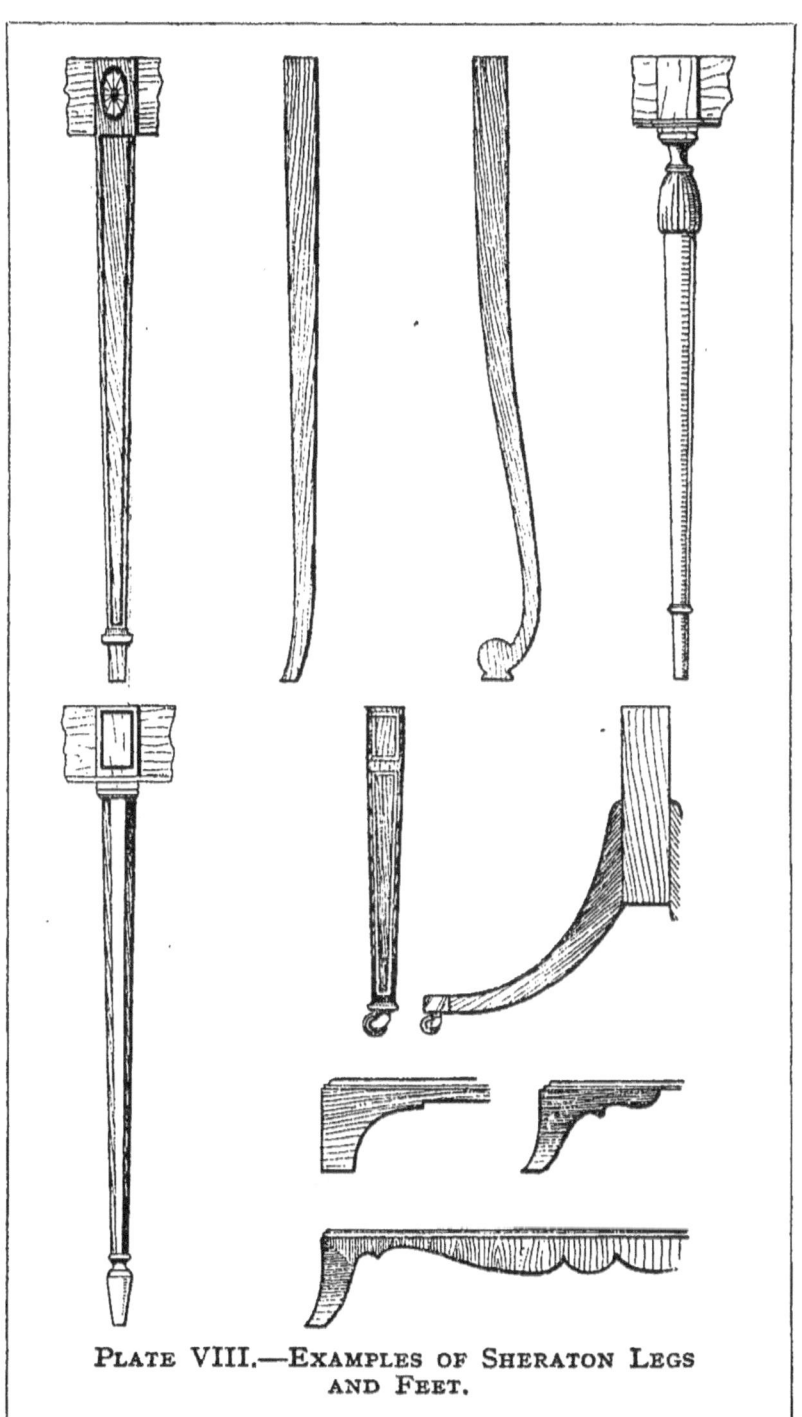

PLATE VIII.—EXAMPLES OF SHERATON LEGS AND FEET.

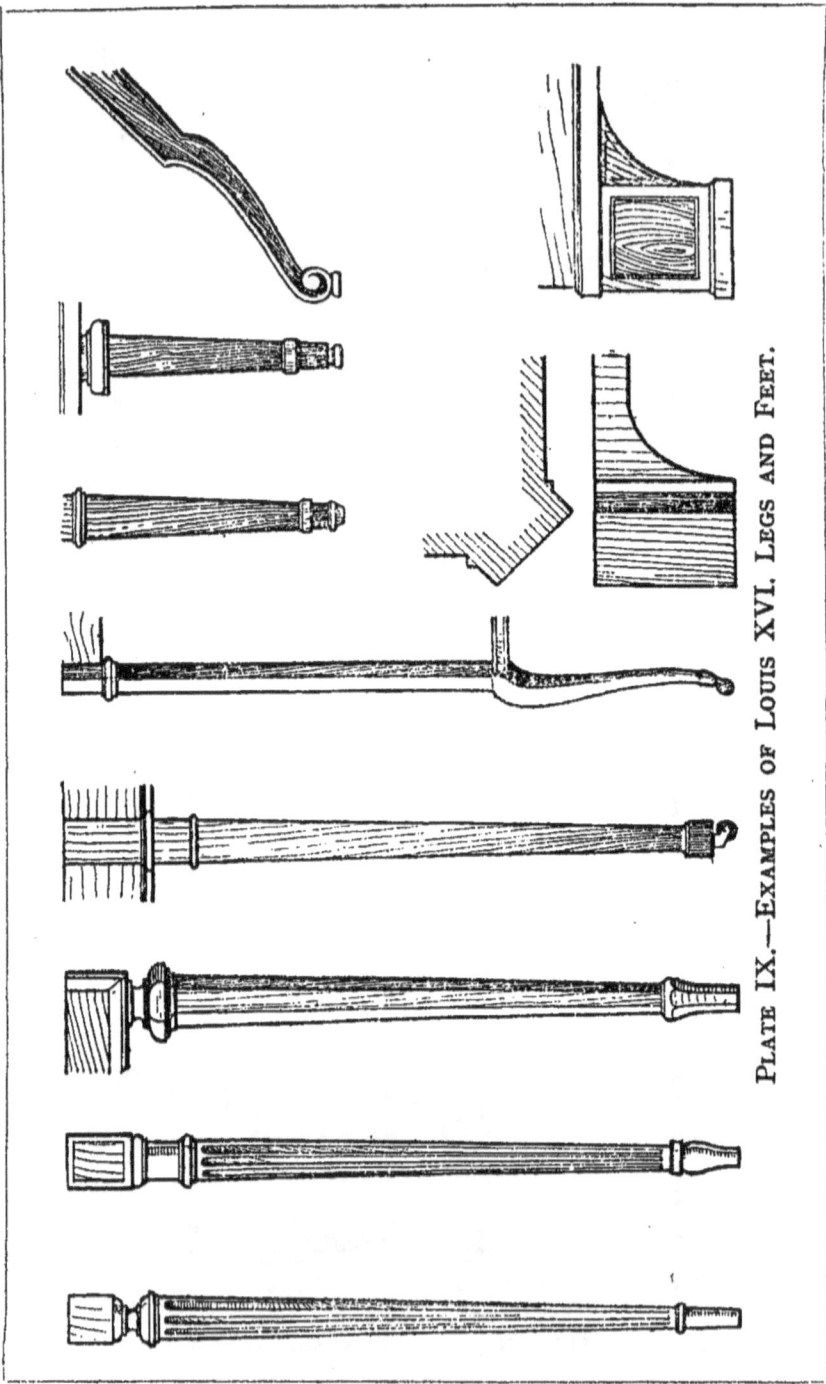

PLATE IX.—EXAMPLES OF LOUIS XVI. LEGS AND FEET.

PLATE X.—CHIPPENDALE BARRED DOORS.

PLATE XI.—SHERATON BARRED DOORS.

RENASCENCE MOTIF.

PIERCED GOTHIC.

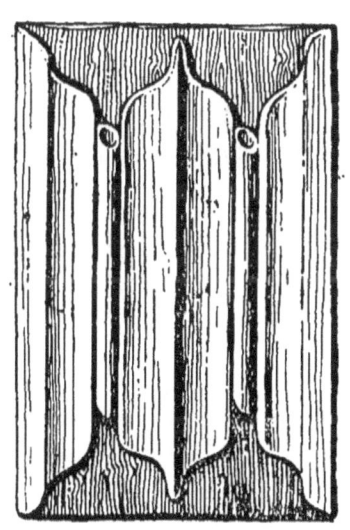
LINENFOLD.

TUDOR GOTHIC.

PLATE XII.—CHARACTERISTIC CARVED TUDOR PANELS.

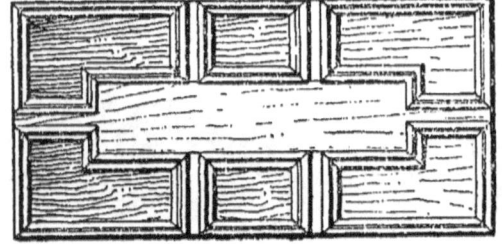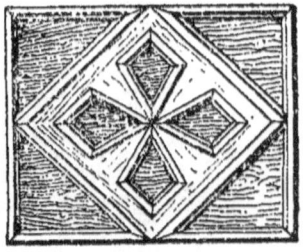

JACOBEAN PANELS.

The Mouldings which form the chief decorative motif are worked separately.

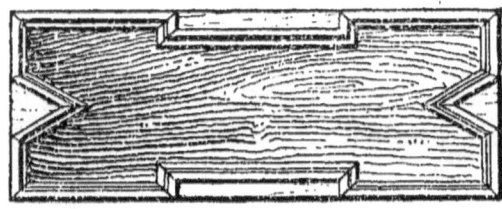
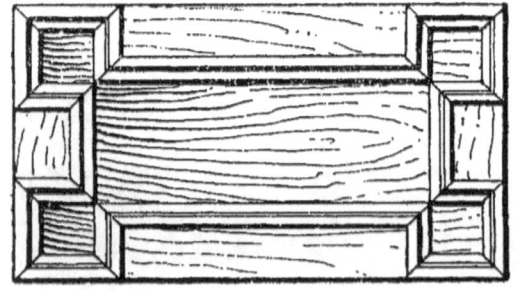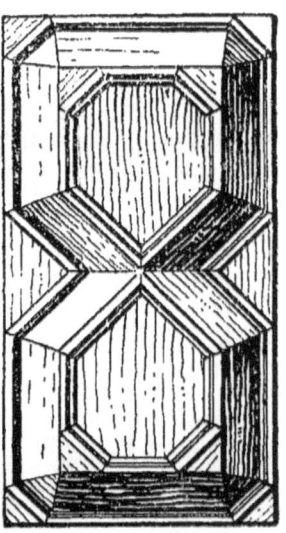

JACOBEAN DRAWER FRONTS.   RAISED PANEL.

PLATE XIII.—EXAMPLES OF JACOBEAN PANELS.

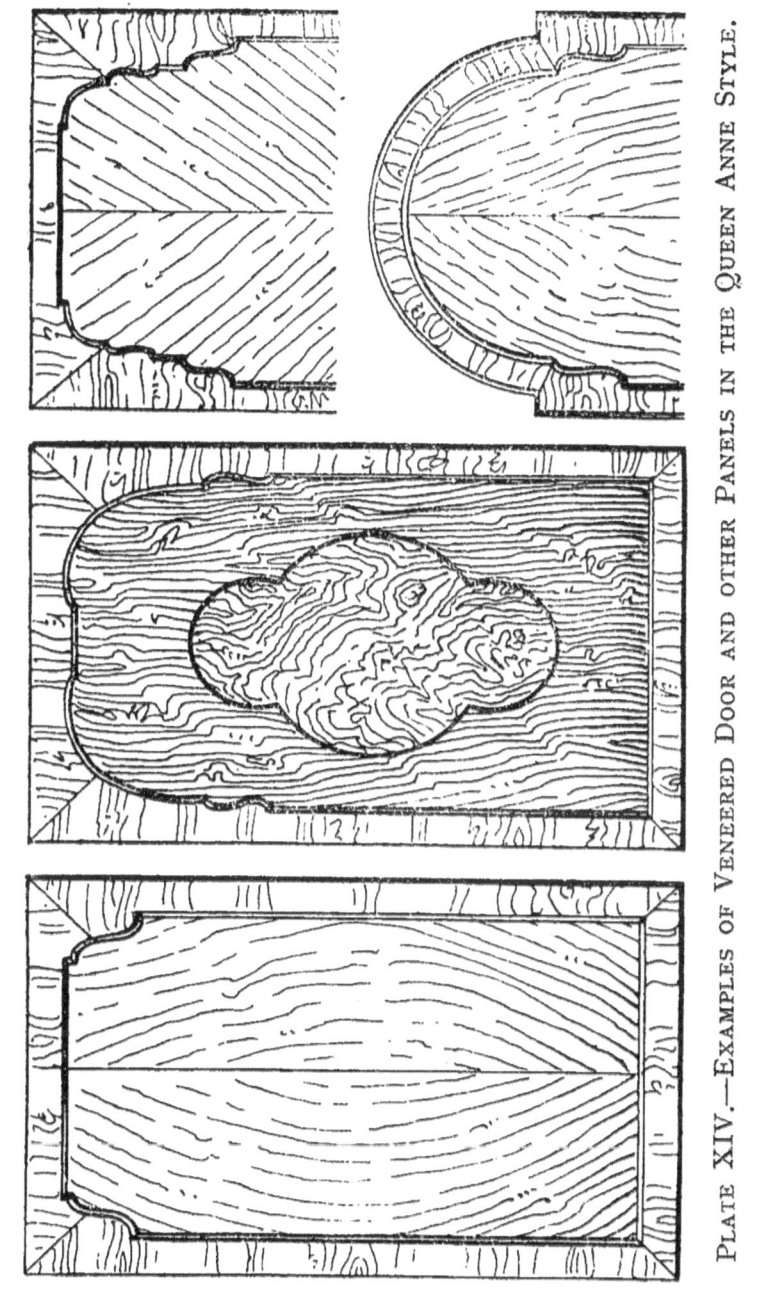

PLATE XIV.—EXAMPLES OF VENEERED DOOR AND OTHER PANELS IN THE QUEEN ANNE STYLE.

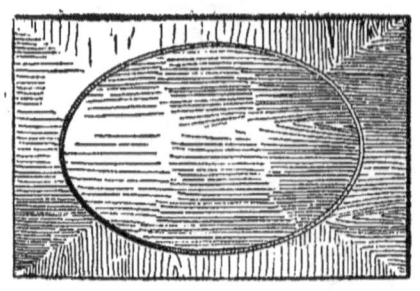

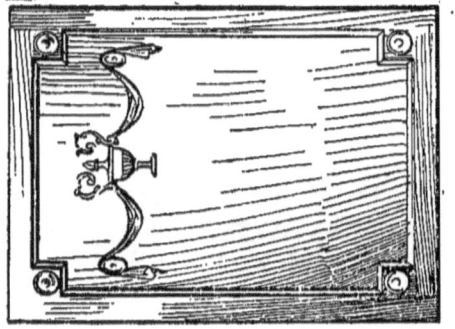
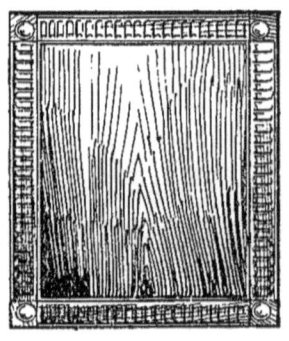
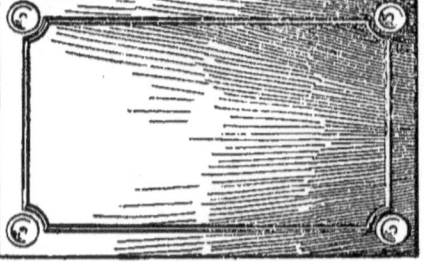

PLATE XV.—THE ADAM STYLE: EXAMPLES OF TYPICAL DECORATIVE PANELS.

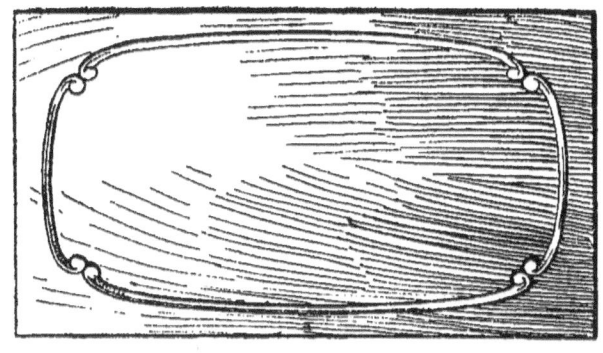
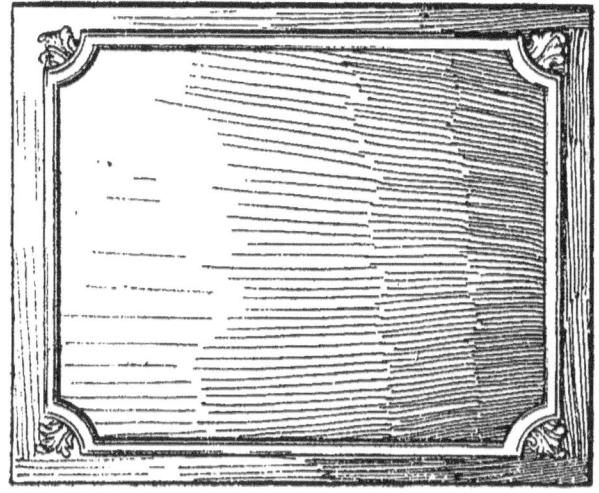
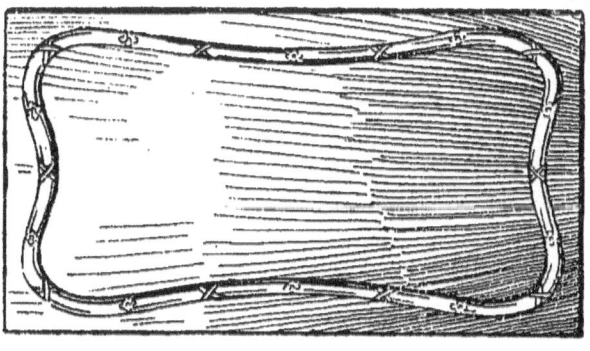

PLATE XVI.—EXAMPLES OF DOOR AND OTHER PANELLING IN THE CHIPPENDALE STYLE.

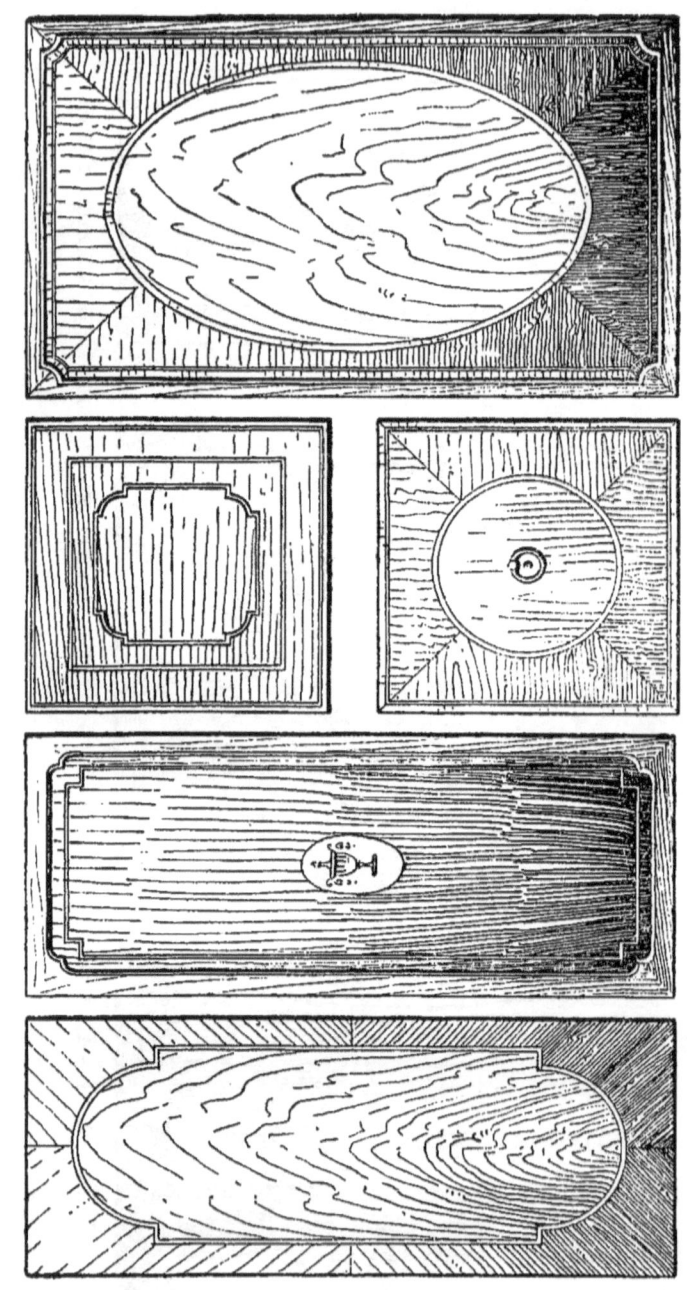

PLATE XVII.—TYPES OF DOOR AND OTHER PANELS OF THE SHERATON PERIOD.

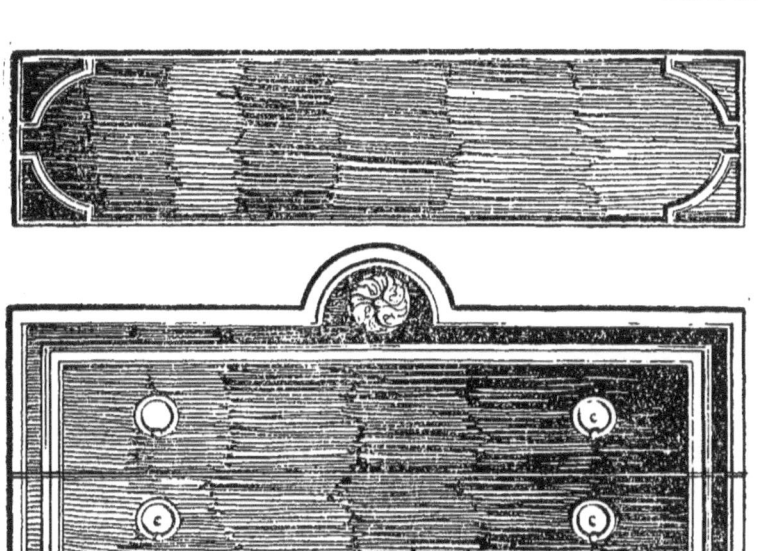

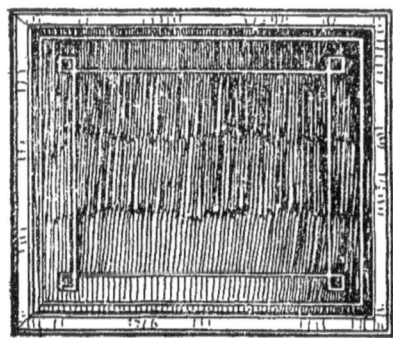
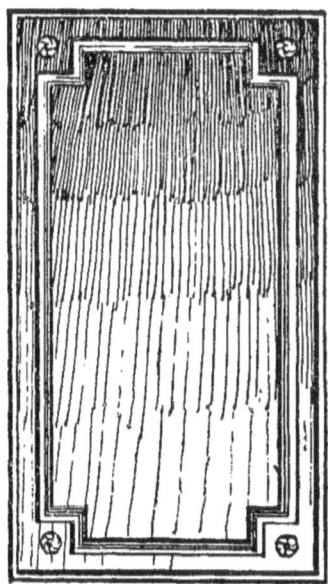

PLATE XVIII.—LOUIS XVI. PANELS, ETC.

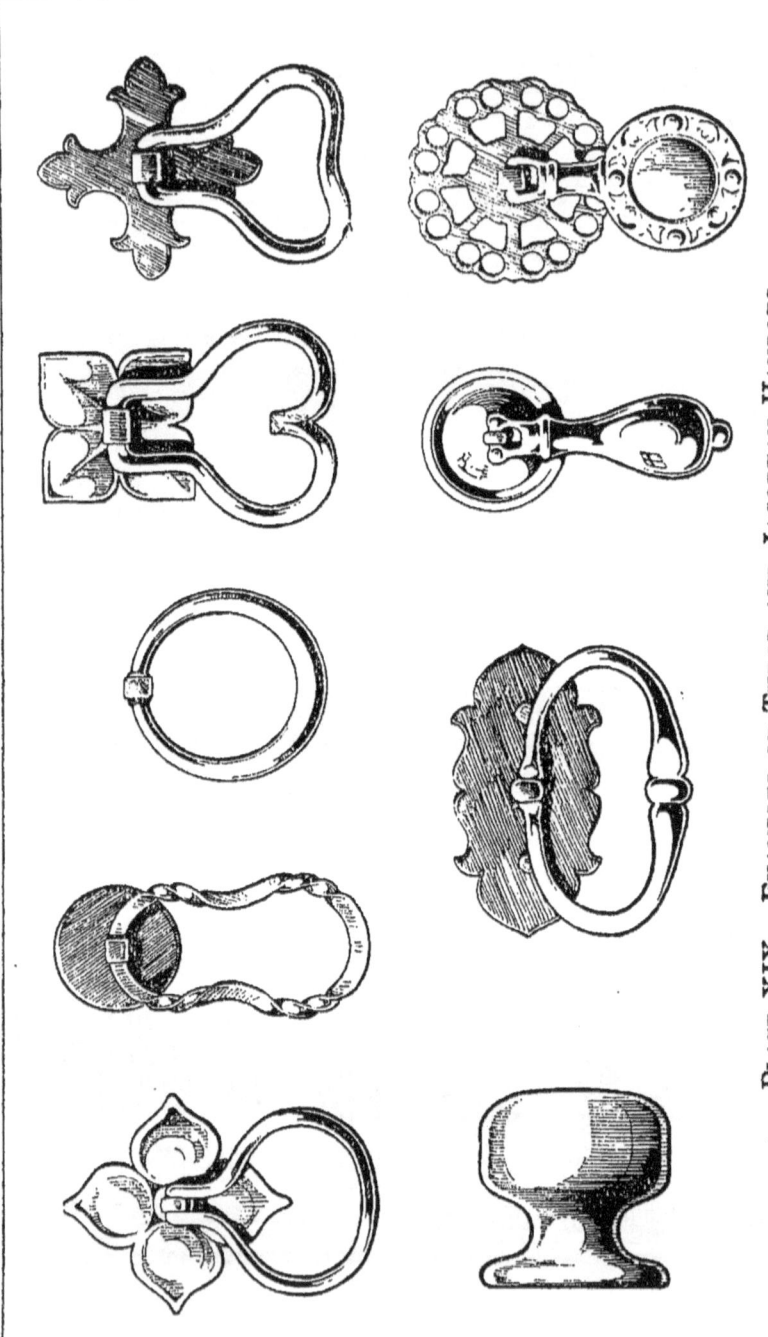

PLATE XIX.—EXAMPLES OF TUDOR AND JACOBEAN HANDLES.

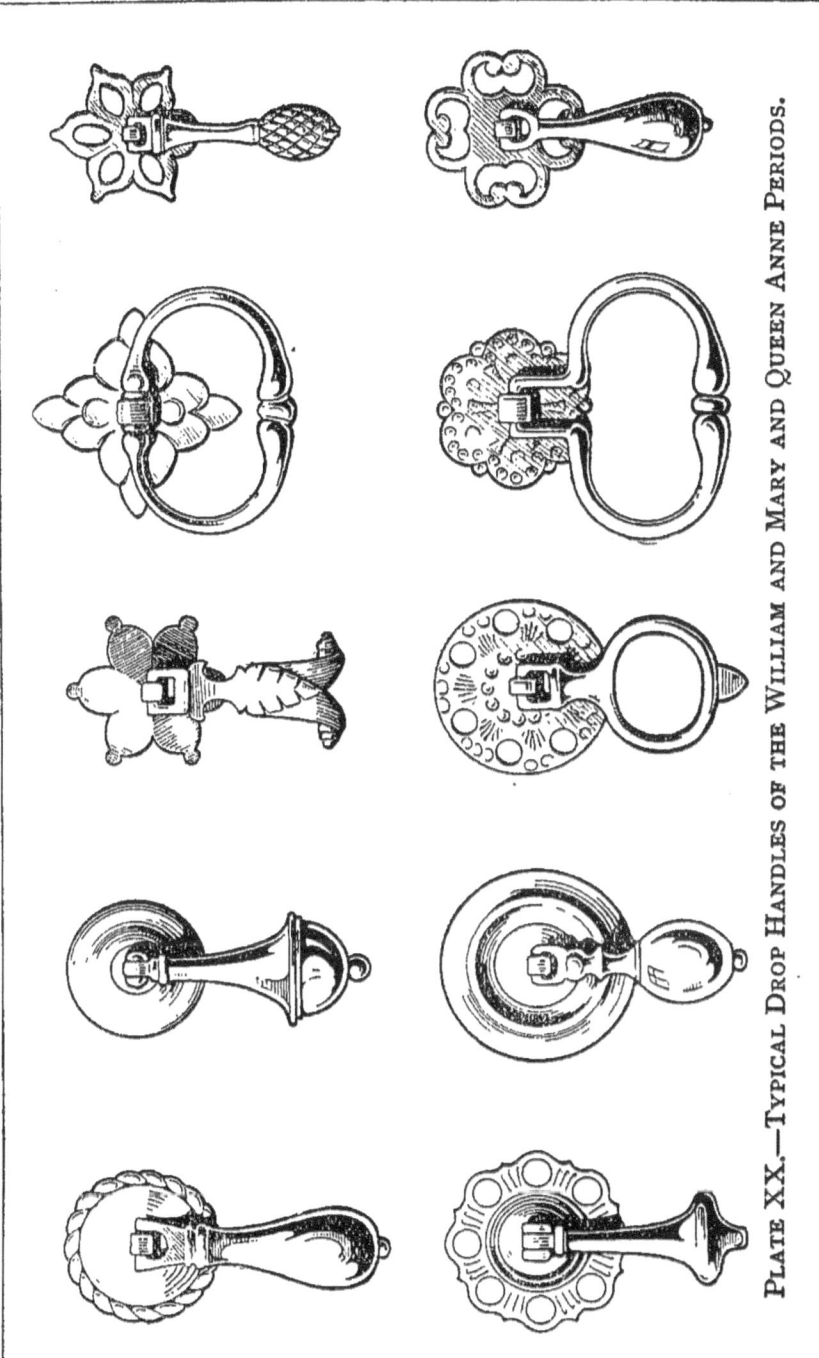

PLATE XX.—TYPICAL DROP HANDLES OF THE WILLIAM AND MARY AND QUEEN ANNE PERIODS.

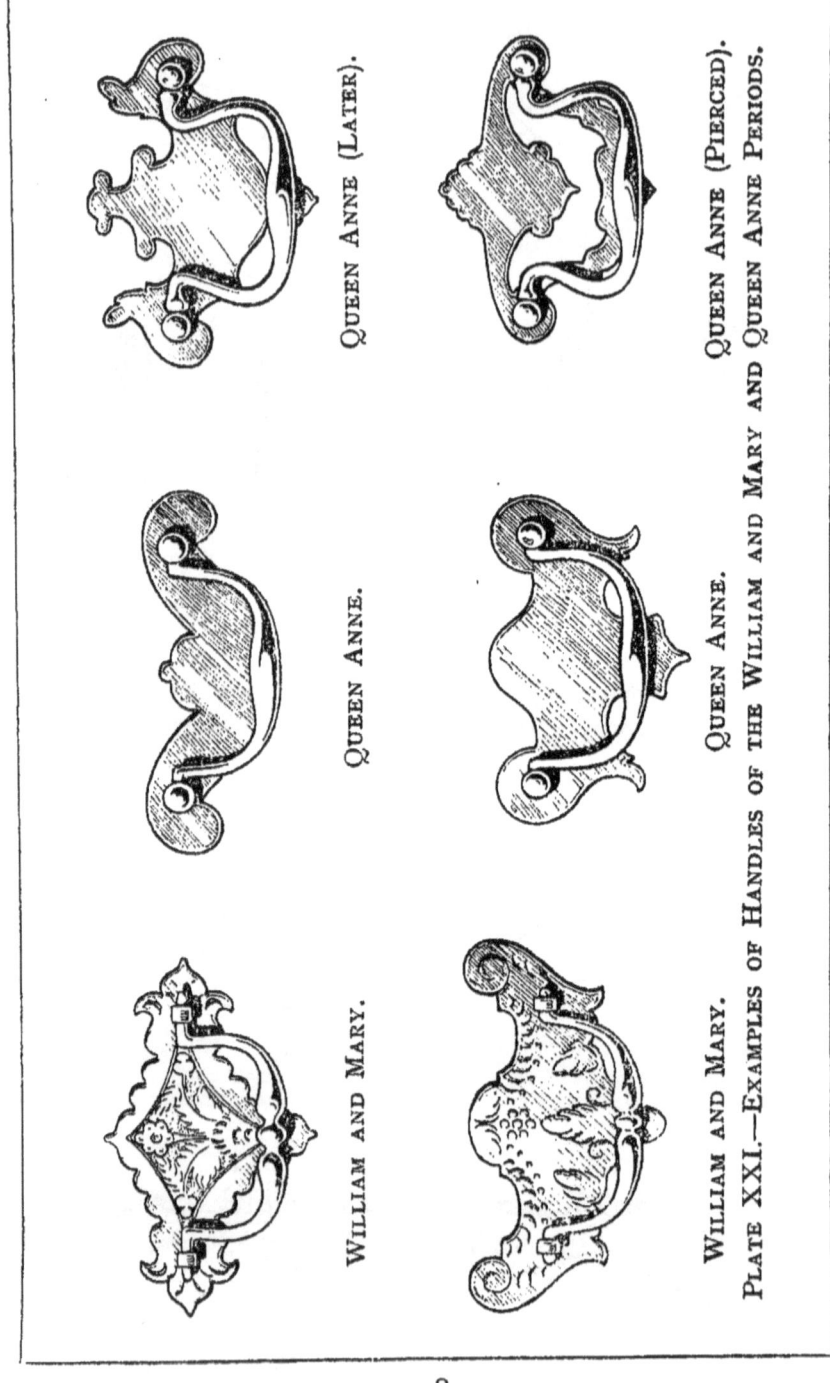

PLATE XXI.—EXAMPLES OF HANDLES OF THE WILLIAM AND MARY AND QUEEN ANNE PERIODS.

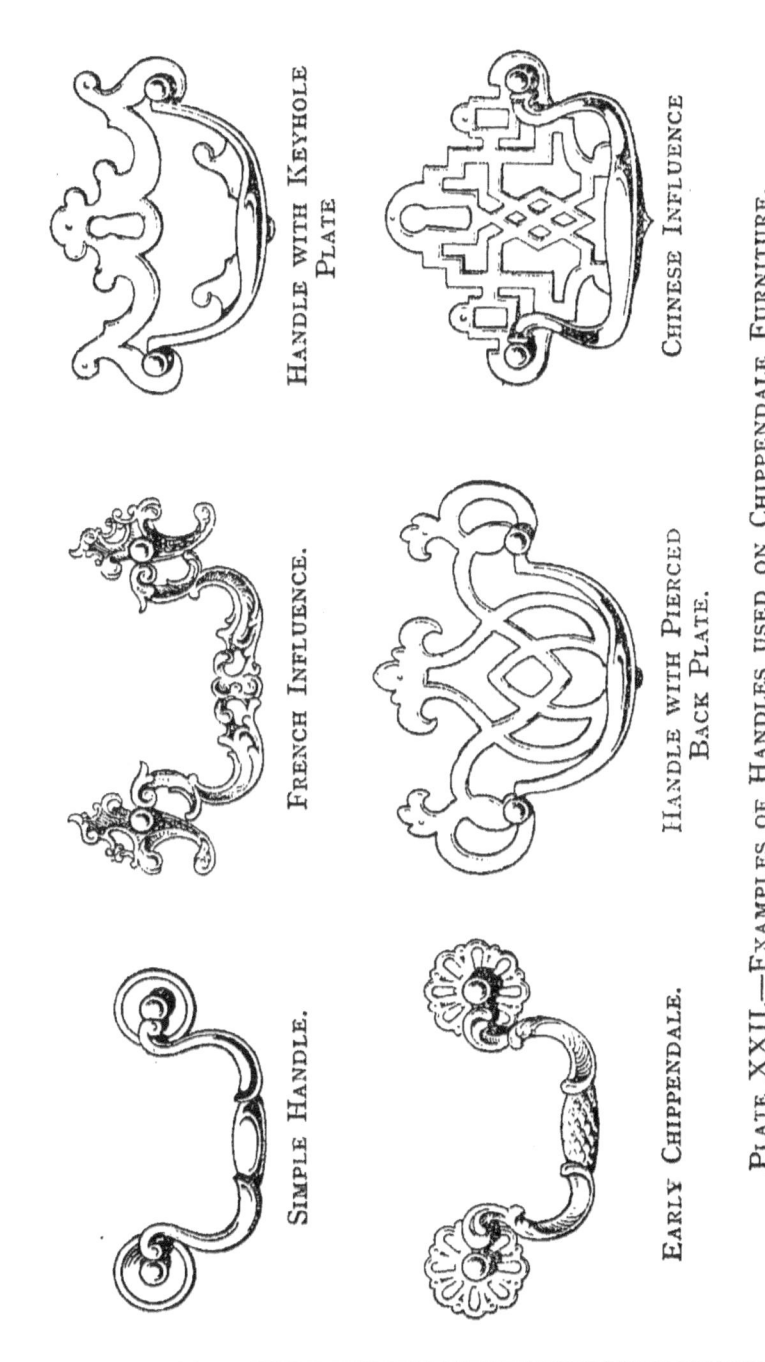

Plate XXII.—Examples of Handles used on Chippendale Furniture.

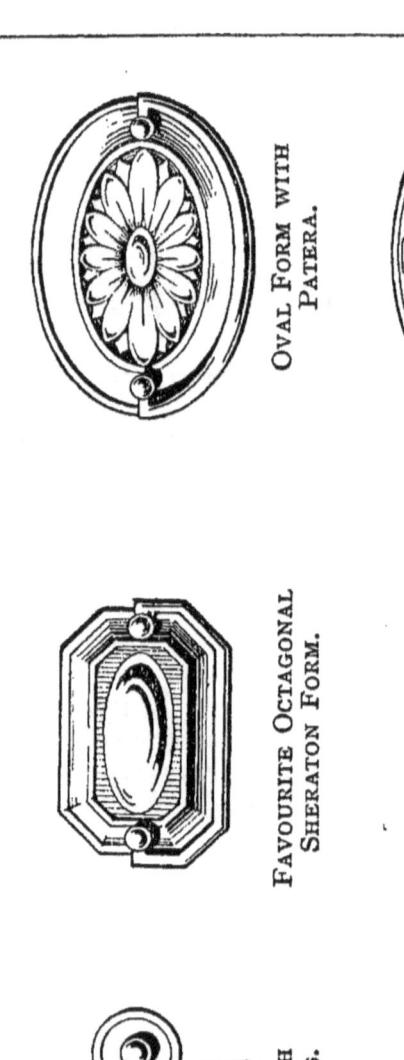

PLATE XXIII.—SIX TYPICAL SHERATON HANDLES.

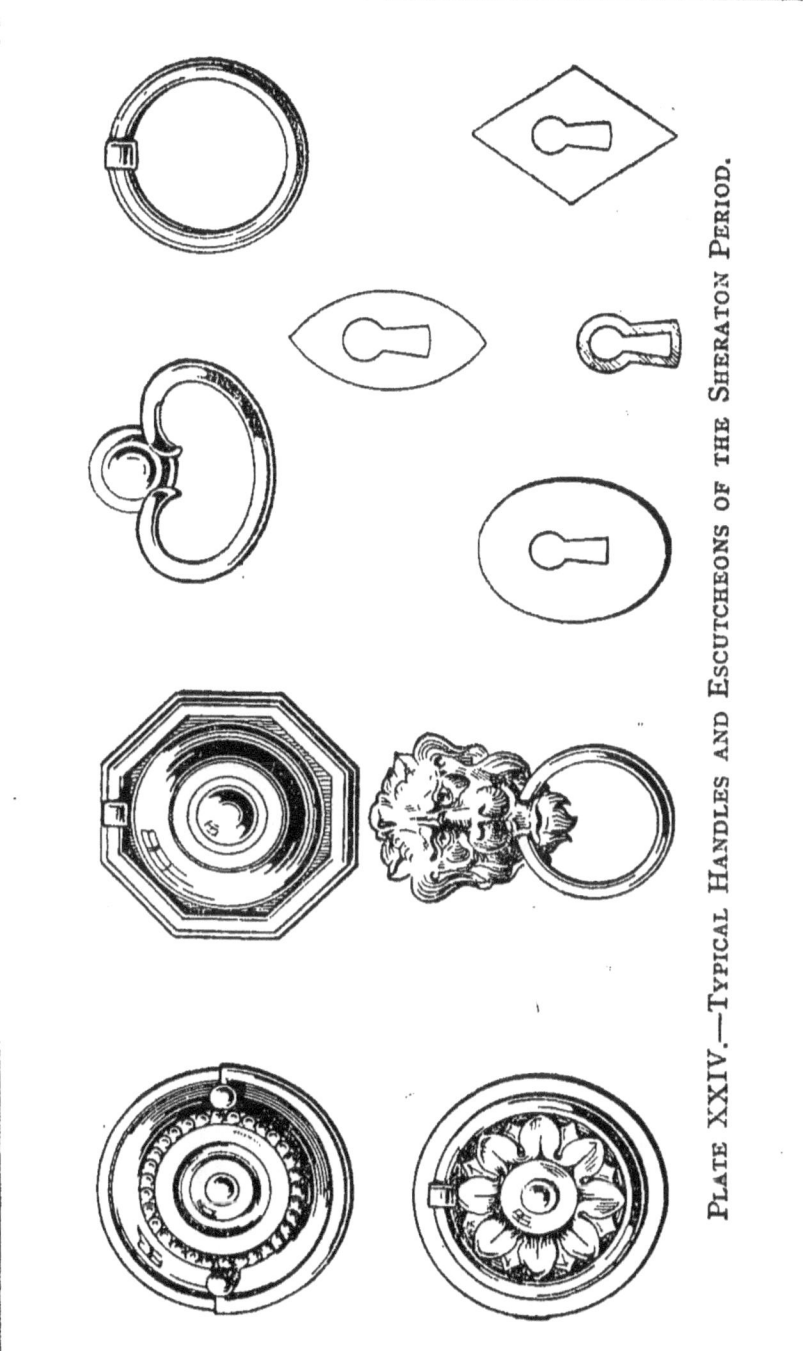

PLATE XXIV.—TYPICAL HANDLES AND ESCUTCHEONS OF THE SHERATON PERIOD.

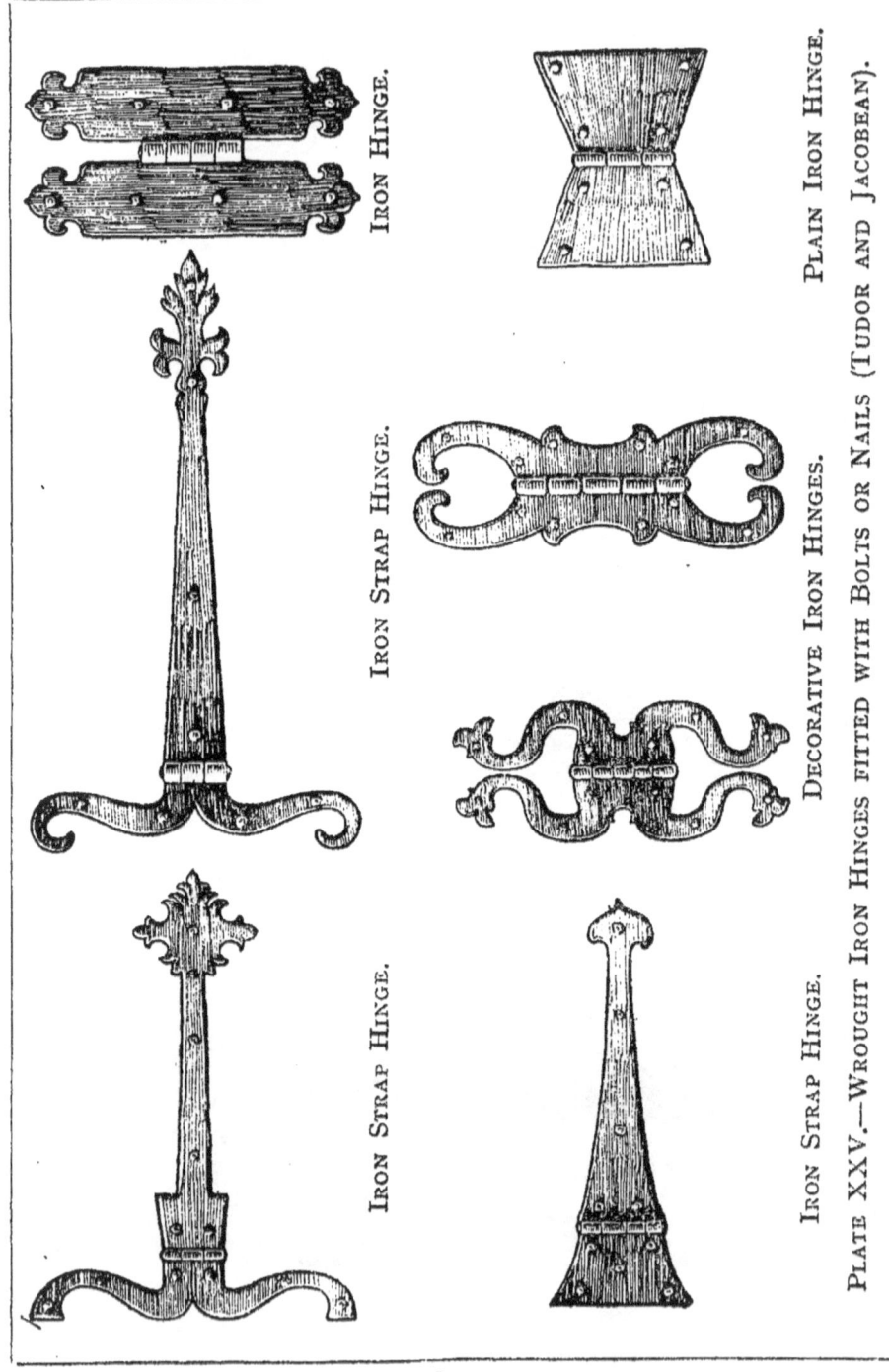

PLATE XXV.—WROUGHT IRON HINGES FITTED WITH BOLTS OR NAILS (TUDOR AND JACOBEAN).

INDEX

ADAM legs, etc., 192, 193
Adam panels, 202
Apron pieces, shaped, 103
Astragals, 53

BACKS, cabinet, 149
Bandings, inlaid, 128
Barred doors, 59
Barred doors, Chippendale and Sheraton, 197, 198
Battened table tops, 25
Bead, cocked, 72, 74
Bolts, metal, 144
Bridle jointing, 41
Boards, setting-out, 167
Bureau ends, setting-out, 18
Butting joints, 2
Buttoning, 36

CABINET backs, 149
Cabriole legs, 42
Cappings, 85
Carved Tudor panels, 199
Castors, 145
Catches, metal, 144
Cauls, 173
Chair and table legs, 31
Chair seats, loose, 112
Chippendale barred doors, 197
Chippendale handles, 209
Chippendale legs and feet, 194
Chippendale panels, 203
Corner cabinet joints, 14
Corner joints, 3, 14
Cornices, 89
Cornices, receding, 96
Cutters for stringings, 125

DOORS, backs to mirrored, 161
Doors, barred, 59
Doors, cabinet, 45
Doors, Chippendale and Sheraton barred, 197, 198

Dovetail housing, 27
Dovetail joints, 8, 67
Dovetailing drawers, 67
Dowelled joints, 7, 35
Drawer rails, 78
Drawers, making, 66
Drop leaves, rule joint for, 113

ESCUTCHEONS, 145, 211

FACING, 110
Feet :—
    Adam, 192, 193
    Chippendale, 194
    Louis XVI., 196
    Queen Anne, 191
    Sheraton, 195
    Tudor, 189
Fillets for shelves, 19
Framing, back, 149
Framing, carcase, 1
Friezes, Adam, 192, 193

GLASS, cutting, for leaded lights, 64
Glueing veneers, 179

HAMMER, veneering, 172
Handles, 145
Handles :—
    Chippendale, 209
    Jacobean and Tudor, 206
    Sheraton, 210, 211
    William and Mary, and Queen Anne, 207, 208
Hinge, the rule joint, 113, 142
Hinges, various, 137, 212
Housed joints, 13

INLAID strings and bandings, 124

Index

Inlaid workbox, 126
Inlaying (*see also* Veneering).

JACOBEAN handles, 206
Jacobean hinges, 212
Jacobean panels, 200
Jacobean turnings, 190
Joint, the rule, 113
Joints, carcase, 1
Joints for back framing, 133
Joints for doors, 46
Joints for legs, 133

KEYHOLE plates, 145, 211

LAMINATED doors, 57
Leaded lights, 63
Legs, etc. :—
    Adam, 192, 193
    Chippendale, 194
    Jacobean, 190
    Louis XVI., 196
    Queen Anne, 191
    Sheraton, 195
    Tudor, 189
    William and Mary, 191
Legs, cabriole, 42
Legs, table and chair, 31
Lining, 110
Lipping, 110
Locks, 146
Louis XVI. legs and feet, 196
Louis XVI. panels, 205

MATCHED backs, 153
Matching joints, 4
Metal fittings, 137, 206–212
Mirrored doors, backs to, 161
Mirrors, fixing, 163
Mirrors, frameless, 164
Mitred dovetails, 11
Mitred joints, 1
Mortises, cutting, 34, 47
Moulded table tops, 29

Mouldings, how to work, 117
Mouldings on drawers, 74

NECKINGS, 38

OVOLO moulding, working a, 120

PANELLING, exposed, 163
Panels :—
    Adam, 202
    Chippendale, 203
    door, 52
    Jacobean, 200
    Louis XVI., 205
    Queen Anne, 201
    Sheraton, 204
    Tudor, 199
    veneered, 178, 186, 187, 201–205
Pediments, 107
Plane, toothing, 173
Planes, hollow and round, 118
Planes, how to work mouldings with, 118
Plywood backs, 150
Pocket screwing, 27, 37

QUEEN ANNE handles, 207, 208
Queen Anne legs and feet, 191
Queen Anne veneered panels, 201

RAIL, stretcher, 5
Rails and runners, drawer, 78
Rails, door, 47
Rails, dovetailed table, 37
Rails, shaped, 103
Rebated joints, 1
Routers for stringings, 125
Rule joint, the, 113
Runners, drawer, 78

Index

SCRIBERS for stringings, 125
Seats, loose chair, 112
Setting-out boards, 167
Shapings, 99
Shapings, how to cut, 104
Shelves, fitting, 19
Shelves, fitting to table legs, 40
Sheraton barred doors, 198
Sheraton handles, 210, 211
Sheraton legs and feet, 195
Sheraton panels, 204
Slot screwing, 25
Split turnings, 190
Stiles, door, 46
Strings, inlaid, 127

TABLE and chair legs, 31
Table tops, 24
Tenon joints, 6, 48
Three-ply backs, 150
Thumb slots, 27, 37
Tongued joints, 1
Tudor handles, 206
Tudor hinges, 212
Tudor legs and feet, 189
Tudor panels, 199
Turnings, Jacobean, 190

UNDERFRAMING, 39

VENEER, how made, 175
Veneered drawer fronts, 75
Veneered panels, Queen Anne, 201
Veneered panels, various, 178, 186, 187, 201–205
Veneering, 171
Veneering, defects in, 184
Veneers, 174
Veneers, cutting, 177

WILLIAM and Mary handles, 207, 208
William and Mary legs and feet, 191

THE WOODWORKER
MAGAZINE

A Free Specimen Copy sent on receipt of postcard.

THE WOODWORKER MAGAZINE provides for the woodworker, cabinet-maker and furniture maker, whether expert or amateur, fresh ideas and up-to-date economical working methods for the making of all kinds of useful furniture and articles such as are needed for every home.

The principal features include practical directions, illustrated by working drawings, for the construction of plain and ornamental furniture and all kinds of indoor and outdoor woodwork. Descriptive features include joint-making, tool manipulation, upholstery, staining and polishing, repairing problems and every-day difficulties.

The contributors are expert craftsmen who know exactly where the woodworker's difficulties lie, and who not only know their craft thoroughly themselves, but are able to impart their knowledge to others.

In this magazine the woodworker will find the exact guidance and suggestions he requires month by month for efficient, economical work.

PUBLISHED MONTHLY.   PRICE 6d.

(*Free Specimen Copy sent on receipt of postcard.*)
THE WOODWORKER ANNUAL VOLUME, 370 pages, 6s. 6d. net.

From any newsagent or direct from

Evans Bros., Ltd., Montague House, Russell Square, London, W.C.1

G. 5058

www.ingramcontent.com/pod-product-compliance
Lightning Source LLC
Chambersburg PA
CBHW031242290426
44109CB00012B/407